P9-AQA-445

Constitutionalism in Asia

Constitutionalism in Asia

Asian Views of the American Influence

Edited by
Lawrence Ward Beer

University of California Press
Berkeley • Los Angeles • London

University of California Press
Berkeley and Los Angeles, California

University of California Press, Ltd.
London, England

ISBN 0-520-03701-4
Library of Congress Catalog Card Number: 78-57303
Printed in the United States of America

1 2 3 4 5 6 7 8 9

Contents

Preface

The purposes of this symposium are to further knowledge of Asian law and to advance the comparative study of law and constitutionalism. This volume presents a wealth of data and expert opinion concerning law and constitutionalism in Asia which hitherto has been unavailable to Americans or difficult to obtain except in indigenous sources. It also sheds light on the degree and manner of the relevance of the Declaration of Independence and the American constitutional experience to the modern legal and political life of Asian nations which stretch in an enormous arc from India and Pakistan to Japan. Asian constitutional and legal realities are here presented, not through the sometimes tinted glasses of Western legal scholars, but as perceived by eminently qualified indigenous jurists and legal scholars: Mr. Justice Abu Sayeed Chowdhury, past President of Bangladesh; Professor Herbert H. P. Ma, College of Law, National Taiwan University, Taipei; Dr. P. K. Tripathi, Faculty of Law, University of Delhi, and past Member, Law Commission of India; Chief Justice Dr. Oemar Seno Adji of the Supreme Court of Indonesia; Professor Nobushige Ukai of Senshu University, Tokyo, and past President, Public Law Association of Japan; Lord President Tun Mohamed Suffian of the Federal Court of Malaysia; Senior Associate Justice Enrique Fernando of the Supreme Court of the Philippines; and Dean S. Jayakumar, Faculty of Law, University of Singapore. (A biographical sketch on each Asian author can be found at the back of this book.) The Committee on Asian Law thanks the Asian contributors for taking time to honor us with their views.

A word of explanation on the background of this symposium and on the Committee on Asian Law is in order. In the spring of 1976, the Committee on Asian Law of the Association for Asian Studies offered a month-long Bicentennial program centered on the theme "Asian perspectives on the American constitutional influence in Asia." The Committee on Asian Law is an elected committee of legal scholars specializing in one of the four subregions of Asia, as Asia is divided for organizational purposes by the Association for Asian Studies (AAS): Northeast Asia (Japan and Korea); China and Inner Asia; Southeast Asia; and South Asia. The Association is the principal learned society for many thousands of scholars in a wide range of academic disciplines who have a special interest in one or more nations of Asia, from Japan to Afghanistan.

The Committee on Asian Law is the primary meeting ground for legal practitioners and academics in the fields of law, political science, sociology, anthropology, and history who share a professional interest in Asian law and legal systems. The Committee's goals include the advancement of research and teaching on Asian law, and the development of reliable information concerning available expertise on Asian law. See, for example, the Committee's annual publication, *Asian Law Forum*, and the *Directory of Persons Interested in Asian Law* (Chin Kim, ed.), which is up-dated periodically by the Committee. Of related interest is a survey of American law schools and Asian Studies programs, "Asian Legal Studies in the United States: A Survey Report," *Journal of Legal Education 29*, no. 4 (1978), a product of Committee collaboration with the International Legal Center.

The Bicentennial program of the Committee on Asian Law consisted in a series of public panel presentations and seminars in March and April, 1976, at the annual convention of the Association for Asian Studies (Toronto), and in Buffalo, New York City, Washington, D.C., and San Francisco. In all, some thirty programs were offered as a group; additional talks and seminars were presented in other cities during the portions of the itinerary when the Asian jurists were traveling singly. Earlier versions of many of the contributions to this volume were presented and candidly discussed on those occasions. The present writer served as program coordinator and an official escort throughout.

The Committee on Asian Law was assisted in this project by the Office of East Asian and Pacific Programs, U.S. Department of State; the Asia Foundation; the Asia Society in New York and Washington,

D.C.; and the Visitor Program Service of Meridian House International. In addition, law schools, the American Bar Association, the Federal Bar Association, Barry Metzger of the Coudert Brothers law firm, and a number of local bar associations and World Affairs Councils lent a helping hand. Generous cooperation was also forthcoming from the White House, Chief Justice Warren E. Burger of the United States Supreme Court, the Committee on the Judiciary of the U.S. House of Representatives, the U.S. Justice Department, and both federal and local courts. To all of these, and to the officers and able staff of the Association for Asian Studies, the Committee and the Bicentennial guests wish to express their deep gratitude.

Members and associates of the Committee on Asian Law have assisted in the preparation of the manuscript for publication, especially the following: Daniel S. Lev and Ronald G. Brown of Seattle; Marc Galanter and Robert Hayden of Madison, Wisconsin; James L. Magavern of Buffalo, New York; Hungdah Chiu of Baltimore, Maryland; and Henry F. Goodnow and Roger K. Paget of Boulder, Colorado.

The views of the Asian authors are their own and are not to be construed as official statements of the policies of their respective nations or as the opinions of the Committee on Asian Law or the Association for Asian Studies or the cosponsors of the 1976 Bicentennial program. In some papers, informational footnotes have been added by the editor and his assistants to clarify the context or to indicate sources to which the reader may turn for further enlightenment on the subject under discussion in the text. Modification and adaptation of English-language phraseology has been necessary in a number of places because English is the second, third, or fourth language of our Asian contributors; in this editing process we have scrupulously avoided any modification of the author's intent. The opinions of the authors of editorial notes before chapters and of the present writer (expressed herein and in chapter 1) do not necessarily mirror those of the Committee on Asian Law or any agency cosponsoring or supporting the Bicentennial program or chapter authors.

The sequence of chapters was determined solely on the basis of the alphabetical order of the names of the countries dealt with herein, in keeping with the system of protocol adopted for the Bicentennial presentations of 1976. The number of Asian countries represented by the writings we offer in this symposium is of necessity limited. Our intent has been, not comprehensive coverage of all the many nations in that vast area encompassing almost two-thirds of humankind, but rather the inclusion of a sufficient number and diversity of nations to provide representation of most Asian legal traditions operative at the present time. For obvious if regrettable political reasons, we do not have the benefit of a contribution by an indigenous scholar of Asian socialist legalism. Final responsibility for the selection of the Asian nations represented and the distinguished contributors rests with the Committee on Asian Law.

Thanks are due, finally, to Ms. Bee Peterson of the Department of Political Science, University of Colorado at Boulder, for typing most of the manuscript; to my parents, Lucile H. Beer of Portland, Oregon, and the late Norman H. Beer, for teaching me to learn from other lands while critically appreciating our own; and to my wife, Keiko, and our children for patience with scholarly absenteeism.

The ideas and institutions espoused in the Constitution of the United States and the Declaration of Independence are among the finest contributions of the United States to the world in the past two hundred years. In the years ahead, Americans may well learn to grasp more deeply the persisting principles of their constitution and legal system by learning from jurists and scholars of Asia who have first honored the United States by studying its legal principles and constitutional experience. This symposium is offered as such a learning opportunity, and in the hope it may stimulate further creative exchanges.

LAWRENCE WARD BEER
Committee on Asian Law
Association for Asian Studies
Boulder, Colorado
May 1978

I

Introduction

Constitutionalism in Asia and the United States

Lawrence Ward Beer

The Constitution and the Declaration of Independence of the United States of America emerged in the particularistic historical context of British North America; but the constitutional values enunciated and institutionalized therein were seen from the beginning as having universal relevance for humankind. These documents still speak forcefully, not only to most citizens of the United States,[1] but also to many peoples of different history and heritage around the world. American constitutionalism is one of the major models available two centuries later.

What is striking is not that some elements of the Declaration and the Constitution are out of tune with the indigenous power structure, legal perceptions, social values, economic systems, or constitutional needs of many nations, but that so much of their spirit has become part of the evolving perennial wisdom of democratically inclined countries

1. The Bicentennial occasioned an outpouring of commentaries on the Declaration of Independence and the constitutional and moral foundations of American government in the American mass media. For some recent scholarly analyses, see Paul Eidelberg, *On the Silence of the Declaration of Independence* (Amherst: University of Massachusetts Press, 1976); Robert H. Horwitz, *The Moral Foundations of the American Republic* (Charlottesville: University Press of Virginia, 1976); Walter Berns, *The First Amendment and the Future of American Democracy* (New York: Basic Books, 1976); and Norman A. Graebner (ed.), *Freedom in America: A 200-Year Perspective* (College Station: Pennsylvania State University Press, 1976).

in so many regions of the world. As the distinguished Ceylonese jurist C. G. Weeramantry has said:

> Aversion for colonialism and all it meant and a respect for the antiquity of Third World tradition must not obscure the fact that one of the grandest intellectual concepts that has emerged in the long history of justice-thinking is the concept of the Rights of Man as developed in the West. The philosophy of natural law, built upon an ancient base by such philosophers as Locke, Rousseau and Bentham in Europe, and Thomas Paine and Thomas Jefferson in America, and their flowering in the American Declaration of Independence and the French Declaration of the Rights of Man—all these are the property, the achievement and the inheritance of all mankind. Third World cultures did not bring their formulations of human rights to this degree of explicitness, and it would be unwisdom indeed to jettison this stream of tradition merely because it had its greatest development in the West. Indeed, the Universal Declaration of Human Rights and the other basic international formulations around these themes, on which the world order of the future needs to be built, draw heavily upon this stream of thought. The very notion of the economic rights and duties of States, on which much of the future of the Third World depends, must rest in the ultimate analysis on a bedrock of natural law.[2]

The United States Bicentennial era of the mid-1970s was ill timed to generate enthusiasm, pride, and confidence in the rule-of-law principles behind the American constitutional endeavor from its inception. The period preparatory to the Bicentennial observance was coincident with the early aftermath of the Vietnam War, probably the most excruciatingly divisive conflict since the American Civil War, and attendant communist victories in Cambodia and Laos. In addition, the balance and cohesion among the elements of the American constitutional structures have been disrupted in recent years by abuses of power symbolized by the Watergate affair. American citizens differed deeply among themselves on what this all meant and on whether the republic emerged strong or weak from the ordeals. The inflation, recession, unemployment, and new concern for energy resources of the mid-1970s provided almost welcome distraction from the exposed national wounds of war and corruption for many Americans.

2. C. G. Weeramantry, *Equality and Freedom: Some Third World Perspectives* (Colombo: Hansa Publishers, Ltd., 1976), p. 67. The Universal Declaration of Human Rights was adopted by the United Nations General Assembly on December 10, 1948. The United Nations Charter, which came into force on October 24, 1945, affirmed human rights particularly in Articles 1 and 55. Some of the other major international documents dealing with human rights are the Convention on the Prevention and Punishment of the Crime of Genocide (adopted in 1948); the International Convention on the Elimination of All Forms of Racial Discrimination (1965); the International Covenant on Economic, Social and Cultural Rights (1966); and the International Covenant on Civil and Political Rights (1966). The United States has chosen not to participate in some such covenants.

Some noted that the number of nations abroad adhering to principles, laws, and governmental practices compatible with those of American constitutionalism seemed to be shrinking perceptibly year by year, and nowhere perhaps more noticeably than in Asia.[3] Moreover, setting aside for present purposes the merits of the conflicting positions taken in the American debate over the causes and effects of the Vietnam War, Asian peoples and leaders seemed to see America as either an enemy defeated, a disturbingly unskilled great power, an unreliable ally, or in some other light unflattering to the American ego. The winds were not favorable for human rights and limited government.

It was a good time for mature reflection on the nation's foundations in light of the experience and knowledge of some of Asia's most able jurists and legal scholars. President Jimmy Carter had not yet been nominated, and his controversial and dramatic emphasis on human rights had not yet become an essential element of American foreign policy. Given the costs of three American conflicts in Asia since 1941, and the complexities of wise implementation of the current human rights policy, legal scholars and policy makers might well bend their efforts to understand accurately what friend, foe, and neutral in Asia say and do with respect to law and constitutionalism. Little information, let alone perspective, has been readily available in America on the law and constitutionalism of many Asian nations.[4] Knowledge will not necessarily bring agreement, but it can lead to a valuable state of mind that is difficult to achieve—genuine disagreement. Those who stand in alleged disagreement in Asia and the United States often lack an accurate understanding of their respective positions. One must understand what the other party is saying before he can correctly say he disagrees with that party; this applies with force to dialogue between those of contrasting legal cultures. This symposium serves the causes of both understanding and disagreement between the legal systems of the United States and of some Asian countries. This chapter briefly sketches the colonialist background of constitutionalism in modern Asia,

3. For example, during the early 1970s South Korea, the Philippines, and India joined the list of Asian nations which systematically increased restrictions on public liberties. See "Authority, Emergency, and Development: A Symposium," *Asian Survey*, April, 1978; Raymond D. Gastil, "Comparative Survey of Freedom," *Freedom at Issue* (this periodic survey, the Freedom House Survey of Human Rights, focuses on political rights, not socioeconomic rights); and the following journals which review progress in this field: American Bar Association, *Human Rights*; and International Institute of Human Rights (Strasbourg), *Revue des droits de l'homme*; and United Nations, *Yearbook on Human Rights*, from 1946.

4. A brief bibliography on Asian law and constitutionalism is at the end of this book. Concerning the debate on human rights, see, for example, Stanley Hoffman, "The Hell of Good Intentions," *Foreign Policy*, no. 29 (Winter, 1977-78), p. 8, and Mumtaz Soysal, "Reflections on Peace and Human Rights," 1977 Nobel Peace Prize Lecture, *Matchbox*, Winter, 1978.

comments on a few problems attendant on comparative studies of Asian law and constitutionalism, and identifies views held in common by a number of the Asian authors regarding Asian and American constitutionalism today.

Colonialism and Constitutionalism in Modern Asia

Obviously there is no such thing as "Asian" constitutionalism and law. Asia is a vast region with many countries and over 60 percent of the world's population; each Asian nation—and indeed, each of many subgroups within some Asian countries—has its own separate history and distinctive laws, customary law, and constitutional system. Moreover, many Asian nations have shared as little in common with each other in premodern times as they share now with the United States. Each of the Asian contributors relates history to the law of his country, but some brief comments on the modern colonial setting in Asia are in order here for the reader who is not an Asia specialist.

Elements of cross-national similarity—in traditional governmental system, legal concepts, religion, and colonial history—do loosely link some Asian countries, in sentiment if not often in practical politics. For example, the majority of the world's Muslims live in Asia, as the primary religious grouping in Indonesia, Malaysia, Bangladesh, and Pakistan, and as significant minorities in India, China, the Philippines, and Singapore; the Islamic legal tradition remains an important force in most of those nations. Confucian legal concepts and assumptions continue to affect social, legal, and political life in varying ways in Japan, Korea, China, Vietnam, Singapore, and Malaysia. Particularly in the area of law and constitutional ideas, the British colonial system has left a common mark on India, Pakistan, Bangladesh, Malaysia, Sri Lanka (Ceylon), Burma, Singapore, and Hong Kong. Much earlier, Hindu notions of kingship spread from India over a period of centuries into the Southeast Asia region, and either Mahayana or Theravada Buddhism entered deeply into the life of many East, Southeast, and South Asian peoples. But kaleidoscopic variety greets the student of modern Asia more often than clues to commonality.

The United States and its law have had very little in common with most Asian nations; the context of "revolution" in late-eighteenth-century America bears little resemblance to the circumstances of Asian revolutions and independence movements of the twentieth century. In most parts of Asia, the very discussion of the principles of democratic constitutionalism imbedded in the Declaration of Independence, the United States Constitution, and other Western legal-political documents did not begin until the nineteenth century; independence and consideration of these principles as a desirable or possible alternative approach to law and government usually came much later.

The patterns of colonial history in East Asia differ from those in Southeast and South Asia. Japan fared best in the confrontation with the West during the nineteenth century. After its forced opening in 1854 by the United States, Japan achieved by the early 1900s full independence from the unequal treaty system imposed by the Western imperialist nations, rose to a status of significant international power, and established new legal and constitutional systems based on European civil law models.[5] But Japan's laws and constitution went through fundamental alteration short decades later during the American-dominated Allied Occupation (1945-1952) following World War II.[6]

The territory now divided into the Republic of Korea (South Korea) and the Democratic People's Republic of Korea (North Korea) was an ancient state, unified since A.D. 668, when the "hermit Kingdom" reluctantly opened to intercourse with Japan and the West in the 1870s;[7] it was annexed by Japan in 1910, and remained in that status until the "Liberation" and tragic fissure of 1945, at the hands of the United States, Russia, and other Allied Powers. North Korea and South Korea became opposing independent nations in 1948.[8] The communist North Korean Constitution was changed formally in late 1972, and in effect it enhances the position of Kim Il-sung, leader of that nation since 1948.[9] South Korea's political history has been turbulent, with constitutional modifications attending changes of national leadership in 1960

5. A good analysis of legal developments in pre-1945 modern Japan is Dan Fenno Henderson's "Law and Political Modernization in Japan," in R. E. Ward (ed.), *Political Development in Modern Japan* (Princeton: Princeton University Press, 1968), pp. 387-456. On the history of China, Japan, Korea, and Vietnam generally, see John K. Fairbank et al., *East Asia: Tradition and Transformation* (New York: Houghton-Mifflin, 1973).

6. See J. A. A. Stockwin's survey of the Occupation period in *Japan: Divided Politics in a Growth Economy* (New York: W. W. Norton, 1975), pp. 35-61. Among notable early assessments are Thomas L. Blakemore, "Postwar Developments in Japanese Law," 1947 *Wisconsin Law Review*, pp. 632-653; and *Washington Law Review*, "Legal Reforms in Japan during the Allied Occupation," special reprint volume, 1977. See also, Theodore McNelly, "American Political Traditions and Japan's Postwar Constitution," *World Affairs* (Summer, 1977), pp. 58-66.

7. Pyong-choon Hahm, *The Korean Political Tradition and Law* (Seoul, Korea: Hollym Corporation, Publishers, 1967).

8. Takashi Hatada, *A History of Korea*, trans. W. Smith and B. Hazard (Santa Barbara: ABC Clio Press, 1969); Gregory Henderson, *Korea: The Politics of the Vortex* (Cambridge: Harvard University Press, 1968).

9. A translation of the Constitution of the Democratic People's Republic of Korea (DPRK) of September 9, 1948 (as amended October 22, 1962), can be found in S. Kim and C. Cho, *Government and Politics in Korea* (Silver Spring, Maryland: Research Institute on Korean Affairs, 1972), p. 316. The new Constitution of the DPRK, proclaimed on December 27, 1972, is in *Journal of Korean Affairs*, 2, no. 3 (January, 1973): 46-57; useful articles on law and constitution in North Korea by Sung Yoon Cho and Ilpyong J. Kim appear in the same issue of that journal.

and 1961,[10] and solidifying Park Chung-hee's hold on power in the 1970s.

China's law and government had been evolving within a perennial framework controlled by the Imperial Court and scholar-gentry elites for thousands of years when the Opium War (1839-1842) wrenched open China's doors to trade and led to disruptive challenge of Chinese legal assumptions.[11] After seventy years of encroachments by many Western nations and Japan, the Republic of China was formally established in 1912; but China was still wracked by warlordism, imposed upon by foreign powers under unequal treaties, and then torn by war with an aggressive Japan from 1937 to 1945.[12] All this was followed soon by a costly civil war in fact suspended, but officially continued on either side, with the establishment in 1949 of Mao Tse-tung's People's Republic of China and the migration to Taiwan of the Republic of China under Chiang K'ai-shek and Sun Yat-sen's "Three Principles of the People." The Kuomintang (Nationalist Party) and the Constitution of the Republic of China (1947) on Taiwan, and the Chinese Communist Party and the Constitution of the People's Republic of China (1954, 1975, and 1978) on the mainland, continue to direct their respective peoples along widely separated legal paths. Each regime disputes the legitimacy of the other's claim to rule all China's land and people.[13]

Thus, the present political order in East Asia took shape between 1946 and 1949 after a century of colonialism and internal constitutional

10. Concerning the constitutional developments of 1959 to 1961, see Sungjoo Han, *The Failure of Democracy in South Korea* (Berkeley and Los Angeles: University of California Press, 1974). The "Text of the South Korean Constitution" adopted by referendum on November 21, 1972, is published in *Journal of Korean Affairs*, 3, no. 1 (April, 1973): 39-53. The previous Constitution of the Republic of Korea (1948, as amended through 1969) can be found in Kim and Cho, op. cit., pp. 294-315.

11. See Derk Bodde and Clarence Morris, *Law in Imperial China* (Cambridge: Harvard University Press, 1967).

12. Li Chien-nung, *The Political History of China, 1840-1928* (Stanford: Stanford University Press, 1956).

13. Concerning Republican Chinese law and constitution, see Herbert H. P. Ma's chapter and the works cited therein. An English translation of the Constitution of the Republic of China (December 25, 1946) can be found in Ch'ien Tuan-sheng, *The Government and Politics of China, 1912-1949* (Stanford: Stanford University Press, 1970), pp. 447-461. Also of interest for perspective on earlier legal history is Harold S. Quigley, "Constitutional and Political Development in China under the Republic," *The Annals of the American Academy of Political and Social Science*, no. 211 (November, 1925), pp. 8-14. In general, see Jerome A. Cohen (ed.), *Contemporary Chinese Law: Research Problems and Perspectives* (Cambridge: Harvard University Press, 1970). On law in the People's Republic of China (PRC) of the 1970s, see James L. Seymour, *China: The Politics of Revolutionary Reintegration* (New York: Thomas Y. Crowell Company, 1976), particularly chap. 3; the 1975 Constitution of the PRC is included as an appendix, pp. 287-295.

redefinition. The colonial period there was characterized by shared and partial control by many foreign powers (Great Britain, the United States, France, Russia, Italy, Germany), for varying time periods, of the relatively homogeneous peoples of China, Japan, and Korea, and by the rise of Japan to full participation in colonialist exploitation and eventual outright control of Taiwan, Korea, and much of Manchuria. In contrast, the patterns in the colonial history of South Asia and Southeast Asia show numerous Western nation-states individually asserting exclusive colonialist rights over different specific regional segments, most of which are characterized by ethnic, linguistic, and religious heterogeneity. Great Britain was the paramount power not only in South Asia but also in Singapore and Malaya, following long periods there of first Portuguese and then Dutch colonialism. France dominated the Indochinese area of present-day Vietnam, Cambodia, and Laos, and the Netherlands pursued colonialist profit in that great sprawl of thousands of islands across the southern seas, the Dutch East Indies. The late-coming United States replaced the Spanish as colonial masters of the Philippines at about the turn of the century. What is now the independent state of Papua-New Guinea was under German, British, and finally, until 1975, Australian administration. Much of Southern Asia was also briefly but significantly affected during World War II by Japan, the Asian colonialist that broke the back of Western exploitation and domination in Asia for both Pan-Asian and self-centered motives.[14] To this day, many Asians are much more knowledgeable about their former colonial masters than they are about neighboring Asian nations.

Under dramatically various circumstances post-colonial independent government has come to South and Southeast Asian countries only since 1945. Independence, earned sometimes by rebellion and sometimes through negotiations and cooperation between Asian and Western men, was achieved at different points in the decades following World War II. Where a few colonial empires once prevailed in South and Southeast Asia, today there stand independent (since the year in parentheses) the Philippines (1946),[15] Vietnam (1954), Cambodia (1953),

14. On the South Asian and Southeast Asian contexts, see Keith Buchanan, *The Southeast Asian World* (Garden City, N.Y.: Doubleday and Company, 1968); Robert N. Kearney (ed.), *Politics and Modernization in South and Southeast Asia* (Cambridge: Schenkman Publishing Company, 1975); and Joel Steinberg (ed.), *In Search of Southeast Asia* (New York: Praeger Publishers, 1971). For recent developments and data on all Asian nations, see the annual *Asia Yearbook* published by the *Far Eastern Economic Review* (Hong Kong), *Asiaweek* (Hong Kong), and the monthly *Asian Survey* (University of California Press).

15. Concerning the modern constitutional and legal development of the Philippines, and for related comment on other Asian nations, see chapter 8 and works cited therein.

Laos (1953), Burma (1948), Indonesia (1945),[16] Malaysia (1963),[17] Singapore (1965),[18] Bangladesh (1972),[19] India (1947),[20] Sri Lanka (Ceylon) (1948),[21] Pakistan (1947),[22] and Papua-New Guinea (1975).[23] Monarchical Thailand, the exception, had retained a significant measure of independence throughout the trying colonial period.[24] Attainment of independence did not imply political stability; over the past three decades, major changes of regime and territorial definition in South and Southeast Asia have obstructed efforts to nurture new legal orders in these regions.

Although Asian nations can boast of a richness of cultural heritage equal to that of countries in any world area, all Asian legal systems are, at least in important part, of relatively recent origin. The legal impact of the Western world on Asia has been great. Indigenous legal institutions and ideas have developed alongside of or been deftly integrated or replaced with newer concepts, forms, and processes derived from the Western world.[25] One aspect of these Asian legal developments has been an explosion of innovative, significant, and fascinating constitutional thinking as Asian nations have made, amended, and occasionally remade their constitutions. This phenomenon has been part of a worldwide pattern. The period since World War II has seen more constitution-making and legal change than any comparable time span in world history.

> Over two-thirds of the [world's] existing national constitutions were drafted and promulgated in the last three decades; in the same period

16. Concerning Indonesian constitutionalism, see chapter 5 and works cited therein. Also, Daniel S. Lev, *Islamic Courts in Indonesia* (Berkeley and Los Angeles: University of California Press, 1972).

17. On Malaysia, see chapter 7 and works cited therein.

18. Concerning Singapore's law and constitution, see chapter 9 and works cited therein.

19. Regarding constitutionalism in Bangladesh, see Justice Chowdhury's chapter 2 in this volume.

20. See chapter 4 and writings cited therein.

21. T. Nadaraja, *The Legal System of Ceylon in Its Historical Setting* (Leiden: E. J. Brill, 1972), and Joseph A. L. Cooray, *Constitutional and Administrative Law of Sri Lanka (Ceylon)* (Colombo, Sri Lanka: Hansa Publishers, Ltd., 1973).

22. Concerning Pakistan and the split with East Pakistan, now Bangladesh, see Kearney, op. cit. (n. 14 above).

23. On the diverse law of pre-independence Papua and New Guinea and constitutional developments there, see B. J. Brown (ed.), *Fashion of Law in New Guinea* (Sydney: Butterworth and Company Ltd., 1969).

24. See David M. Engle, *Law and Kingship in Thailand* (Ann Arbor: CSSEAS Publications, 1975); and D. D. Nash and S. Valaisathien, "Thailand: The Courts and the Legal Profession," *Lawasia*, 5 (December 1974), p. 61. Other monarchical nations and principalities in South and Southeast Asia include Nepal, Brunei, Sikkim, Bhutan, and, until it was incorporated into China, Tibet.

25. Henry W. Ehrmann, *Comparative Legal Cultures* (Englewood Cliffs, N.J.: Prentice-Hall, 1976), chap. 1.

> constitutions of many old established nations were either partly or totally revised to fit the new era and its new needs and values.[26]

Sudden twists and turns in constitutional politics having profound impact on legal life continue unabated in the late 1970s, in Asia as in many areas of the world.

The Comparative Study of Constitutionalism and Law: Asia

Because of the colonial era and a continuing interest among Asian elites in Western legal institutions and processes, Asian legal scholars are commonly familiar with Western legalism and constitutionalism, while their legal counterparts in the West are generally ignorant of law and constitutionalism in Asia. Not only are the Asian authors of this book eminently qualified to comment as scholars on the constitutional struggles and legal characteristics of their respective countries, they have also experienced these revolutionary changes personally and directly. However, as in the rest of the world, so also in Asia and about Asia, there has been too little cross-national dialogue on constitutional and legal issues. Detailed studies of specific problems or aspects of individual nations—or, in some cases, of a specific ethnic subgroup within a given country—are a necessary basis for the development of constitutional theory and comparative perspective on legal doctrines; and too few such studies yet exist. Moreover, even when the scholarly stage has been carefully set for the exploration of modest binational, bilegal comparative speculation on a specific issue, it is difficult for the social scientist or legal scholar to see the terms of the comparison in accurate perspective and avoid the temptation to attribute meanings to words, institutions, and sociopolitical contexts that are characteristic of his own country or peculiar to the experience of only one of the nations being compared. Presumptuous and hasty data interpretation and theorizing from a weak basis in knowledge of foreign systems may be encouraged by an academic climate in the social sciences or the legal profession which presumes a priori, as some Americans do, sometimes unwittingly, that the theoretical model necessary for transcultural qualitative judgments on laws, constitutions, politics, and judicial behavior already exists in refined form in the Western world. Indeed, American scholars sometimes assume that their own are precisely the practical standards against which the legal and constitutional behavior

26. Ivo D. Duchacek, *Rights and Liberties in the World Today: Constitutional Promise and Reality* (Santa Barbara: ABC Clio Press, 1973), p. 4. See also, by the same author, *Power Maps: Comparative Politics of Constitutions* (Santa Barbara: ABC Clio Press, 1973); and Richard P. Claude (ed.), *Comparative Human Rights* (Baltimore: Johns Hopkins University Press, 1976).

of other nations may best be judged, without reference to what might be called the ecology of the specific constitutional issue in a foreign society—its history, social environment, and legal background, and the direct effects and probable by-products of alternative solutions to the problem. A further obstacle to the development of a transcultural understanding of constitutionalism and law is the contrary assumption that each cultural system is so unique and separate from the world community that virtually all apparent similarities unearthed by careful, country-specific, and comparative legal studies must be regarded as illusory or insignificant.

Admittedly, the comparative study of legal systems, constitutionalism, and constitutional law is still in its infancy; it will never advance into childhood until the experience of the Asian two-thirds of humankind, as well as that of Africa, is routinely incorporated into comparative discussions of law and constitution. During their Bicentennial visit, data and perspectives on Asian constitutionalism were exchanged by the Asian authors in the process of considering the influence in Asia of America's constitutional ideas and legal institutions. Although each participant spoke or wrote primarily of his own country, some similar concerns and convictions emerged, regarding both Asian and American law and constitutionalism. The remainder of this chapter will indicate the nature and limits of the influence of American law and constitutionalism in Asia, and will highlight some of the common views expressed in the other chapters or in oral dialogue during the Bicentennial program of the Committee on Asian Law in the spring of 1976.

Constitutionalism in Asia and the United States: Some Comparisons

Americans tend to regard the United States as a young country and European and Asian nations as ancient and mature civilizations. If one disregards the antiquity of the foundations of American civilization, this may be a tenable position; but, as was pointed out by Chief Justice Seno Adji, in the history of documentary constitutionalism the United States can more accurately be considered a hoary-headed pioneer of venerable status.[27] The Declaration of Independence, the Constitution of the United States of America, and other early and basic American documents antedate most of the world's foundation documents of constitutional government. The antiquity and relative success of these documents as guides in American constitutional and legal development is one basis for the unfeigned respect shown for American constitutionalism by the Asian contributors and many other Asians. For

27. See chapter 5.

example, former Justice C. G. Weeramantry, mixing praise with criticism, notes:

> America, the first country in the modern world wherein the formulations of human rights and dignity received State recognition without reservation or class distinction, has thus many claims to leadership concerning human rights. It would be ungracious indeed for the Third World to discount the importance of this fact, which contributed so signally to the stream of revolutionary thought which coursed through the nineteenth and twentieth centuries into the liberation movements of our age. The links between Thoreau and Gandhi, between the American Constitution and the Indian and the host of others patterned on it are too real to pass without due recognition.
>
> It is a pity this debt has tended to be obscured by the fact that such a country, for generations the apostle of liberty, independence and the rights of man, has in some of its relationships with the Third World shielded dictatorial regimes against the claims of the oppressed.[28]

But have the Declaration and the Constitution of the United States been relevant to the constitutional and legal needs of contemporary Asian nation-states? If so, in what manner and degree is this relevance manifested? Where it is not considered a suitable set of general guidelines or a model for the constitutionalism of a particular Asian country, what precisely about American constitutionalism, in theory or practice, is found irrelevant or repugnant in which Asian country covered herein? What alternative systems have been preferred by Asian constitutional states? These and similar questions were put to the Asian symposium participants, not only as they prepared to write their papers, but also in public and private discussions with American legal scholars, judges, and lawyers, and with each other.

It is of course impossible to make many salient generalizations about such a diversity of nations, and those that are hazarded here are made with reference to some but not all Asian nations considered. First, let us look at some of the *modes* of American constitutional influence in Asia. One form of influence is found in the fact that some constitution makers consulted as seminal, relevant *documents* the Declaration, the U.S. Constitution, and other American documents when they were in the process of drafting or debating the details and principles of their own nations' constitutions. This mode of recognition as a forerunner in documentary constitutionalism is found in the cases of Indonesia, India, Bangladesh, the Republic of China, the Philippines, and Japan.[29] The latter two used American models out of the political necessities attendant upon American occupation and tutelage, but with general acceptance of most constitutional principles suggested in both cases.

28. Weeramantry, op. cit. (n. 2 above), pp. 67-68.
29. See the chapters on these countries herein, passim.

Moderate nationalist resentments remain in some circles, but adoption of American constitutional and legal ideas was a step that smoothed the way to independence at the time.

A second context for American influence has been the *consultation* of American experts on constitutionalism and law during the process of drawing up, applying, interpreting, or amending a national constitution. Concretely, the views of individual American judges and legal scholars have been solicited during visits by Asian constitutionalists to America; American legal literature (including judicial precedents) has been studied, and one or more Americans have been directly involved in some Asian constitution-making. As noted in the chapters below on Bangladesh and Malaysia and elsewhere, British rather than American influence was of course significant. In the case of Japan, historically a civil law country, Americans wrote most of the Constitution of Japan (1947), Japanese judges often study (even if they do not often cite) precedent of the United States Supreme Court in constitutional cases, and many influential Japanese legal scholars continue to be well informed about American laws and judicial decisions touching on constitutional issues. This or analogous patterns of consultation are found in a number of other Asian systems. A fascinating example of indirect American influence on the Constitution of India (1950) is in Article 21 of that constitution, which adopts the wording in Article 31 of the Constitution of Japan in providing: "No person shall be deprived of his life or personal liberty *except according to procedure established by law*" (the phrasing adopted is in italics).[30] Other instances of consultation will be found in the chapters concerning India and the Philippines. As Justice Fernando makes clear, even in those systems of constitutional law which were not directly affected by the United States there will be found recognition of principles, such as the concepts of judicial review and the supremacy of the constitution, deriving their historical influence in fair part from American constitutionalism.[31]

What are some of the other specific issues and constitutional characteristics in terms of which American influence has been notable in Asia?[32] All of the Asian jurists stressed the rights, equality, and

30. See chapter 4. See Article 21 at p. 15 in Jagdish Lal, *The Constitution of India, as Amended by Forty-second Amendment* [1976] (Delhi, India: Delhi Law House, 1977). Article 31 of the Constitution of Japan: "No person shall be deprived of life or liberty, nor shall any other criminal penalty be imposed, except according to procedure established by law" (H. Itoh and L. W. Beer, *The Constitutional Case Law of Japan* [Seattle, University of Washington Press, 1978], p. 260.)

31. See, for example, chapter 8.

32. Some of the views herein attributed to the Asian participants are a distillation of many discussions with or in the presence of the present writer during the month-long Bicentennial program in the spring of 1976. They do not necessarily represent the views of this writer. Those of the authors contributing to this symposium who were present are

religious values enunciated in the Declaration of Independence: "We hold these truths to be self-evident: that all men are created equal; that they are endowed by their Creator with certain unalienable rights; that among these are life, liberty and the pursuit of happiness." This Declaration is considered by the participants to be one of the few most important human documents enunciating these values. Although there are profound differences of religious concept among the Asian nations represented, all protect freedom of religion; the Islamic states (Malaysia, Indonesia, Bangladesh, Pakistan) and the Christian Philippines emphasize monotheism, as do prevalent American religious concepts. In discussing appropriate *constitutional relationships between religion and the State*, the visiting Asians agreed that the American constitutional doctrine of strict separation is unreasonable, extremely rigid, and in effect possibly inimical to religion and the community.[33] They felt that the central concern should be, not the nonestablishment of a particular religion or religions, but rather the equal and friendly treatment of all religions by the State, without discrimination against any religion. In fact, they found rather strange, even puzzling, the secularist and implicitly antireligious legal bias of some current American constitutional law, in light of the commitment to religious values in the Declaration of Independence and the apparent intent of the Constitution. Can, they ask, a "wall of separation" between Church and State and full exercise of religious freedom coexist? In another context, Professor Ukai, an influential Christian from non-Christian Japan, speculated that perhaps the long-term success of democratic constitutionalism in Japan requires a Christian religious foundation. Whatever the merit of that view, it suggests the broader question: What are the necessary characteristics of a legal, social, philosophical, or religious basis for democracy? In the diversity of Asia, how relate democratic rule-of-law values to Buddhism, Hinduism, Islam, Christianity, and animism?

A second issue on which a number of the contributors agree is the centrality of equality. *Equality was stressed more than freedom*, not because the Asian jurists do not value freedom, but because many Asian nations suffer from serious poverty, maldistribution of goods, and a deep gap between a small, privileged elite and most other citizens. In part, the economic problem is seen as a direct result of colonial systems that restructured traditional economic life to produce com-

---

Chief Justice Seno Adji, Professor Ukai, Tun Suffian, and Justice Fernando; in addition, a paper by Dr. Tripathi (unable to attend owing to a last-minute complication) was read at a number of public panel presentations.

33. This view is also expressed in this volume; see, for example, chapter 5 and chapter 7.

modities in kind and quantity desired by colonialist traders and functionaries. For example, Sri Lanka was forced to cut back on rice production and to grow tea for export, while Burma became a major rice exporter under British rule.[34] The tendency today is to put *less emphasis on individual private property rights than on economic justice*, and more stress on policies leading toward economic prosperity for the generality of citizens. The Asian jurists were particularly sharp in their criticisms of America's allegedly excessive emphasis on private property to the detriment of economic equality. The contention was that the U.S. Constitution, as it has developed through legislative, administrative, and judicial interpretation, has come to serve special economic interests much more assiduously than it has pursued the contrary ideals of equality, life, and the pursuit of happiness in the Declaration of Independence. Interpretations of the Constitution which in effect protect economic "liberty," for example, at the expense of economic viability and education for all citizens are seen as a possible betrayal of the spirit of the Declaration by the United States. At the same time, the "state action theory" of some American law, and also government entry into the private sector to regulate the use of resources and to correct discrimination in housing and employment, and into the political arena to equalize political campaign financing, were seen as doctrines in keeping with the true spirit of the Declaration of Independence and the best in the U.S. Constitution.

Third, the necessary linkage seen by many Americans between economic liberty in a free enterprise system and civil liberties is not easily accepted by many of the Asian jurists. *Political liberties and civil rights are separable from economic liberty and property rights* and are to be more vigilantly protected; but this socialist leaning does not imply "pro-communism."

Fourth, a common view expressed is that *freedom of speech and freedom of the press should be protected*, but only insofar as they do not excessively disrupt the development and functioning of the political or the economic order. Given the fragility and youth of some political arrangements and economic systems in Asia, as well as patently existing internal or external sources of possible threat to some regimes, such views are not necessarily self-serving prevarications. As our Bicentennial guests from Asia found through personal exchanges in the United States, relatively few American constitutional lawyers and political observers are likely to refrain from harsh attributions of authoritarianism and political evil whenever they perceive restraints of liberty, whether it be economic liberty, free speech, freedom of assembly, or

34. Buchanan, op. cit. (n. 14 above), pp. 24 and 78-86; and Weeramantry, op. cit. (n. 2 above), pp. 38-68.

freedom of the press. Torture or prolonged incarceration without trial for peaceable acts of dissent from political policy are of course incompatible with any system of genuine constitutionalism; but interpretations at variance with common American views of rights in areas of other issues were not rare. America does not face political and economic problems analogous to those of most Asian nations which affect the status of freedom and law. Moreover, like scholars in some European democracies, most of the Asian jurists took issue with the absolutist tone of some legal interpretations of the First Amendment to the U.S. Constitution, as being both unpersuasive and unrealistic. On the other hand, Professor Ukai felt that a near absolutist posture was needed in Japan in order to encourage citizens to exercise rights and liberties granted only some thirty years ago, in light of Japan's prior modern history of governmental and social restrictions.[35] The relative stability of Japan's economic and sociopolitical order adds to the plausibility of Professor Ukai's position; but other Asian jurists critically contrasted the "social responsibility theory" of freedom with American "absolutist theory."

Fifth, the status of individual *rights and liberties under "martial law" regimes and "emergency" declarations* was discussed on a number of occasions and is touched on here and there in this volume. The suspension of legal or constitutional rights or both has occurred under many constitutional traditions, legal provisions, and political situations in Asia since World War II; but reliable generalizations about the empirical status of rights in such circumstances—the degree and consistency of restraints, popular support or resentment of the same, the significance of their effects on the system, and the intent of ruling elites in restricting certain types of activity normally thought lawful in a country—are not easily arrived at. For example, Lord President Tun Suffian noted in public session that although the King of Malaysia has utilized his constitutional power to declare an "emergency" on the advice of the Prime Minister three times in recent decades, an emergency has not in fact implied a suspension of civil liberties. He added that this may seem unusual, particularly in a nation where civil liberties are generally less of a preoccupation than are socioeconomic and cultural rights. (He might have added that the critical importance of a semblance of communal harmony among the majority Malays, and the Chinese and Indians of Malaysia, suggests the rationality of quiet restraint on speech likely to foment violence, judging from past tragedies.) Tun Suffian also pointed out that Malaysian law concerning emergencies derives from British legal practice in India prior to Inde-

35. Relevant to this point is Richard H. Mitchell, *Thought Control in Prewar Japan* (Ithaca and London: Cornell University Press, 1976).

pendence, which copied British legal thinking on an earlier Palestinian situation, which in turn goes back finally to English policy during the Irish "troubles" of the early twentieth century. Justice Chowdhury in his paper maintains that the *suspension* of rights and of Superior Court jurisdiction to protect them by the emergency proclamation of late 1974 did not *abrogate* rights, but left them in a temporary state of "animated suspension." Justice Fernando, while emphasizing the great importance of the issuance of writs of *habeas corpus* in the Philippines system of judicial review, said that recent denials of such writs to political prisoners under the presidential emergency powers of the present "Martial Law Constitution" of the Philippines rely on American legal precedent and constitutional doctrine of both the Civil War period and the colonialist era in the Philippines. Professor Ma of National Taiwan University points out that the principles of *habeas corpus* have been incorporated into Chinese law and constitution under American influence, but that the interpretation of the relevant provisions requires intelligent adaptation of foreign legal techniques, both European and Anglo-American, to the Chinese legal context.[36]

The severity of the threats to a system and the rigidity of governmental restraints on individual rights can be balanced only by regard both for theory and for detailed studies of the ecology of rights and freedom in each nation. Groping for a fair assessment of some Asian systems, Michael Brecher has maintained that a clear democratic thrust exists in the regimes and elites of most "middle zone" Asian states, which sets them off from the less open Asian communist systems:

> But in none of these states is authoritarianism total; this is one vital distinction between communist governments and those of the "middle zone." Another difference is the commitment in principle to "democracy," though this has lessened in recent years; but even among those who seek alternative paths to a stable political system, there is acceptance of the idea of change in the political elite, protection for individual and minority rights, the notion of choice by the governed as to who shall be the governors, and other components of "democracy." Because of these commitments and the possibility of change in the political system, these authoritarian regimes are potentially closer to the substance of democracy than to the rigid closed political system of communism.[37]

In the contributions to this symposium, one of the American constitutional institutions most frequently cited as important and relevant is the *judicial review* of laws and other acts of government in light of constitutional requirements. Judicial review directly inspired by American precedent was written into the 1947 Constitution of Japan

36. See chapter 3.

37. Michael Brecher, *The New States of Asia: A Political Analysis* (New York: Oxford University Press, 1966), p. 48; see also the symposium cited in n. 3 above.

(Chapter VI, Articles 76 to 82) during the Occupation; but, as in other Asian nations such as Indonesia, the coexistence of judicial independence and judicial review powers with aspects of civil law tradition limits in theory, law, or practice or all three the judicial assertion of review powers.[38] Continental German, Swiss, French (e.g., in Japan, China, Korea) and Dutch (in Indonesia and Sri Lanka) legal thinking and interpretive approaches have been notable formative factors in modern Asian law. Dr. Tripathi's chapter explicates the American influence on incorporation of judicial review into the Constitution of India and indicates the negative effects on legislative development and on rights protection itself of subsequent citizen reliance on judicial review for the solution of an excessive range and number of problems.[39] The Federal Court of Malaysia has and makes moderate use of the power of judicial review, a constitutional feature adapted from the Constitution of India.[40]

An American type of *federalism* has not been characteristic of constitutionalism in Asian countries; but the U.S. pattern has been consulted in the process of devising systems of limited local autonomy in India and Japan.[41] Indonesia's "United States of Indonesia" (January to August, 1950) experimented briefly with federalism but found it impossible in a system composed of hundreds of ethnic groups and over 13,000 islands.[42] Professor Ma of China notes the importance of American influence on the federalist strain of early republican constitutional thinking, and the movement in the 1920s for "United Autonomous Provinces."[43] The Federation of Malaysia, building unity out of long-existing autonomous sultanates, operates under a distinctive system contrasting clearly with the American federal modes. For example, federal subjects for judicial review include education and police matters, and Malaysia's king (the Yang Dipertuan Agung) is elected for a five-year term from among the hereditary sultans of the federal states by a Conference of Rulers; he is a constitutional monarch, not a president.[44] All other nations in Asia are unitary in constitutional structure.

38. See chapter 5. Concerning the differences between law and judicial practice in civil law and common law countries, see John Henry Merryman, *The Civil Law Tradition* (Stanford: Stanford University Press, 1969). An accurate American assessment of the status of judicially protected rights, for example, in a civil law country must take into account the contrasts in judicial function and powers flowing from the two major Western legal traditions.

39. See chapter 4.

40. Oral comments of Tun Suffian. See also his *An Introduction to the Constitution of Malaysia*, 2nd ed. (Kuala Lumpur: Ibrahim Bin Johari, Government Printer, 1976), pp. 105-110.

41. See chapters 4 and 6. 42. See chapter 5. 43. See chapter 3.

44. See chapter 7, and Tun Suffian, *An Introduction* (chap. 3).

The *executive systems* of governmental Asia owe little to the American presidency, except in the cases of the Philippines and Indonesia; but with respect to his powers, the President of the Republic of China resembles the American President.[45] The Indonesian President's position was originally modeled in part on the American system, Chief Justice Seno Adji points out, but the office is not balanced against legislative and judicial organs in the American manner.[46] In 1975, constitutional amendments under Martial Law Regulations by Parliament made the President of Bangladesh more powerful than the American President, and reduced the considerable powers vested in the Prime Minister by the 1972 Constitution.[47] Most democratically elected Asian executives are parliamentary prime ministers in a cabinet system deriving its forms, at least in part, from the British Parliament. In addition, a rich tradition of distinctive *monarchical systems* continues to live in the constitutions, written and unwritten, of a number of Asian nations. The unique kingship system of Malaysia has been mentioned. In Japan, the Emperor Hirohito is the latest of an ancient line of hereditary monarchs; he is now a symbol of national unity in the Constitution of Japan, is explicitly denied any governmental powers, and is technically not a head of state. Except during the period from 1868 until 1945, and then only formally, the Emperor has very rarely held any significant political power in the past thousand years.[48] Other kingship systems are found in Thailand, Laos, Nepal, and the Himalayan principalities. In Thailand, for example, perhaps the most stable and popular element in constitutionalism, despite changes in government and in constitutional document, is the hereditary kingship system.

Patterns of *written constitutional change* vary strikingly in Asia, but American influence on amendment processes has rarely been significant. Constitutions have been amended often in India and Malaysia, but never in Japan. Indonesia too has been reluctant to employ its amendment process.[49] The Constitution of India, already the longest constitution in the world, can be amended by a majority vote with "a majority of not less than two-thirds of the members" of each house "present and voting."[50] Forty-two amendments have been passed, with complications analyzed in this volume by Dr. Tripathi.[51] The amendment process under the Constitution of Malaysia is modeled on that of India, but establishes different requirements for different categories of amendment; in all, there had been seventeen amendments in seventeen

45. See chapter 3. 46. See chapter 5. 47. See chapter 2.

48. David A. Titus, *Palace and Politics in Prewar Japan* (New York: Columbia University Press, 1974).

49. See chapter 5. 50. Article 368, in *Constitution of India*, p. 173.

51. See chapter 4.

years by the beginning of 1976.[52] On the other hand, the fear that any amendment will imply wholesale anti-democratic revision of the Consituation has rendered politically impossible any utilization of the amendment provisions of Japan's Constitution.[53] *Replacement* of one constitution with another as a means of change has occurred in the Philippines (1972), Indonesia (1966, a returning to the 1945 Constitution), Burma (1974),[54] and the People's Republic of China (1975 and 1978).

In summary, the American influence in Asian constitutionalism is manifest in the utilization of American sources, from the Declaration of Independence and the Constitution of the United States to the Gettysburg Address to more recent judicial decisions, and in the direct or indirect adaptation of American institutions such as legally protected liberty and judicial review. Federalism and the American system of separation of powers have not been exported to Asia. In the area of individual rights and liberties, the Asian contributors have found fault with American notions of absolute freedom of expression, property rights, and separation of religion and the State, but much inspiration in the emphasis on the equality of persons, the right to self-government, human dignity, and the pursuit of economic justice found in America's constitutional documents and experience. All express commitment to the principle of the supremacy of the law of the constitution in their respective countries.

As the United States picks her way through the next century of constitutional development, the constitutional strains and wisdom arising from the current era of experimentation in Asia's politico-legal cultures will deserve the attention of American judges and constitutional lawyers. One measure of the constitutional maturity of the United States in the twenty-first century may well be the degree of American openness to the reception of legal and constitutional influences flowing from Asia and other non-Western regions.

52. Oral comments of Tun Suffian, and his *Introduction*, pp. 337-343.

53. Article 96, Constitution of Japan, in Itoh and Beer, op. cit. (n. 30 above), p. 268.

54. The Constitution of the Socialist Republic of the Union of Burma, adopted January 3, 1974.

II

Bangladesh

Editorial Note

Prior to August 1947, when India was still part of the British Empire, one of its large and populous states was known as Bengal. Its capital and its center of transportation, communication, commerce, industry, and education was the city of Calcutta. The first university in India of the English type was established in Calcutta in 1857. Bengal had a substantial Muslim population whose ancestors had been converted to that faith in the twelfth century as an aftermath of the Turks' capture of Delhi in 1191. In August 1947 these Muslim majority districts of Bengal became the eastern wing of Pakistan—separated by more than a thousand miles from the western segment of Pakistan. By 1971—some twenty-four years later—East Pakistan had demanded its autonomy and, with the aid of the Indian Army, achieved its independence after the Pakistan Army surrendered on December 16, 1971. This new nation was called Bangladesh.

Bangladesh is the most densely populated nation in the world except for the very small nation of Singapore. Its population in 1978 was estimated at 87 million—an average of about 1,500 persons for each of its 55,000 square miles (a little larger than England). Its capital is Dacca, a city with a population of over one million. Bangladesh is bordered on the west, north, and east by India; to the south lies the Bay of Bengal; it shares a short border with Burma to the southeast. No point in Bangladesh is more than a hundred miles from the border of India. Most of the country is a flat, alluvial plain—never more than five hundred feet above sea level. It is a nation of rivers flowing south into the Bay of Bengal and adding more silt to the extensive delta.

Bangladesh has a tropical monsoon climate with heavy rainfall. About 94 percent of the population lives in villages; 80 percent depends on agriculture for subsistence. It is difficult land on which to build substantial structures: foundations are soft and floods are frequent. Calcutta, which once provided extensive services to this area, now lies across the border in India.

The citizens of East Pakistan (as the area was called from 1947 to 1971) were never satisfied with their treatment by the national government in the west. Although the population of East Pakistan exceeded that of the western segment, Pakistan's national government never placed a high priority on the development of its eastern province. The people of West Pakistan dominated the armed forces, the civil services, industry, and commerce. The two parts of Pakistan spoke entirely different languages. Although the eastern province earned most of the nation's foreign exchange through jute sales, it was the west that decided how to spend it. In 1978 Bangladesh continued to have an agricultural economy that relied principally on rice, tea, jute, and sugarcane. Its annual per capita income was approximately $70 (U.S.). Only 20 percent of the population was literate.

Bangladesh shares with the rest of the Indian subcontinent a common governmental heritage. In the eighteenth century the British East India Company became the principal commercial organization in India and, after victory in two military engagements, had emerged as the undisputed ruler of Bengal by 1764. A century later the Company had been replaced by the British government, and Bengal was governed in the name of the Crown. A penal code, a code of criminal procedure, a civil code, an administrative code, and a civil service system were prepared by the British for India. The system and its procedures were carefully designed to facilitate British control of the subcontinent and also to give the natives an opportunity to learn self-government. At times these two objectives seemed inconsistent. The Government of India Act of 1935 set the pattern for the original constitutions of independent India, Pakistan, and even Bangladesh.

The immediate events in Pakistan which led to the independence of Bangladesh may be recounted briefly. Military officers and retired civil servants had been running Pakistan for most of its brief history. In 1970 Pakistan scheduled its first general election. The results of the voting in that election showed massive support in East Pakistan for the Awami

League and its leader, Sheikh Mujibur Rahman. Surprisingly, the Awami League also won a majority of the seats in the National Assembly without winning a single seat in West Pakistan. Thus the logical head of government would be Mujibur Rahman except for the fact that he had campaigned on a platform of autonomy for East Pakistan and was therefore unacceptable to the leaders of West Pakistan.

The new National Assembly never met. No compromise could be reached; there were strikes and riots in East Pakistan. On March 25, 1971, the Pakistan Army attacked. There was devastation. Mujibur Rahman was arrested and flown to West Pakistan. An estimated ten million refugees fled to India, and ultimately the Indian Army entered East Pakistan and forced the surrender of the Pakistan Army on December 16, 1971. The following month Mujibur Rahman was released from prison and became Prime Minister of the newly created nation of Bangladesh; Abu Sayeed Chowdhury became President (see footnotes 5 and 10). By the end of 1972 a Constitution had been prepared by a Constituent Assembly consisting of those elected from East Pakistan in the 1970 elections. In March 1973 elections were held under the new Constitution, and Mujibur Rahman's Awami League party won 305 of 313 seats.

President Abu Sayeed Chowdhury resigned in December 1973 and was succeeded by Professor Mohammadullah. By the end of 1974 the deteriorating political situation caused the President, at the request of Prime Minister Mujibur Rahman, to proclaim emergency rule and suspend the fundamental rights contained in the Constitution of 1972. The Constitution was also amended to provide for a system of presidential supremacy. On August 15, 1975, Mujibur Rahman was assassinated and Khondakar Mushtaque Ahmed was named President (see footnote 11). In November 1975 he resigned in favor of a former Chief Justice of the Supreme Court, Abusat Mohammad Sayem. A little more than eighteen months later, on April 21, 1977, President Sayem resigned for health reasons and nominated Major General Ziaur Rahman, who continued to hold the posts of Chief of Army Staff and Chief Martial Law Administrator, to succeed him as President. The new President immediately ordered the amendment of the Constitution to eliminate a reference to Bangladesh as a secular state and inserted in its place an expression of absolute faith in Allah. Other changes made the Constitution amendable by a simple majority vote of the membership of Parliament and provided a procedure by which Supreme and High Court judges could be removed by the President.

In a referendum held in May 1977, 85 percent of the electorate reportedly went to the polls, and almost 99 percent voted in support of

General Ziaur Rahman as President of Bangladesh. Nevertheless, the situation remains unstable. In early October 1977 an abortive coup occurred and was promptly suppressed, but five hundred persons were said to have been tried as a result, and ninety-two received the death penalty.

May 16, 1978 HENRY F. GOODNOW

The Bangladesh Constitution in American Perspective

Mr. Justice Abu Sayeed Chowdhury
Past President of Bangladesh

The American Experience

American celebration of the bicentenary of its independence is in effect renewal of its determination to pursue a way of life as visualized in the declaration of its independence and in its Constitution. It reminds the world of its pledge for democracy founded on the basic principle of consideration for others. America derived benefit of the experiences acquired since the discovery of the New World from men and women from all over the world and built it up by dedicated and collective efforts for the welfare of the people of America and the peace and happiness of the peoples of the world.

The way of life cherished in its Constitution is mainly based on its well-founded and well-recognized principle of the "government of laws and not of men." Implicit in this American concept is that nothing can happen without due process of law, and the United States has provided its judiciary with all facilities to do justice in all circumstances, and the mechanism is laid on a foundation, solid and stable.

Americans wanted liberty. When that was denied, they were left with no other course than to demand complete and full independence, which they achieved by their determination and steadfast adherence to and firm faith in the cause they were upholding. Liberty, it is well established, consists in the power of a person to perform an act which would not infringe on the right of another. The principle of common good as conceived in a civilized society implies limitation of the power of an individual in that he is free to act in any manner—so long as he does not stifle the natural rights of another person. None of his actions claimed to be in pursuance of his fundamental rights can encroach upon those of others.

There is an eternal human yearning for an individual to be free to act, think, and move about with his head erect and conscience clear so long as he does not violate other supervening principles established for the common good of the people. Limitation on such powers can be discerned in the police power, taxation power, eminent domain, and such other powers limiting the fundamental rights in the interest of the State as a whole.

Salient features of the United States Constitution such as the doctrine of *ultra vires*, separation of powers, the enumeration of inalienable human rights, and well-planned checks and balances have influenced many written constitutions since the adoption of the Constitution in Philadelphia in 1787. Since that year these principles designed to uphold human liberty have been adopted in varying degrees in written constitutions adopted in many parts of the world, including Bangladesh.

It is true that for some time America became indifferent to other nations of the world. After a period of isolationism America was brought by force of circumstances to play its destined role in the development of the modern world; and the Second World War led America to be a founding member of the United Nations and enshrine the principles upholding human dignity and honor in its Charter. These formulations placed man above everything else, and the world body was entrusted with the solemn and historic duty of upholding the cherished ideals of civilization and the dignity of man.

The nations that believed in a representative form of government, whether presidential or parliamentary, gained much from the American experiences and the fruits of the struggle to make the world "safe for democracy." In fact, President Woodrow Wilson when declaring war on Germany in 1917 emphasized the philosophy of life which guided the thoughts and deeds of the great American people. In his ringing voice he told the Congress that America would enter the war "for the rights and liberties of small nations, for a universal dominion of right by such a concert of free peoples as shall bring peace and safety to all nations and make the world at last free. To such a task we can dedicate our lives and fortune." It was in fact a reiteration of cherished goals of mankind as contemplated in the U.S. Constitution and its various amendments.

The Path to Bangladesh Independence

Bangladesh is a new country with an ancient civilization and culture. As its mighty rivers flow down one can hear, in their murmurs, the music that was heard thousands of years ago. The enchanting beauty of its vast green fields spreading to the distant horizon and its azure blue sky still reveal the beauty witnessed since the dawn of civilization. The people inhabiting the land are well known for emotion, a strong sense of values, hospitality, friendliness, a capacity to face challenges, endure sufferings, bear losses calmly, meet the demands of the occasion, and retain firm faith in God.

The territory now known as Bangladesh was a part of British India, and on the achievement of independence in 1947, it became a province of Pakistan and was called East Pakistan. People of this area took a remarkable part in the quest for independence during British days and acquired considerable political consciousness.[1] They became fully aware of their legitimate rights and privileges.[2]

The first British step according some recognition to the struggle for independence was the Government of India Act (1919), which declared that its aim was to establish "a responsible government as an integral part of the British Empire." This naturally failed to satisfy the growing aspirations of the sub-continent. The Act was to be reviewed after a period of ten years, but the time was shortened and a commission headed by Sir John Simon was appointed to report about constitutional reforms. There was no one from the sub-continent itself on the commission, and it was claimed that such a task could not be accomplished without someone having intimate and close association with the thoughts and prevailing ideas in the sub-continent; so the commission suffered from lack of cooperation. It submitted its report on May 27, 1930. Thanks to the good efforts of Lord Irwin, three successive round-table conferences could be held to find an acceptable solution; but unfortunately they failed to work out an agreed framework for the constitution.

The British Parliament, however, rightly felt that it was high time to act and, if necessary, to act unilaterally. And so it did, by enacting a valuable document called the Government of India Act (1935). Elaborate and detailed in its provisions, the Act provided the foundation on which all constitutional exercises were made in the sub-continent. This Act introduced a federal form of government to which princely states were also to accede.

Although the part relating to the federation could not be put into operation at all, the provincial governments as provided in the Act came into existence and worked satisfactorily. The federal form provided therein worked as a model to the framers of constitutions in both India and Pakistan after the achievement of independence in 1947.

1. Leonard Gordon, *Bengal: The Nationalist Movement, 1876-1940* (New York: Columbia University Press, 1974).

2. Concerning the modern constitutional development of India, see R. G. Aggarwala, *Constitutional History of India and National Movement* (Delhi: S. Chand & Co., 1964); Sankar Ghose, *The Western Impact on Indian Politics (1885-1919)* (Bombay: Allied Publishers, 1967); Granville Austen, *The Indian Constitution* (New York: Oxford University Press, 1966), and chapters 4 and 6 of this work.

When the Second World War was raging, renewed efforts were made to arrive at a constitutional settlement satisfactory to the sub-continent. With that end in view, a mission led by Sir Stafford Cripps, an eminent British jurist and statesman, went to India in 1942, but again no accepted formula could be found. It was felt that Sir Stafford was very genuine in his efforts, and naturally high hopes were raised, but as the political parties failed to reach agreement, these hopes were dashed to the ground.

Soon after cessation of hostilities, the question of framing a suitable constitution for the sub-continent was again taken up. Lord Pethick-Lawrence, the then Secretary of State for India, led another mission for the purpose. It presented a scheme of its own in May 1946. It recommended that an elected Constituent Assembly should be entrusted with the work of framing a constitution for the sub-continent. It also brought into existence an interim government at the centre. But a constitution could not be framed without settling the demand for partition between India and Pakistan, which had grown into a gigantic mass movement.[3]

The British government by then became anxious to transfer power to the sub-continent, for it knew when to leave, and the British Parliament enacted the Indian Independence Act in 1947. As the political parties by then had agreed to partition the sub-continent, Britain handed over its responsibilities to two independent dominions, India and Pakistan, amidst universal friendliness for Britain, without bitterness, without rancour. The American attitude at the time of the severance of its connection with Britain was perhaps not the same.

The two wings of Pakistan were separated by more than twelve hundred miles. They had, however, many things in common. As was already noted, the people of East Pakistan, now known as Bangladesh, took full part in the struggle for independence from Britain. Such a politically conscious people now clamoured for equality of rights and opportunities as visualized in the United States Constitution, and the struggle which started soon after achievement of Pakistan in 1947 culminated in the emergence of Bangladesh as a sovereign and independent republic on December 16, 1971, after twenty-four years of working together.[4]

3. Khalid B. Sayeed, *Pakistan: The Formative Phase, 1857-1948* (London: Oxford University Press, 1960); G. W. Choudhury, *Constitutional Development in Pakistan* (London: Longman, 1969, 2nd ed.); and Sir Ivor Jennings, *Constitutional Problems in Pakistan* (Cambridge: Cambridge University Press, 1957).

4. Rounaq Jahan, *Pakistan: Failure in National Integration* (New York: Columbia University Press, 1972); Wayne Wilcox, *The Emergence of Bangladesh* (Washington, D.C.: American Enterprise Institute, 1973); G. W. Choudhury, *The Last Days of United Pakistan* (Bloomington: Indiana University Press, 1974).

Independent Bangladesh then adopted a parliamentary Constitution on the fourth day of November, 1972;[5] the first election under this Constitution was held in the beginning of 1973.[6]

The 1972 Constitution of Bangladesh and the Emergency

This Constitution when first adopted in 1972 provided for a parliamentary form of government, although the Prime Minister and not the Cabinet was made all powerful, deviating from the theory of collective responsibility. In fact, by virtue of Article 55 (2) of the Constitution, all executive authority was to be exercised by the Prime Minister.

Suddenly, at the end of 1974, an Emergency was declared;[7] fundamental rights were suspended, and the Superior Courts, which were to enforce them, were divested of the authority to do so against any executive action infringing them. Suspension, however, does not mean abrogation; it means that these rights remain in a state of animated suspension. The moment the suspension order is removed, they would be revived. Even before the proclamation of the Emergency, the Prime Minister in reality possessed all the powers, and as such its need was widely doubted.

The Prime Minister possessed unlimited powers even otherwise by reason of a number of Presidential Orders or Ordinances which were later protected by the Parliament by a saving clause of the Constitution. A list of these Orders and Ordinances was given in a schedule of the Constitution as passed by the Parliament prohibiting by a constitutional provision any attack on them; many of their provisions were violative of the fundamental rights.[8]

5. *The Constitution of the People's Republic of Bangladesh*, passed by the Constituent Assembly of Bangladesh on Nov. 4, 1972, and authenticated by the Speaker on Dec. 14, 1972 (Dacca: Constituent Assembly of Bangladesh, 1972). See Rounaq Jahan, "Bangladesh in 1972: Nation Building in a New State," *Asian Survey*, Feb. 1973, pp. 199-210; M. M. Sankhdher, "Bangladesh Constitution: A Content Analysis," *Journal of African and Asian Studies*, 4, no. 1 (March-April 1973): 23-34; and Abul Fazl Huq, "Constitution-Making in Bangladesh," *Pacific Affairs*, 46, no. 1 (Spring 1973): 59-76. The latter author notes, at p. 60: "Justice Abu Sayeed Chowdhury, a former High Court Judge and Vice-Chancellor of Dacca University (one of the few intellectuals who had actively participated in the liberation movement and yet was not aligned with any political party), became the new president of the Republic. If integrity and impartiality are considered essential qualities of the head of the state, there could have been no better choice for the presidency."

6. Concerning the March elections and other 1973 developments, see Rounaq Jahan, "Bangladesh in 1973: Management of Factional Politics," *Asian Survey*, Feb. 1974, pp. 125-135.

7. On events of 1974 and the emergency decree of December 28, see Talukder Maniruzzaman, "Bangladesh in 1974: Economic Crisis and Political Polarization," *Asian Survey*, Feb. 1975, pp. 117-128, and "Bangladesh," *Keesing's Contemporary Archives*, Jan. 20-26, 1975, pp. 26924-26925.

8. *Keesing's*, p. 26925.

The Constitution also made it a unitary form of government and it continues to be so.

The United States Constitution and the Bangladesh Constitution

Geographically, Bangladesh is a homogeneous territory inhabited by a people speaking the same language, inheriting the same traditions, culture, thoughts, and ideas. The question of a federal form of government therefore did not arise, and the framers of the Constitution were therefore relieved of the many problems which confronted the Convention at Philadelphia.

We may now have a closer look at the Bangladesh Constitution and the American impact thereon. The U.S. Constitution declares in its Preamble:

> We the people of the United States, in order to form a more perfect union, establish justice, insure domestic tranquility, provide for the common defense, promote the general welfare, secure the blessings of liberty to ourselves and our posterity, do ordain and establish this Constitution for the United States of America.

The Bangladesh Constitution, also in its Preamble, pledges that its aim is to realize a society free from exploitation and that fundamental human rights and freedom and equality and justice will be secured for all citizens. Resemblance between the two is apparent.

The Bangladesh Constitution is an all-embracing document providing for a mechanism of administration practically in all constitutional spheres.[9] It consists of 153 Articles in 11 Parts. Part I deals with the republic, declares Bengali the State language, provides for citizenship, and other matters. Part II is devoted to fundamental principles of State for the guidance of the government and the Parliament, but these are not enforceable by courts. Part III is the most important, relating to fundamental rights recognized by the Parliament and enforceable by Superior Courts when there is no suspension order on account of any proclamation of emergency. Part IV is divided into five chapters and deals with the executive branch of the government. Part V provides for Parliament, and for legislative and financial procedures and ordinance-making powers. Part VI provides for the judiciary, Part VII deals with elections, Part VIII provides for the Comptroller and Auditor General, and Part IX deals with the armed services of Bangladesh. The procedure for amendment of the Constitution is to be found in Part X. Miscellaneous matters have been laid down in Part XI. This outline should give an idea of the structure of the Constitution itself.

9. See note 5 above.

As was already noted, the Bangladesh Constitution has enumerated fundamental rights in a chapter. A study of these rights would at once make it clear that in their formulation Magna Carta (1215), the Petition of Rights (1628), the Bill of Rights (1689), and the Constitution of the United States of America, together with its amendments, were kept in mind. It is in this part of the Constitution that the full benefit of the written Constitution of the United States was taken as a model, and in fact, in dealing with these provisions the courts in Bangladesh freely refer to the judicial pronouncements of the Superior Courts of Britain, America, and the Commonwealth countries. Bangladesh is a sovereign and independent republic, and these decisions are certainly not binding on Bangladesh courts, but the views expressed by them are taken into consideration as and when similar questions arise, just as those courts also refer to judicial pronouncements of Superior Courts of other countries.

The chapter on fundamental rights begins by adopting the doctrine of *ultra vires*, for it expressly declares that all existing law inconsistent with those rights as enumerated therein shall be void to the extent of inconsistency; it incorporates a prohibition to the effect that the State shall not make any laws inconsistent with those rights, and if so made they would also be void. It is clear that an order made by the State, if challenged, has to be referable to some law of the land, and if there is no law supporting the executive order, or even if there is one and that law is inconsistent with fundamental law, the law must be declared void, and the executive order set aside.

Perhaps the most important of all rights enumerated therein is Article 27 of the Bangladesh Constitution, which reads: "All citizens are equal before law and entitled to equal protection of law." Broadly speaking, this Article confers the right to equality as visualized in the Fourteenth Amendment to the U.S. Constitution.

The principle of equality before the law contemplates that the courts must treat all citizens as subject to the ordinary law of the land and they must enjoy equal protection of law. It will therefore be seen that the obligation imposed on the State is to secure to a person equality before the law and also to give equal protection thereof. It is true that in the Fourteenth Amendment to the U.S. Constitution the expression "equality before the law" does not occur; but it must be remembered that the expression "equal protection of the laws" occurs therein; and in this context one has to bear in mind that the expression "due process of law" is so elastic in its ideas that in its application it does include "equality before the law" as well.

This Article of the Bangladesh Constitution prohibits discrimination in any shape or manner. One cannot arbitrarily pick and choose any person or class of persons under the law. In other words, the law should be equal and equally administered, and the like should be treated alike. Without going into detailed examination of this principle, one would say that it is one of the most important of all the rights conferred on a citizen, for it is an injunction against discrimination in applying the law. Moreover, Article 28 prohibits discrimination on grounds of race, colour, sex, or place of birth.

Similarly, Article 29 provides for the equality of opportunity in public appointment. Article 32 guarantees that no person shall be deprived of life and personal liberties except in accordance with law. Article 33 provides that a person who is arrested shall not be detained unless informed of the grounds of arrest and shall have the right to be defended by a lawyer of his choice. A person so detained has to be brought before a court of law within twenty-four hours.

Articles 39, 40, and 41 provide for freedom of thought and conscience, freedom of profession and occupation, and freedom of religion. Articles 42 and 43 provide for the rights to property and protection of home and correspondence. A study of the Amendments to the U.S. Constitution would show that these cherished principles were incorporated therein.

In a parliamentary form of government provision is made for a head of state who represents the State as distinguished from the government; as such, after election the President belongs to the country as a whole and not to a party and is looked upon as a symbol of national unity and national dignity. Bangladesh also provided for a President to be elected by the Parliament; by virtue of Article 48 (2), as head of the state "he shall take precedence over all other persons in the State." It was also provided that all executive actions of the government were to be expressed as taken in the name of the President. He was by another Article made Supreme Commander of the armed forces, and the officers of the government were to hold office during his pleasure. He is also to appoint constitutional functionaries like the Prime Minister, Ministers, Judges of the Superior Courts, Attorney General, and Auditor General. He was invested with legislative functions as well when the Parliament was not in session.

But, by one single Article, namely, Article 48 (3), all these functions were rendered ceremonial inasmuch as the advice of the Prime Minister was made constitutionally binding on him in the discharge of all his functions except the appointment of the Prime Minister. This was a mandatory constitutional provision as distinguished from a convention in a parliamentary form of government such as is found in Britain.

The Constitutional Changes of 1975

But this discussion about the functions of the President in the Constitution that was originally adopted in 1972 is merely academic now. Without again ascertaining the opinion of the country, which earlier gave its verdict for a parliamentary form of government, drastic and sweeping changes were brought about by the Parliament in the beginning of 1975,[10] empowering the President to discharge all his functions at his own discretion or in his individual judgment, and the Prime Minister and all other Ministers were made to function subject to the direction of the President.

A number of amendments to the Constitution had to be effected now by Martial Law Regulations in order to make it workable. Briefly stated, by sweeping amendments made by the Parliament, the President was vested with much more power than the President of the United States, without any of the well-thought-out checks and balances obtaining in the U.S. Constitution. As was already stated, the Cabinet was retained; so also was the office of the Prime Minister, but he had none of the powers or functions of a Prime Minister in a parliamentary form of government. Ironically enough, this time it was the Prime Minister's office which was made a ceremonial one.

Then on August 15, 1975, the Constitution as it existed on that date, as was indicated above, was kept in force but with necessary amendments made by Martial Law Regulations.[11] It continues in force today, subject to Martial Law Regulations, which may bring about amendments as and when thought necessary.

The present Constitution provides for a unicameral legislature as distinguished from a bicameral one. The Parliament consists of three hundred members; for a period of ten years there shall be fifteen women members of the Parliament, to be elected by the three hundred members already elected.

Illustrative of its legislative functions are provisions that no tax can be levied without parliamentary sanctions, and the budget is to be

10. Mr. Justice Chowdhury, a confidant of Mujibur Rahman, had resigned from the presidency in December 1973 to devote himself to service in the foreign affairs of Bangladesh. The constitutional changes were adopted by the Parliament (Jatiya Sangsad) on January 25, 1975. See "Bangladesh," *Keesing's Contemporary Archives*, March 3-9, 1975, p. 26997, and Aug. 25-31, 1975, pp. 27296-27297.

11. On August 15, 1975, President Mujibur Rahman, together with his family, was killed in a coup d'état by a group of military officers. He was succeeded as President by Khandaker Moshtaque Ahmed. On August 20, 1975, President Moshtaque Ahmed assumed the power to issue martial law regulations which could not be questioned in any court. See "Bangladesh," *Keesing's Contemporary Archives*, Oct. 13-19, 1975, pp. 27381-27383; and Talukder Maniruzzaman, "Bangladesh in 1975: The Fall of the Mujib Regime and Its Aftermath," *Asian Survey*, Feb. 1976, pp. 119-129.

passed by the Parliament. As the Parliament stands dissolved now, the budget can be authenticated and certified by the President.

The Constitution as it now stands provides for a Supreme Court and a High Court. It is also provided, as in Article III of the U.S. Constitution, that Chief Justices of the Supreme Court and the High Court and other judges shall be independent in the exercise of their judicial functions. The Supreme Court originally had an Appellate Division and a High Court Division; but recently the Constitution has been amended, and a High Court has been established with a Chief Justice with distinct status and functions.

The Supreme Court is empowered to hear appeals from the High Court. The High Court is entrusted with original powers of issuing orders directing a functionary to refrain from doing anything which he is not permitted in law to do, or declaring an act illegal if it is in contravention of a statute. These are, in fact, powers of issuing writs analogous to the American writs of *mandamus*, prohibition, *quo warranto*, *certiorari*, or *habeas corpus*.

Although the power of enforcing fundamental rights has been in suspension by proclamation of emergency since 1974, the High Court is empowered to issue directions as contemplated in Article 102 of the Constitution if the order against which a complaint is brought is in violation of any statutory provision. Appeals from such orders are made to the Supreme Court.

A brief reference can now be made to the question of separation of powers. The principle postulates that the same person or body of persons should not be entrusted with unrestricted powers. The idea is that the three different organs of the State, the executive, the legislature, and the judiciary, should function independently of each other. Here we may refer to the words of James Madison, who said: "The accumulation of all powers, legislative, executive and judiciary in the same hands, whether of one, a few or many and whether hereditary, self-appointed or elected, may justly be pronounced the very definition of tyranny."

The United States Constitution, therefore, in Article I gave legislative power to the Congress, executive power to the President, and judicial power to the Supreme Court and such inferior courts as the Congress may from time to time establish. Although the U.S. Constitution greatly succeeded, without entering into an elaborate discussion it may be said that it has also been found that the watertight compartments were neither possible nor desirable.

A study of the Bangladesh Constitution would show that the Parliament, while acting as the Constituent Assembly, adopted the principle of separation of powers but did not make effective provision for its implementation.

Bangladesh is a new country and as such it has to go through constitutional experiments with a view to securing peace and happiness for the people, who are looking forward to enjoyment of the fruits of independence. It has been aptly said that a constitution is best which works best. A nation vibrating with enthusiasm and continuously looking for prosperity and a higher standard of living has to adopt a mechanism suitable to the changing circumstances and needs of society. This is particularly true of a country like Bangladesh, which is still in the process of constitutional experimentation, in order to secure for its people peace, happiness, and prosperity.[12]

12. "Bangladesh," *Keesing's Contemporary Archives*, Jan. 16, 1976, pp. 27521-27522; Oct. 15, 1976, pp. 27989-27992; March 4, 1977, p. 28223; and July 29, 1977, p. 28480. See also Maniruzzaman, "Bangladesh in 1975," and by the same author, "Bangladesh in 1976: Struggle for Survival as an Independent State," *Asian Survey*, Feb. 1977, pp. 191-200; M. Rashiduzzaman, "Bangladesh in 1977: Dilemmas of the Military Rulers," *Asian Survey*, Feb. 1978, pp. 126-134.

III

Republic of China

Editorial Note

Geography: The Republic of China (ROC), located in East Asia, exercises control over the island of Taiwan (Formosa), the Penghu (Pescadores) islands, the Quemoy and Matsu islands. It also controls Pratas and some of the Nan-sha (Spratly) Islands, such as T'ai-p'ing (Itu Aba) Island, in the South China Sea. Although the ROC continues to claim legal sovereignty over other parts of China under the Communist rule, it has since 1958 renounced the use of force to achieve that goal.

Taiwan Island lies 80 to 125 miles off the southeastern coast of the China mainland. It is about 245 miles long and from 60 to 90 miles wide. A north-south mountain range forms the backbone of the island, with the highest peak, Yü Shan, rising to 13,110 feet above sea level. The eastern slope of this range is exceedingly steep and craggy, but the western half of the island is generally flat, fertile, and well cultivated.

Population and education: The ROC has a population of 17 million, including about 120,000 on the Penghu islands and 75,000 on other islands (excluding the military). Population density is about 1,200 per square mile, which is almost five times higher than that of mainland China and is the second highest in the world, only after Bangladesh. In 1977, the population growth rate was about 2 percent.

Over 27 percent of the population (about 4.4 million) are in school. Since 1968 a nine-year free education system has been in effect. There are about 300,000 undergraduate (including junior college) and graduate students. The literacy rate in the ROC is over 95 percent.

History: China is one of the oldest of the world's civilizations. The earliest Chinese dynasty began in about 2205 B.C., and under successive dynasties Chinese culture prospered and advanced to a point where achievements in literature, philosophy, art, and craftsmanship were among the highest attained by man. But China was weak in science, and there was no industrial revolution similar to what happened in the West. As a result, China was falling behind the West in technology, especially with respect to weapons, in the nineteenth century.

The foreign Ch'ing (Manchu) rulers adopted an isolation policy to prevent foreign penetration into China. However, after its defeat in the Opium War (1839-1842) by Great Britain, China was forced to open to the Western powers. Continued encroachment on China by Western nations and Japan led to other unequal treaties which included foreigners' extraterritoriality, foreign control of tariff and customs administration, and other matters which the Chinese considered humiliating. Some unequal treaties continued into the 1940s.

After decades of painful experiences and frustration, the Chinese people began to take a keen interest in the revolutionary movement led by Dr. Sun Yat-sen, which finally overthrew the Ch'ing Dynasty (1644-1911) and established the Republic of China in 1912. The new republic was soon beset with warlordism, foreign intervention, and domestic social disorder.

In the 1920s a new leader arose, Chiang Kai-shek, a follower of Dr. Sun Yat-sen. Chiang reorganized the Kuomintang (Nationalist Party) and established a party army. In 1929, Chiang almost unified China. At that time, the Communist movement began to spread in southeast China, and Chiang moved to eliminate the Communists. He succeeded in destroying most of their party organization and virtually paralyzed their ranks throughout China. The remnants of Communist forces of several thousand fled to Shenshi Province in the northwest in 1936. In 1937, Japan invaded China, and a provisional truce was made between the ROC government under Chiang and the Communists led by Mao Tse-tung.

During the Sino-Japanese War, when the Chiang government was preoccupied with resisting the Japanese aggression, the Communists took the opportunity to expand their military forces from roughly thirty thousand in 1937 to a million in 1945. After the defeat of Japan, civil war broke out and finally culminated in the Communist defeat of the ROC forces in 1949. On October 1, 1949, the Communists established the People's Republic of China on the mainland. Chiang Kai-shek moved his government and the remnant of his forces and his supporters to Taiwan in late 1949.

Economy: During the past three decades, Taiwan has changed dramatically from an agricultural to an industrial economy. The gross national product (GNP) in 1977 was about \$19 billion and per capita income was about \$1,000 (U.S.). The economic growth rate since 1970 has been about 8 percent annually. Foreign trade, both ways, in 1977 was about \$18 billion, with a favorable balance (surplus) of \$850 million. Trade between the United States and the ROC in 1977 was about \$6 billion.

The economic system is a mixture of socialism and free enterprise. The government controls electricity, petroleum, railways, highways, steel, shipyards, salt, tobacco, wine, postal service, and a few other major enterprises. All others are open to private enterprises.

The economic policy is also directed toward a more equitable distribution of income among the population. In 1976, the 20 percent of families with the highest income received 37.3 percent of the total personal income, while the 20 percent of families with the lowest income received 8.9 percent of the total personal income. The ratio between the highest income group and that of the lowest was 4.2. Such discrepancy in income distribution between the two groups is one of the lowest in the world.

Constitutional development and government structure: Modern constitutionalism was unknown in traditional China. The emperor possessed all legislative, executive, and judicial powers. However, his rule was not absolute, and there were some limitations on his authority in practice, usage, and the teachings of ancient sages. Beyond that, the censorial institution formed another check on the Chinese emperor. The censors had the duty to watch and criticize any member of the entire official system, including the emperor. Therefore, China did have in its tradition something similar to modern constitutional limitation on the government.

Modern Western constitutional concepts were introduced to China in the late nineteenth century. After decades of effort, the Constitution of the ROC was adopted on December 25, 1946, by the constitutional National Assembly. This Constitution is still in effect in Taiwan.

A popularly elected National Assembly is the supreme organ. The Assembly elects the President and Vice-President, who serve six-year terms. The main legislative body is the *Li-fa-yuan* (Legislative Yuan), composed of popularly elected members. The cabinet—the Executive Yuan, appointed by the President with the consent of the *Li-fa-yuan*—is responsible to the latter. Under the central government, there are the Taiwan Provincial Government, Taipei Special Municipality, and Fukien Provincial Government (in charge of Quemoy and Matsu islands). A provincial assembly, city councils, and mayors are all popularly elected.

Legal system: Under the traditional Chinese legal system, the written law was predominantly penal, and the traditional society was not legally oriented. There were no independent judiciary, no professional lawyers, no formal legal education in the modern sense. One of the results of Western intervention in China has been the modernization of its legal system on the Western model. A legal reform movement started in the late Ch'ing Dynasty at the turn of the century. However, it was not until the Kuomintang assumed nation-wide power in the 1930s that a complete set of modern laws was enacted and promulgated by the ROC government and has become known as the Six Codes (Organic and Administrative Law, Commerical Law, Civil Code, Criminal Code, Code of Civil Procedure, and Code of Criminal Procedure). These codes are essentially modeled upon continental Europe's civil law systems, but they also retain some of the traditional Chinese legal rules or principles.

The ROC government under the Kuomintang also began to establish modern court systems throughout China. Under the 1946 Constitution, the highest judicial organ is the Judicial Yuan, composed of the Council of Grand Justices—primarily responsible for interpretation of the Constitution—the Supreme Court, the Administrative Court, and the Commission on the Discipline of Public Functionaries. Below that there is a high court (court of appeal) in each province or special municipality and a district court at the county or city level. Modern law schools are established to train lawyers and judges. The constitution also guarantees the independence of the judiciary. Since late 1949, the Six Codes and the judicial system have operated only in Taiwan and other islands under ROC control.

HUNGDAH CHIU

American Influence on the Formation of the Constitution and Constitutional Law of the Republic of China: Past History and Future Prospects

Herbert H. P. Ma
Professor of Law, National Taiwan University

I

China's first attempt to emulate Western political and legal institutions dates back to the last years of the last dynasty, the Manchu reign, in the 1800s. However, serious efforts to make a permanent constitution began only after the founding of the Republic of China in 1912. As a result, a number of drafts were introduced leading to the May 5th Draft Constitution of 1936, which in turn formed the basis of the present Constitution of 1947.

Both the May 5th Draft Constitution and the present Constitution are founded on the unique political theory of the Three Principles of the People and the doctrine of separation of five powers as taught by Dr. Sun Yat-sen, founder of the Chinese Republic. However, Western influence has always been present.

The purpose of this paper is twofold: first, to try to show what influence the United States Constitution and constitutional law had on the Republic of China during the formation of her constitution; second, to try to see in a modest way what prospects there are for developing the constitutional law of the Republic of China in light of American experience. It is convenient to begin with what is historically relevant.

II

When Japan first defeated China in 1894 and then Russia in 1905, the Manchu rulers of the Ch'ing dynasty were convinced by loyal political reformers that a constitutional government was the only way to be strong again. A concrete step was taken in 1908 when the Emperor Kuang-shü declared the 23-article General Plan of the Constitution aiming at transforming the body politic into a constitutional monarchy patterned after the Meiji Restoration in Japan. However, it was a time when the revolutionaries led by Dr. Sun Yat-sen had determined to bring down the dynasty as a prerequisite to the successful reconstruction of China. As a last attempt to survive, the Manchu imperial house further promulgated in 1911 the Nineteen Constitutional Principles to take effect immediately as a temporary constitution. These Principles were obviously meant to copy the British cabinet system, with the Emperor as a mere figurehead. But it was too late to turn the tide. The next year saw the fall of the last dynasty in China's long monarchical history, and the first Chinese republic came into being.[1]

It is interesting to note that supporters of the Chinese revolution in their attempts to establish a republic often referred to the experiences of the United States of America in her constitution-making. In late 1911, when the governors of Kiang-su and Chekiang provinces called upon all other provinces which had declared independence to send delegates to a meeting in Shanghai to form a provisional government, they had this to say in a joint proposal:

> A Republican form of government is now recognized by national opinion. However, success will not be easily had unless there is a model to be followed. The system of the United States of America should be the future pattern of our country. At the beginning of the founding of the United States, the country was rife with crises of internal disruptions although declaring herself a union. That she managed to achieve final victory after eight years of bitter struggle was primarily because the thirteen colonies formed a Congress which ably conducted business and enforced order unitedly. The first and the second Congress of the American colonies meant to assist the legislatures of the respective colonies. . . . It was not until the third Congress that a national Congress was established for permanent order and lasting peace. This is also a necessary course of history. It is appropriate for us urgently to emulate the method of the first Congress of the American colonies and set up a provisional congressional organization in Shanghai to discuss proper measures for internal and external affairs in order to preserve the unification of our land and to regain peace.[2]

Delegates from ten and later seventeen provinces did meet in Shanghai and elsewhere, and the result was the 24-article General Plan for Organization of the Provisional Government. Though quickly drawn up and short-lived, these articles are nevertheless fruits of the first attempt at constitution-making of the first Chinese Republic. These articles bore some striking similarities to the original United

1. For a general history of the formation of the Chinese Constitution (1908-1934), see W. Y. Tsao, *The Constitutional Structure of Modern China* (Melbourne: Melbourne University Press, 1947), chap. 1, pp. 1-22.

2. See Hsieh Cheng-min, ed., *The History of Legislation of the Republic of China* (in Chinese) (Shanghai: Cheng-chung Book Company, 1948), pp. 45-46.

States Constitution. Among other things, they made the provisional President the real chief executive, and there was no mention of the people's basic rights and duties.

It was most unfortunate that the Chinese Republic had to face in her infancy successive crises of internal disruptions, to repeat the words of the above-quoted joint proposal used to describe the United States of America in her initial stage. The fact was, shortly after the installation of the provisional government, there arose warlordism, which kept the country divided and irresolute. It started with Yuan Shih-kai, the most influential figure during China's transition from a monarchy to a republic. When Sun Yat-sen, the revolutionary leader, was made the provisional President, no one feared he would abuse that powerful position. But the members of the Senate did have grave concern over the ambitious incoming President, Yuan Shih-kai—so much so that the Senate strongly proposed a Provisional Constitution of fifty-six articles,[3] which replaced the General Plan for Organization of the Provisional Government and changed the American type of presidential system to the cabinet system based on the French model. However, the official explanation was best given by one of the senators as follows:

> When the provinces were first united, the situation was very much likened to the Union of the thirteen colonies of America. Because the circumstances made it natural for us to have a federal state, the American presidential system was adopted. Since, after the establishment of the provisional government, the unification of the south and the north was felt so necessary, it is appropriate for us to have a unitary state such as the centralized government of France. So we should adopt the French cabinet system.[4]

When an elected Congress worked out a draft for a permanent constitution in 1913, it adhered to the cabinet system, which requires all the President's acts to be countersigned by a member of the government. This greatly angered Yuan Shih-kai, who had by then become dissatisfied with his already dictatorial presidential power.

What is significant here is the fact that, primarily in fear of a single person, the early constitution-makers of China forsook the American presidential system, which, as later developments attested, never was considered by the subsequent Chinese constitution-makers with the same force.

After disbanding the Congress by force, Yuan Shih-kai sought to put himself on the throne. In this he failed. But great damage was done to the cause of republicanism in China, because, although the Congress

3. In this Provisional Constitution, the rights and duties of the people were for the first time itemized, but the rights of the people are subject to legislative restrictions. See Hsieh Cheng-min, *History of Legislation*, p. 362.

4. These words were Ku Chung-Hsiu's; see Hsieh Chung-min, p. 49.

was soon reassembled and the constitution-making efforts were made to continue in the following ten years, warlords began to vie with one another for control of the central government in Peking. Since they were not genuinely willing to see China embrace constitutionalism, which would threaten their own positions, the constitutional drafts drawn up in 1919, 1923, and 1924, respectively, were either abortive or never enforced. These drafts all adopted the French cabinet system, but each time in a more elaborate form.

However, two things that came up during this agonizing period of constitution-making had obvious American influence. First a bicameral Congress comprised of a Senate and a House of Representatives based on the American model was adopted by the constitutional draft of 1913 and followed by the subsequent drafts mentioned above.[5] Second, when the governors of Kiang-su and Chekiang sent out a joint proposal calling for a meeting of the provincial representatives to discuss the formation of some kind of national government, they explicitly indicated that "the system of the United States of America should be the future pattern of our country." This pronouncement had no small impact on the later movement for "united autonomous provinces" that began to gain ground during 1920-21. Frustrated by political and military strife, many provinces advocated a kind of federalism by the making of provincial constitutions, on the one hand, and a constitution of united provinces, on the other. At one time, it was openly proclaimed that all provinces should first enact their own constitutions and then, following the American example, seek to create a constitution for the Republic of China.[6] But the movement did not go very far, because it soon met with strong opposition from many sources.

At the time when the warlords battled against each other in the north, Dr. Sun Yat-sen, the founder of the Republic, rallied the revolutionary forces of his Nationalist Party in South China to oppose them. He was not to see China unified before he died in 1925. The unification of China was left for his devoted disciple, Generalissimo Chiang Kai-shek, to complete when in 1926 he successfully carried through the northern expedition which wiped out the major warlords. The capital was moved to Nanking, and a new epoch began in China's efforts to make a permanent constitution, this time on the basis of the theory of Dr. Sun Yat-sen's Three Principles of the People and the doctrine of separation of five powers.[7]

5. Ibid., pp. 364-365.

6. Ibid., p. 176.

7. This was also the time when basic Chinese laws were codified, following in general the European continental system. For an introduction to prevailing Chinese laws and legal system in English, see Herbert H. P. Ma, "General Features of the Law and Legal System of the Republic of China," in *Trade and Investment in Taiwan: The Legal*

III

Often translated as the Principle of Nationalism, the Principle of Democracy, and the Principle of People's Livelihood, these three principles provide the theoretical bases for the cause of revolution and national construction. Since so much has been written about them, it is sufficient for our purpose to say that they aim at national unity and independence, a government of popular sovereignty and the general welfare of the people.[8] The separation of five powers as a direct guideline for constitution-making is meant to implement the three principles. While this theory and doctrine are unique in many senses, they are not cut off from the main currents of political thought underlying any democratic form of government. Indeed, it has been asserted that Dr. Sun Yat-sen's Three Principles of the People were in the main of American origin. The immediate inspiration of the three principles was said to be Lincoln's Gettysburg Address, particularly his "government of the people, by the people and for the people."[9] However, since Dr. Sun Yat-sen in elaborating his three principles obviously resorted to many sources, Eastern as well as Western, European as well as American, the above assertion is only true to the extent that Lincoln's words probably gave a powerful impetus to Dr. Sun's forming the idea of three principles of the people.

On the other hand, the separation of five powers as a foundation of China's constitutional structure is not a departure from, but an improvement on, Montesquieu's doctrine of separation of powers. The ingenuity of separating the powers of examination and impeachment, traditionally highly developed in China, from the executive and legislative powers and according them independent status marks the uniqueness of the doctrine. In this way, a government of qualified persons chosen by means of competitive civil service examinations may be ensured. On the other hand, the power of impeachment may no longer be used to achieve partisan purposes in parliament, but may be exercised independently to help bring about a clean and efficient government. Dr. Sun Yat-sen believed, however, that a five-power

---

and Economic Environment in the Republic of China, edited by Richard Cosway, Herbert H. P. Ma, and Warren Shattuck (Taipei: Mei-ya Publishing Company, 1973), chap. 1, pp. 1-50; Herbert H. P. Ma, "The Legal System of the Republic of China," *Lawasia*, 5 (December 1974): 96-127; Herbert Han-Pao Ma, "Legal System of the Republic of China," in *Rables Zeitschrift für auslandisches und internationales Privatrecht*, 37. Jahrgang 1973, Heft I Paul Siebeck, Tubingen, pp. 101-110.

8. For an authoritative interpretation of Dr. Sun Yat-sen's teachings, see Ts'ui Shu-chin, *New Commentaries on the Three Principles of the People* (in Chinese), 4th ed. (Taipei, 1959).

9. See Arthur N. Holcombe, *The Chinese Revolution: A Phase in the Regeneration of Power* (Cambridge: Harvard University Press, 1930), pp. 134-135.

government plan would not be able to substantiate popular sovereignty as advocated by him unless the demarcation of political powers and administrative (government) powers were realized. In short, Dr. Sun Yat-sen would push the idea of direct democracy to the extent possible by installing a popularly elected National Assembly armed with the political powers of election, recall, initiative, and referendum, so that the five-power government would function according to the will of the people.[10] On the basis of these doctrines, the Organic Law of the National Government was formulated in 1928 to create the first five-power national government under the leadership of the Nationalist Party (Kuomintang).

In the subsequent years constitution-making efforts continued steadily. In 1931 a Provisional Constitution was adopted, consisting of eighty-nine articles to be divided into eight chapters. This document recognized the supremacy of the Kuomintang during the period of political tutelage in that "the National Congress of the Kuomintang delegates shall exercise the powers on behalf of the National Assembly." But this period of party rule was supposed to be of short duration. Hence, after 1932, drafts of the permanent constitution began to be proposed and released to the public for comment and criticism. It was only after six revisions that the draft became final on May 5 in 1936. Hence the popular name, "May 5th Draft Constitution."[11]

Unfortunately, the constitution-making task was interrupted, first by the Sino-Japanese war, which broke out the next year and lasted for eight years, then by the political crises started by the Chinese Communists who, taking advantage of the war, had been made so strong as to threaten the existing government and its determination to introduce a permanent constitution. To keep the country united the government agreed to a Political Consultation Conference to settle the differences of all major political parties with regard to constitution-making. Although certain agreements were reached, the Communists and leftist parties still refused to participate. The National Assembly finally met to pass a revised version of the May 5th Draft Constitution as guided by the agreements, on December 25, 1946.

Since the present Constitution differs from the May 5th Draft Constitution in both form and substance, it is pertinent to point out the highlights of that draft before dealing with the present Constitution in more detail. The May 5th Draft Constitution is by and large in conformity with the guidelines bequeathed by Dr. Sun Yat-sen. As far

10. For a general explanation in English of Dr. Sun Yat-sen's five-power theory of government, see Hsieh Kwan-sheng, *A Brief Survey of the Chinese Constitution* (Taipei, 1954), pp. 1-17.

11. An account of this laborious procedure is found in W. Y. Tsao, *Constitutional Structure of Modern China* (n. 1 above), pp. 17-19.

as government structure is concerned, it entrusted the four political powers with a popularly elected National Assembly, which elects and recalls, among other officials, the President and Vice-President of the Republic. The President of the Republic, on the other hand, possesses actual power, and the office resembles to a large extent that of the President of the United States of America. He appoints all the top officials of the executive department of the central government, who are individually responsible to him. Though his acts must be countersigned by the president of the Executive Yuan, the fact that the President of the Republic chairs the meetings of the Executive Yuan Council gives him every opportunity to exert his influence.[12]

IV

The Constitution in its present form consists of 175 articles divided into 14 chapters.[13] It was meant to cover all the major points of Dr. Sun Yat-sen's constitutional theories and the principles agreed upon at the Political Consultation Conference participated in by leaders of the then existing political parties. For this reason, some deviations from the May 5th Draft Constitution were unavoidable. Consequently, there has been much argument as to whether as a result the present constitution is not less conformative to Dr. Sun Yat-sen's teachings than the May 5th Draft Constitution. However, the following introduction to the present Constitution of the Republic of China will be done only in terms of whatever relationship its provisions may have with the United States Constitution and constitutional law.

First of all, the Chinese Constitution, like the U.S. Constitution, has a preamble setting forth the theoretical bases and the major aims of the fundamental law of the land. And nothing in the Chinese Constitution shows more affiliation with the United States of America than its Article 1, which declares that "The Republic of China, founded on the Three Principles of the People, shall be a democratic republic of the people, to be governed by the people and for the people." While the origin of Dr. Sun Yat-sen's Three Principles of the People may have derived from Lincoln's famous words, there has been criticism against the advisability of equating the two and qualifying national polity with those obvious "foreign slogans."[14]

12. For a detailed analysis of the May 5th Draft Constitution, see W. Y. Tsao, *Constitutional Structure*.

13. It should be noted that to meet the unexpected needs of the period of war with the Communists a few Provisional Clauses were added to the Constitution by the National Assembly from 1945-1966. An official English translation of the Chinese Constitution and the Provisional Clauses may be found in the appendix of the *China Year Book*. For a general introduction to the present Constitution in English, see Hsieh Kwan-sheng, *op. cit.*

14. See Hsieh Ying-chow, *The Constitution of the Republic of China* (in Chinese), 6th ed. (Taipei, 1954), pp. 26-27.

Under the chapter on Rights and Duties of the People there are articles corresponding to the Bill of Rights in the United States Constitution. For example, the people are guaranteed (1) freedom of speech, lecturing, writing, and publication (Article 11, first amendment), (2) freedom of religious faith (Article 13, first amendment), (3) freedom of assembly and of association (Article 14, first amendment), (4) freedom of person (Article 8, fourth amendment), (5) right to present petitions, to file complaints, and to institute legal proceedings (Article 16, first amendment). Article 22 of the Chinese Constitution is strikingly similar to the Ninth Amendment to the U.S. Constitution. That Article provides that "all other freedoms and rights of the people that are not detrimental to social order or public welfare shall be guaranteed under the Constitution."

However, while the Chinese Constitution, like its American counterpart, guarantees individual freedoms and rights without qualification, restriction of them is allowable under conditions set forth in Article 23, namely: (1) to prevent infringement upon the freedoms of other persons, (2) to avert an imminent crisis, (3) to maintain social order, (4) to advance public welfare.

The governmental structure as found in the present Constitution is based in general on Dr. Sun Yat-sen's demarcation of political and administrative powers and the separation of five administrative powers. There are a National Assembly, a President, and five Yuan: the Executive Yuan, the Legislative Yuan, the Judicial Yuan, the Examination Yuan, and the Control Yuan. Compared with the National Assembly as defined in the May 5th Draft Constitution, the present National Assembly is so limited in its powers that in practice it only elects the President and Vice-President of the Republic. For this reason, it has been derogatively likened to the American presidential electoral college.[15]

Of particular relevance to our purpose is the frequent question whether the central government structure adopted by the Chinese Constitution is modeled on the American presidential system or on the British cabinet system. This question can best be answered in light of the triangular relationship between the President, the Executive Yuan, and the Legislative Yuan. Article 57 reads:

> 1.The Executive Yuan has the duty to present to the Legislative Yuan a statement of its administrative policies and a report on its

15. The present Constitution provides for initiative and referendum only for constitutional amendments, not for ordinary legislation, and limits election and recall to the offices of President and Vice-President of the Republic (Article 27). However, in 1966 the National Assembly, on the basis of the Provisional Clauses to the Constitution, enacted a set of rules in accordance with which the National Assembly may initiate principles and practice referendum for central government legislation. These powers and the power to recall are seldom practiced.

administration. While the Legislative Yuan is in session, Members of the Legislative Yuan shall have the right to question the President and the Ministers and Chairmen of Commissions of the Executive Yuan.

2. If the Legislative Yuan does not concur in any important policy of the Executive Yuan, it may, by resolution, request the Executive Yuan to alter such a policy. With respect to such resolution, the Executive Yuan may, with the approval of the President of the Republic, request the Legislative Yuan for reconsideration. If, after reconsideration, two-thirds of the Members of the Legislative Yuan present at the meeting uphold the original resolution, the President of the Executive Yuan shall either abide by the same or resign from office.

3. If the Executive Yuan deems a resolution on a statutory, budgetary, or treaty bill passed by the Legislative Yuan difficult of execution, it may, with the approval of the President of the Republic and within ten days after its transmission to the Executive Yuan, request the Legislative Yuan to reconsider the said resolution. If, after reconsideration, two-thirds of the Members of the Legislative Yuan present at the meeting uphold the original resolution, the President of the Executive Yuan shall either abide by the same or resign from office.

If the above provision gives one the initial impression that the system contained therein appears to be both cabinet and presidential, a closer look indicates that it is neither the one nor the other. While the President of the Executive Yuan (the Prime Minister) is made responsible to the Legislative Yuan, Article 57 expressly prohibits members of the Legislative Yuan from holding government posts concurrently, and the President of the Executive Yuan is not given the power to dissolve the legislature. On the other hand, while the President of the Republic, subject to the consent of the legislature, does nominate and appoint the President of the Executive Yuan,[16] his power of appointment ceases there and does not reach down to the Vice-President of the Executive Yuan and the various heads of the ministries and commissions.[17] And unlike the American system, where the President is the ultimate decision maker, the Executive Yuan meeting, which the President of the Yuan himself chairs, makes the decisions on all important matters of the State.[18] Article 57 does adopt the veto power, the prerogative of the American President, but it is exercised by the President of the Executive Yuan. The President of the Republic only reserves the power of approval. So analyzed, the Chinese government system is of a unique type taking after both the British cabinet system and the American presidential system.

One may next ask whether the American judicial review system, which has been adopted by many countries, obtains in the Chinese Constitution. If by judicial review is meant the power vested in the judiciary to interpret the Constitution and to repudiate the applicability of laws

16. Constitution, Article 55. 17. Article 56. 18. Article 58.

inconsistent with the Constitution, it has its counterpart in the Chinese Constitution.

According to the provisions of Articles 78, 79, 171, and 173 of the Constitution, the Council of Grand Justices, a component part of the Judicial Yuan, is vested with the exclusive power of judicial review and the power of interpreting the Constitution and unifying the interpretations of laws and ordinances.[19] Among other things, the Council alone is to determine whether a law or an ordinance is in conflict with the Constitution. However, interpretation can be given only upon request by governmental organs or the people and not of the Council's own initiative.[20]

On the other hand, the ordinary courts, unlike their American counterparts, have no power of judicial review as to whether a law is in conflict with the Constitution. Only if a judgment is deemed to be in conflict with the Constitution does the litigant concerned have the right to state this in the reasons for his appeal to a higher court while the proceedings for the case are still in progress.[21] It is not made clear whether a higher court must necessarily accept this as a fact, nor what the higher court can do if it affirms the allegation in the appeal.

Finally, a few words about the Control Yuan may be in order. Although based on the traditional Chinese censorial system, the Control Yuan as found in the present Constitution is to a certain extent in its organization modeled on the United States Senate.[22] For example, members of the Control Yuan are basically elected by provincial and municipal councils, the number being five from each province and two from each municipality. They are prohibited from occupying any other public office during the time for which they are elected.[23] One of the major functions of the Control Yuan is to exercise the power of consent in the appointment of the President, Vice-President, and Grand Justices of the Judicial Yuan, and the President, Vice-President, and Members of the Examination Yuan.[24] In fact, it was on the basis of its similarity to the upper house of a Western parliament or congress, such as the United States Senate, that the Control Yuan, the National Assembly, and the

19. Article 78 provides: "The Judicial Yuan shall interpret the Constitution and shall have the power to unify the interpretation of laws and orders." Article 79 provides: "The Judicial Yuan shall have a certain number of Grand Justices to take charge of matters specified in Article 78 of this Constitution." Article 171 provides: "Laws that are in conflict with the Constitution shall be null and void." Article 173 provides: "The Constitution shall be interpreted by the Judicial Yuan."

20. Law governing the Council of the Grand Justices, Articles 2, 3, and 4.

21. Interpretation of Council of Grand Justices, *Shih Tzu* No. 9, 1952.

22. For an introduction to the Chinese Control Yuan, see Herbert Han-Pao Ma, "The Chinese Control Yuan: An Independent Supervisory Organ of the State," *Washington University Law Quarterly*, no. 4 (December 1963), pp. 401-426.

23. Constitution, Articles 93 and 103.

24. Articles 79 and 84.

Legislative Yuan jointly were regarded by the Council of Grand Justices as being equivalent to a "parliament" of a Western democracy.[25]

V

In the above paragraphs, instances of American influence exerted and felt during the extended period of Chinese constitution-making were given. These instances, large or small, mostly refer to the formation of the Constitution as a document—whether it be the language used, institutions adopted, or theories preferred.

Once the Constitution is framed, the next task is to work out a technique of interpretation and application of the Constitution in order that a law of the Constitution may be developed. This is based on the assumption that a constitution, like any code, could not provide a solution for all controversies that might arise, no matter how carefully it was drawn up. In other words, a written constitution is not the whole of constitutional law, and many questions can only be answered by means of judicial decision or interpretation aided by doctrinal exposition. In this way the constitution is put on a working basis, and a law of the constitution may be developed. It is with this understanding that attempts will be made in the following to see whether and how the American experiences may be resorted to in the development of the constitutional law of the Republic of China.

First, a mention of some historical facts is pertinent in this connection. Two years after the promulgation of the Constitution of 1947, the Chinese Communists overran the country and the Nationalist government retreated from the mainland to the island province of Taiwan. It brought with it the Constitution, the laws, and the legal system intact, and they have since been in force within the present territories of the Republic of China. In other words, there is a continuation in the Constitution proper since it was framed in 1947, but the interpretation and application of the Constitution are limited to the experiences after the Nationalist government moved to Taiwan in 1949.[26]

25. Interpretation of Council of Grand Justices, *Shih Tzu* No. 76, 1957.

26. Because the Chinese Communists across the Taiwan Strait have continued to threaten to take the island province of Taiwan by force, the Republic of China has been continually kept under martial law. However, the economic growth and the prevailing peace and stability enjoyed by the society as a whole have made it unnecessary to apply such measures as are authorized by martial law, except in a few special cases. In other words, to conform to the actual situation of the country, a set of rules has been enacted to limit the jurisdiction of military courts to certain specific categories of serious crimes, leaving most other cases to ordinary courts. It is now a well-known fact that the government has not stopped making efforts to relax existing restrictions. Under these circumstances, developing the law of the Constitution, even in the area of guaranteed freedoms and rights of the people, is not absolutely impossible, as this paper will show later.

It should first be remembered that the Chinese Constitution, while based on Dr. Sun Yat-sen's unique political theories, has incorporated provisions taken from both continental European and Anglo-American constitutional systems together with their respective legal techniques. It should also be emphasized that there is great diversity in training of the people who participated in the framing of the Chinese Constitution and people who have interpreted and applied it. These people were trained in Germany, in France, in England, in America, in Japan, or in China by teachers with a like diversity of training. When they come to interpret and apply the Constitution, they are likely to do so from different standpoints and with different techniques. This will inevitably lead to an unsystematic interpretation and application of the Constitution, which is detrimental to the development of constitutional law in the Republic of China. Therefore, there has been felt an imperative need for a unified interpretation and application of the Constitution, which can be brought about by intelligent use of the doctrinal and judicial development of European and Anglo-American constitutions which have contributed to the framing of the Chinese Constitution. By intelligent use is meant an adaptation of these foreign experiences, theoretical and technical, to the basic ideas and techniques of Dr. Sun Yat-sen and the general constitutional and legal framework developed on the basis of them.[27]

On this assumption, any provision in the Chinese Constitution which is of American origin should therefore be interpreted and applied in light of an adaptation of the American doctrinal and technical development concerned to the basic Chinese teachings and constitutional and legal framework. This is often easier said than done. But as a general guideline to be borne in mind in the development of Chinese constitutional law, the approach is sound and workable. An example would serve to show the direction. However, the adoption of a more basic approach in the U.S. Constitution should perhaps first be considered.

As is well known, the United States Constitution is both a legal and a political document. But in America the Constitution is more a legal than a political document. It is enforced and applied in the courts as the "supreme law of the land," binding legally not only all private

27. For this basic assumption the present writer is indebted to Dean Roscoe Pound, who served as Advisor to the Ministry of Justice of the Republic of China in Nanking between 1946 and 1948. During these two years he commented often on the Chinese law and legal system and suggested how to better apply them. His comments have been published in different places, for example, *Some Problems of the Administration of Justice in China* (Nanking: National Chengchi University, 1948); *The Law in China as Seen by Roscoe Pound*, edited by Tsao Wen-yen (Taipei: China Culture Publishing Foundation, 1953). In particular, his opinions on how to develop a true constitutional law on the basis of the then newly framed Chinese Constitution are full of insight and foresight. The subsequent discussion in this paper is mainly enlightened by them.

persons but all officials and government agencies. Like the U.S. Constitution, the Chinese Constitution is also both a legal and a political document in the sense that it is not only a frame of government, a declaration of national policies, but also a body of the supreme law of the land. Article 8, which guarantees personal freedom by the privilege of *habeas corpus*, and Article 24, under which wrongful exercise of authority may create a liability enforceable in the courts, attest to this.

What is significant in making this comparison is that there is the need of a body of principles derived from the Chinese Constitution by a legal technique to deal with controversies arising under it. For instance, disputes over the jurisdictional lines between the several Yuan are likely to rise as the operation of the Constitution increases. How is legislation in contravention of the Constitution to be made void by Article 171? How are administrative ordinances in conflict with the Constitution invalidated by Article 172? And how may guaranteed rights and freedoms of individuals be infringed? These and other matters are questions of law and should be solved by judges and jurists with legal methods rather than by politicians over conference tables. In other words, so far as constitutional law can be made a body of interdependent principles and rules, it is important to make it such. And in this respect American experience as a whole is invaluable.

VI

From here it is convenient to go back to the above assumption that the interpretation and application of any provision in the Chinese Constitution which is based on the American model should be done in light of an adaptation of the relevant American doctrinal and technical development to the basic Chinese constitutional and legal environment. Article 8 of the Chinese Constitution is a good example. In definite terms it provides:

> Personal freedom shall be guaranteed to the people. Except in case of flagrante delicto as provided by law, no person shall be arrested or detained otherwise than by a judicial or a police organ in accordance with the procedure prescribed by law. No person shall be tried or punished otherwise than by a law court in accordance with the procedure prescribed by law. Any arrest, detention, trial, or punishment which is not in accordance with the procedure prescribed by law may be resisted.
>
> When a person is arrested or detained on suspicion of having committed a crime, the organ making the arrest or detention shall in writing inform the said person, and his designated relative or friend, of the grounds for his arrest or detention, and shall, within 24 hours, turn him over to a competent court for trial. The said person or any other person may petition the competent court that a writ be served within 24 hours on the organ making the arrest for the surrender of the said person for trial.
>
> The court shall not reject the petition mentioned in the preceding

> paragraph, nor shall it order the organ concerned to make an investigation and report first. The organ concerned shall not refuse to execute, or delay in executing, the writ of the court for the surrender of the said person for trial.
>
> When a person is unlawfully arrested or detained by any organ, he or any other person may petition the court for an investigation. The court shall not reject such a petition, and shall, within 24 hours, investigate the action of the organ concerned and deal with the matter in accordance with law.

That this Article adopted the privilege of the writ of *habeas corpus* as found in Article 1, Section 9, of the U.S. Constitution is beyond doubt. In fact there had been in force before the introduction of the present Constitution a law entitled the Habeas Corpus Act, which now serves to strengthen the provision in the Constitution.[28]

What calls for discussion is this expression in the above Article: "No person shall be tried or punished otherwise than by a law court in accordance with the procedure prescribed by law." It was argued that, from the standpoint of the Anglo-American legal system in which the writ of *habeas corpus* originated and long operated, this sounds very good. But to the Chinese, who are more accustomed to the French regime of police handling of petty police offences informally, interpretation and application of this portion of Article 8 to the letter will lead to awkward results. A preferable way is to change "a law court" to "a judicial authority" and to prescribe by legislation the procedure in case of minor infractions of police regulations, thus bringing the customary practice within the Constitution. The dissatisfaction and inconvenience in the American system of traffic courts for petty cases in large cities have also been advanced as reasons for rephrasing this portion of Article 8 of the Chinese Constitution.[29] However, the actual development in the past two decades seems to uphold the system as defined in the Chinese Constitution, which is in conformity with its Anglo-American archetype. As a matter of fact, years ago the constitutionality of the Law for the Punishment of Police Offences, which has been in force since 1943, was formally challenged, and the case eventually ended up in the Council of Grand Justices awaiting an interpretation. This is a strong indication that the court rather than the police station is thought to be the place where better protection for personal freedom is afforded.

28. Enacted in 1935 and enforced since 1946, this Act has ten articles specifying the procedural details of the privilege of *habeas corpus*.

29. These arguments were advanced by a person no other than Roscoe Pound himself. (See *The Law in China as Seen by Roscoe Pound*, p. 2.) To promote a rule of law in the Western sense, he would have advised more use of the court in China. That he should have argued otherwise than this in this example might be reputed partly to his concern that unsuccessful molding of established customs by legislation would render the legislation concerned ineffectual. This is also consistent with the basic tenet of his sociological jurisprudence.

It is also interesting to note that, contrary to the American experience alleged above, traffic divisions have been established in the district courts in major cities of this country to govern the rapidly increasing traffic cases, which were formerly exclusively handled by the police. In a country to which constitutionalism and a rule of law in the Western sense are historically unknown and traditionally strange, these tendencies in the development of her constitutional law are healthy and encouraging.

VII

Another example of American influence on the development of the interpretation and application of the Chinese Constitution may be given. Article 24 of the Chinese Constitution provides:

> Any public functionary who, in violation of law, infringes upon the freedom or right of any person shall, in addition to being subject to disciplinary measures in accordance with law, be held responsible under criminal and civil laws. The injured person may, in accordance with law, claim compensation from the State for damage sustained.

This Article, like Article 8, secures the protection of the freedoms and rights of the people and may be directly enforced by the courts. Borrowing from both the European continental system and the Anglo-American system, it has to do, first, with the civil and criminal liability of public functionaries for injuries caused by their acts to individuals in the operations of government, and second, with the liability of the government to answer for damages sustained by the injured individuals. More specifically, the purpose of this Article is mainly to provide compensation for the injured person. As far as this aspect of the Article is concerned, the injured person may either hold the public functionary causing the wrong to be answerable or call upon the government itself for compensation.

The idea of holding the government responsible for the acts of its officers is, in American law, based on the common law principle of *respondeat superior*, that is, let the principal or master be answerable for the acts of his agent or servant.[30] This principle, as a matter of fact, is not completely unknown to Chinese law. Article 187 of the Chinese Civil Code explicitly provides: "The employer is jointly liable to make compensation for any damage which the employee wrongfully causes to the rights of another person in the performance of his duty."

In the case of exacting compensation from the wrong-doing public functionary, the injured person may resort to civil law proceedings, as the first part of Article 24 implies. When the government itself is the

30. See 2 *American Jurisprudence* 270, *Broom's Legal Maxims* 843.

target, the purpose of Article 24 can be achieved only with the help of special legislation, as is obvious from the latter portion of its provisions. This was also modeled on the experiences of both European continental law and American law.[31]

As for the Chinese legislation relevant to Article 24 of the Constitution, it is the Law Governing Compensation for Wrongful Convictions of 1959. As the title indicates, this Law only governs criminal cases in which the innocent has been convicted. The significant thing about this legislation is that it adopted the principle of liability without fault, again following the example of many countries, including the United States of America. Specifically, it includes injuries to individuals in the course of government, which are not due to the wrong-doing of public functionaries or which are not the result of violation of law by public functionaries. This is based on the conviction that the necessary ground for compensation should be whether there has been a wrong or an injury sustained, not whether there is violation of law on the part of public functionaries.[32] Only in this way are the freedoms and rights of the people sustained.

What is of particular interest here is that the remedies provided by Article 24 of the Constitution are available only in cases in which the public functionary concerned has infringed the freedom or right of an individual in violation of law. In other words, Article 24, based on the traditional principle of no fault-no liability, is narrower in scope in providing for compensation for the injured. As a result, the question was raised as to the constitutionality of the Law Governing Wrongful Convictions. However, it is heartening to see that most law teachers and doctrinal writers of importance have in recent years come to support the Law.[33] Outstanding among the opinions expressed is the argument that the Law not only conforms to the general trend of modern legislation but also serves to realize the ultimate purpose of Chapter Two of the Chinese Constitution, namely: the protection of the freedoms and rights of the people.[34] One may even go so far as to say that this piece of legislation also serves to implement the fundamental Principle of People's Livelihood, which in essence is to help bring about a service state for the general good of the people.

31. For instance, special legislation or provisions obtained in Switzerland, Germany, Austria, the states of New York, California, Wisconsin, and North Dakota.

32. See Ho Tso-chih, *A Treatise on the Chinese Law Governing Wrongful Convictions* (in Chinese) (Taipei, 1959), p. 102.

33. Notably, Lin Chi-tung, *Commentaries of the Constitution of the Republic of China* (in Chinese) (Taipei, 1960), p. 164; Ho Tso-chih, op. cit., pp. 102-103, 159-161.

34. See Ho Tso-chih, p. 103.

VIII

In conclusion, it seems clear that the usefulness of comparative constitutional law was not exhausted in the framing of the Constitution. It does and will enter into the interpretation and application of many constitutional provisions. However, it should be remembered that the major laws of the Republic of China were codified on the basis of continental European models, especially German and Swiss codes. Hence, as far as basic concepts, principles, and techniques are concerned, modern Chinese law and the modern Chinese legal system are similar to other legal systems influenced by the reception of Roman law.

As this paper has modestly shown, in the formation of the Chinese Constitution American influence was apparently present though in different degrees. For this reason, in the development of Chinese constitutional law, American influence will have to continue so that borrowings of American origin may be properly adapted to a codification on continental European lines. What is more important, the Chinese Constitution is founded on Dr. Sun Yat-sen's unique political doctrines. Any adaptation of Western institutions, European or Anglo-American, will have to fit into the basic constitutional framework as defined by those doctrines. This calls for a well-developed juristic technique, which Chinese legal scholars and judges must work out for themselves. Inasmuch as such a technique must be developed mainly by judicial decision and interpretation, American experience will prove to be invaluable.

IV

India

Editorial Note

India has a population of approximately 600 million, of whom about 85 percent live in the country's half-million villages. Most are poor: per capita gross national product in 1974 was $98. While most of the Indian people are Hindus, 11 percent are Muslims and another 5 percent are Christians, Sikhs, Buddhists, Jains, and followers of tribal religions. The population is also extremely diverse in language and culture: the Constitution of India confers the status of official languages on fourteen of the country's languages.

Agriculture is the base of India's economy. Self-sufficiency in agricultural production has been attained in some years in the late 1960s and 1970s, but the uncertainties of the monsoons and the sharp rise in the price of artificial fertilizers have left agricultural production unpredictable each year. Since Independence, a number of industries have also been developed. India now makes some of its own steel, vehicles, farm machines, and other heavy goods and exports industrial products to other countries in Asia and to Africa. It must still import some industrial goods, however, and is dependent on other countries for petroleum and artificial fertilizers.

India attained independence from Great Britain in August 1947. After two and a half years as a dominion in the British Empire, India became a republic with the coming into force of the Constitution in January 1950. The government created by this Constitution is patterned largely after the British parliamentary system. Parliament is composed of two houses. Of these, the upper house (Rajya Sabha, or House of the States), like the British House of Lords, has little legislative power. The lower house (Lok Sabha, or House of the People) is the principal legislative body. The executive powers rest with the Prime Minister, who is a member of the Lok Sabha. The President of India, though titular head of state, has very limited powers.

India is a federation. Each of the twenty-three states has its own government, each on a parliamentary model similar to that of the Central government. However, the Constitution envisions a strong central government. It is possible for the President of India to dissolve a state government and rule the state directly from New Delhi, and this step has been taken on a number of occasions.

From Independence until 1977 the dominant party in national politics was the Congress Party, which led the movement for independence from Britain. All national governments until 1977 were Congress governments, under three different prime ministers. There were a number of opposition parties throughout this time, however, and some of them were strong enough to control intermittently several of the state governments. In 1969 the Congress Party split, but in the national elections in 1971 Indira Gandhi, who had been Prime Minister since 1967, and her segment of the Congress Party won a heavy majority in Parliament.

In 1974 there were massive political agitations in several states against Mrs. Gandhi's Congress Party. In early 1975 a High Court judge found Mrs. Gandhi guilty of corrupt practices in the 1971 election campaign for her Lok Sabha seat. This increased the agitation and brought demands that Mrs. Gandhi resign. Instead, citing the civil disturbances caused by the agitations against her, the President of India at Mrs. Gandhi's request declared a State of Emergency, in accordance with Article 352 of the Constitution. Civil liberties were sharply curtailed, and the press was put under heavy censorship. Most opposition political leaders were quickly arrested and held for months without being charged. It was such a detention that was challenged in the *Shivkant Shukla* case, mentioned by Dr. Tripathi.

The overwhelming parliamentary majority attained by Mrs. Gandhi's Congress Party in the 1971 elections made it possible for the government to amend the Constitution without much difficulty: the Forty-second Amendment was passed at this time. In early 1976 the Parliament, whose term would have expired that year, extended its own term for one year, as it was entitled to do under Article 83(2) of the Constitution. The elections were finally called in early 1977; most of the opposition politicians were released from jail to campaign, and the newspapers, which had been subjected to strict censorship throughout the Emergency, were permitted some freedom in covering the elections. Mrs. Gandhi's party was badly beaten in the March 1977 elections and the Emergency was immediately ended by the President. The new government has promised to amend the Constitution again to nullify most of the amendments passed by the Congress Parliament during the Emergency.

At the time of the Bicentennial symposium (1976: see the Preface) the Emergency was firmly established; Parliament had just extended its own term, and it looked as though the Emergency would last indefinitely. At the last minute Dr. Tripathi was not permitted to leave India to attend the Committee on Asian Law sessions in North America. Dr. Tripathi's contribution to this volume was written after the change in government in the spring of 1977.

May 22, 1978

ROBERT HAYDEN
MARC GALANTER

Perspectives on the American Constitutional Influence on the Constitution of India

P. K. Tripathi
Professor of Law, University of Delhi

Introduction

Irrespective of whether recourse to the doctrine of judicial review was intended or "invited" by the framers of the United States Constitution or was plainly a usurpation of power by Chief Justice Marshall and his Court, the doctrine has come to be recognized as an outstanding American contribution to world culture. Based on the seminal English principle of rule of law—or being, in fact, a maturer paradigm of it—the doctrine has realized the utmost potentialities of that great principle. In England, the principle of rule of law ensured that executive action would comply with established standards of legality and propriety, but it stopped short of enforcing those standards against parliamentary legislation. The credit for overcoming that inhibition and subjecting the legislature also to judicial scrutiny for compliance with those standards goes to the United States.

The claim to share with the United States allegiance to the doctrine of judicial review is a cachet of cultural attainment which many nations should be eager to own. Several countries have, in fact, incorporated the doctrine in their written constitutions. But in this respect, constitutional text is not enough, and actual conduct is of the essence.

Even in the United States, the doctrine and its application have not been free from practical and even theoretical difficulties. Crises like the Civil War and the confrontation between President Roosevelt and his Supreme Court have been attributed, at least in part, to the unimaginative application of the doctrine. The anti-majoritarian principle inherent in the exercise of the doctrine has been recognized ever since its very inception.[1] More recently, towards the beginning of the century, James Bradley Thayer warned that exercise of the power of judicial review "is

1. Jefferson's opposition to it is well known.

always attended with a serious evil," namely, that of depriving people of "the political experience and the moral education and stimulus that comes from fighting the question out in the ordinary way, and correcting their own errors" and with the tendency "to dwarf the political capacity of the people and to deaden its sense of moral responsibility."[2]

These should have been serious deterrents to any newly liberated underdeveloped Asian nation inclined to adopt the doctrine of judicial review. Yet, India has not only incorporated the doctrine in her Constitution, but has also lived with it all these years since January 26, 1950, when the operation of the Constitution commenced. During this period thousands of controversies have been presented before and disposed of by the Supreme Court at the Centre and the High Courts in the states, and hundreds of laws whose expression has been defined to include, besides Acts of the Parliament or of the state legislatures, "any Ordinance, order, bye-law, rule, regulation, notification, custom or usage having in the territory the force of law"[3] have been declared unconstitutional and void.

It is not as if such a large-scale application of the doctrine presented no problems in India. By and large, it engendered a sense of security and a respect for the law and for the law courts throughout the country, so vital to a good beginning for a young democracy. But, in the first place, it all began to be unwieldy. Although the numerical strength of judges in the High Courts was doubled or, in some cases, even trebled, often at the cost of quality on the bench and depletion of talent at the bar, arrears continued to mount. High Courts issued writs in several matters in which the courts in the United States or in England (when validity of parliamentary legislation is not involved) would probably not be persuaded to grant relief. Thus, for instance, students who did not complete the required attendance in schools or colleges could often get *ex parte* stay orders enabling them to take an examination, subject, of course, to the final outcome of the litigation in which they sought relief on the basis of such allegations as that they had no notice of the rules, or they were not warned about the condition of their attendance, or, occasionally, that the rules of attendance were not made by the proper authority or in accordance with the proper procedure and so forth. Investigation of tax matters was stayed, and the relevant papers were sealed, and sometimes the ordinary procedure for *mandamus* or injunction was permitted to be utilized for enforcing simple contracts against the state, completely bypassing the regular procedure through a civil suit.

2. J. B. Thayer, *John Marshall* (Boston: Houghton, Mifflin, 1902), pp. 57-84.

3. Constitution of India, Article 13 (3) (a). Ed. note: see Jagdish Lal, ed., *The Constitution of India* (as amended by Forty-Second Amendment) (Delhi: Delhi Law House, 1977), p. 7.

There were more serious problems, too. Chief among them was perhaps the running battle of wits between the Supreme Court and the legislatures on the matter of compensation for property acquired for public purposes. This was characterized by a series of constitutional amendments seeking to attenuate and limit the scope of judicial review for the enforcement of the fundamental right to property, and an equally sustained succession of resourceful judicial opinions frustrating each amendment and reasserting the original norm under which the State must pay not less than the market value of the property acquired.[4] This culminated in the year 1967 in an opinion of the Supreme Court which sought to limit the power of constitutional amendment itself in the same way as ordinary legislation when it attempted to abridge a fundamental right.[5] This opinion was overruled in 1973, but is understood to have been replaced by another which enlarges the power of judicial review by adopting what may be called the doctrine of "basic structure and framework."[6] This doctrine enables the Court to strike down any amendment which, in its judgment, abrogates or damages any provision or principle of the Constitution—not necessarily a funda-

4. The Patna High Court, in 1951, struck down the "Bihar Land Reforms Act, 1950" on the ground that it violated the "equal protection" guarantee in Article 14, inasmuch as it provided for a higher rate of compensation to the smaller landowners (up to twenty times the annual rental) and a lower (discriminatory) rate to the bigger landowners (three times the annual rental); A.I.R. 1851 Pat. 91. This led to the Constitution, First Amendment Act of 1951, which placed certain Acts in the so-called "Ninth Schedule" of the Constitution and immunized them from judicial review on the basis of Articles 14 (equality), 19 (right to acquire, hold, and dispose of property), and 31 (compensation). Then, in 1954, in State of West *Bengal* v. *Bela Banerjee* (A.I.R. 1954 S.C. 170), the Supreme Court pronounced that "compensation" guaranteed in Article 31 (2) of the Constitution must mean "just equivalent" and could not be less than the market value of the property (here a housing site in Calcutta) at about the date of acquisition. This was met by the Fourth Amendment, in 1955. The amendment resulted in an express statement being appended to the right in Article 31 (2) to the effect that "no such law shall be called in question in any court on the ground that the compensation provided by the law is not adequate." This worked for some time; but, in 1970, in *R. C. Cooper* v. *Union of India* (A.I.R. 1970 S.C. 564) the Supreme Court held that the "market price" rule will continue to apply in adjudging the constitutionality of the "compensation" offered or paid for property acquired by the State. This led to the Twenty-fifth Amendment in 1971, which substituted for the word "compensation" the word "amount." This was done in the hope that the difficulties created by the use of the expression "compensation" would thereby disappear. However, in the meantime, a new question cropped up, namely, whether Parliament has the power to amend the fundamental rights in the Constitution. For a full and critical discussion, see P. K. Tripathi, *Some Insights Into Fundamental Rights* (Bombay: University of Bombay, N. M. Tripathi, 1972), chapters 5 and 6.

5. *I. C. Golak Nath* v. *State of Punjab*, A.I.R. 1967 S.C. 1643. For a critique, see P. K. Tripathi, *Some Insights*.

6. *Kesavananda Bharati* v. *State of Kerala*, A.I.R. 1973 S.C. 1461. The present writer has analyzed the opinions in the case and taken the view that there is no majority support in the case for the doctrine that "the basic structure and framework" of the Constitution is immune from the power of constitutional amendment laid down in Article 368. See P. K. Tripathi, "Kesavananda Bharati v. State of Kerala: Who Wins?" *1 Supreme Court Cases*, Journal 3 (1974).

mental right—which the Court may regard as part of the "basic structure or framework of the Constitution."

This exchange, which one may or may not like to describe as a confrontation between the Parliament and the judiciary, continues to this day. The latest shot has been recently fired by Parliament in enacting the Forty-second Amendment to the Constitution which, *inter alia*, reasserts with retrospective effect the power of Parliament to amend each and every provision of the Constitution, and declares that no such amendment "shall be called in question before any court."[7]

Is it any wonder that the operation of the doctrine was attended with difficulties in India? Indeed, it would reflect upon the credibility of the enterprise if no problems arose. What is truly significant is that India has lived with the doctrine for more than a quarter century; and, although recently there has been some effort to contain its operation within certain limits whose reasonability itself is being avidly debated in the country,[8] it can be confidently asserted that the doctrine has been assimilated as a part of India's cultural fabric.

Judicial Review: British Statutes and the U.S. Constitution

The doctrine of judicial review came to be received in India through two distinct channels. Ironically enough, it came to India, in the first instance, through a British statute, namely, the Government of India Act, 1935, which was, in a sense, the precursor of the Constitution of India. Much earlier, the British Parliament had reconciled to the doctrine to a limited extent by enacting federal constitutions for the Dominions of Canada[9] and Australia.[10] Once a detailed scheme of distribution of powers between the central and regional governments on the United States pattern was adopted for each Dominion, judicial umpiring became almost a logical necessity. For these Dominions the British Parliament occupied the position simulative of a constituent assembly, keeping itself beyond the reach of judicial review, but permitting the doctrine to operate upon what the English jurists euphemistically called subordinate legislation by the federal as well as the regional governments functioning under the written constitutions.

These constitutions provided the models for the Government of India Act, 1935. The Act provided for three legislative lists. Two of

7. The Constitution (Forty-second Amendment) Act, 1976, s. 55.

8. The Forty-second Amendment debars the High Courts from questioning the validity of a "Central law," i.e., a law passed by the Parliament or any regulation, rule, by-law, etc., passed by the Union Government. But the Supreme Court remains available for the purpose.

9. The British North America Act, 1867.

10. The Commonwealth of Australia Act, 1900.

these were based on the Canadian pattern and enumerated the matters on which the federal government and the regional governments, respectively, had the exclusive power to legislate. But, like the Australian Constitution, the Government of India Act of 1935 also provided a concurrent list comprising matters over which both governments could legislate; and, as in Australia, in case of "repugnancy" between their laws on the same subject, the federal law was to prevail. The Constitution of India substantially adopted this scheme of distribution of powers between the Union and the states, although there were important modifications aiming at a strong centre.

Thus, even before the Constitution, India was familiar with the operation of the American doctrine in the limited field of judicial umpiring between the central and the regional governments with a view to confining each within the constraints of a written constitution. Important decisions were given by the High Courts, the Federal Court, and the Privy Council on the validity of legislation by the federal and the provincial governments under the Government of India Act of 1935. Many of them are still regarded as authority and are followed in settling disputes under the Constitution.

This is not to say that the framers of the Constitution did not directly consult or benefit from the United States Constitution in the matter of distribution of powers between the central and the regional governments. The Constituent Assembly, which began its deliberations on December 9, 1946, in New Delhi, was not quite unrestrained, initially, in its choice on vital issues like the powers of central government under the new Constitution. The Cabinet Mission Plan of May 16, 1946, which set the process of constitution-making in motion, had envisaged that the Union of India "should deal with the following subjects: 'Foreign Affairs, Defense, and Communications; and should have the powers necessary to raise the finances required for the above subjects,' and that 'all subjects other than the Union subjects and all residuary powers should vest in the Provinces.'"[11] True, these were only "recommendations" from the Cabinet Mission and the Viceroy of India; the British Prime Minister, Mr. Attlee, had expressly stated on March 15, "just before the despatch of the Cabinet Mission to India," that the British government's intention was "of using their utmost endeavour to help her [India] attain her freedom as speedily and fully as possible" and that "what form of government is to replace the present regime is for India to decide."[12] Yet, in view of the fact that no agreement had been possible between the Congress Party and the

11. B. Shiva Rao, *The Framing of India's Constitution, Select Documents* (New Delhi: The Indian Institute of Public Administration), vol. I, p. 209.

12. Ibid.

Muslim League, the two popular organizations without the imprimatur of whose assent the Constitution could have no social acceptance, these recommendations constituted real constraints on the Assembly. The effort of the Congress Party in the Assembly, therefore, was to bloat and expand the powers under the four rubrics of Foreign Affairs, Defense, Communications, and Finance, to cover as many subheads or "items" as possible. In that effort, Sir B. N. Rau, the Constitutional Adviser to the Constituent Assembly, and Sir Alladi Krishnaswamy Ayyar, one of the ablest and most respected lawyer members of the various committees set up by the Assembly, frequently relied on the Constitution of the United States.

In one of the notes prepared for the use of the members of the Assembly, Rau referred to Article 1, Section 8, of the United States Constitution to emphasize that "external matters, whether described as foreign or external affairs or not" included in its embrace commerce with foreign nations, naturalization, regulation of foreign exchange, piracies and felonies committed on the high seas, offenses against the law of nations, declaring war, and making "all laws which shall be necessary and proper for carrying into execution the foregoing powers."[13] In his second note, Rau referred to the ambiguity in the Cabinet Mission Plan's statement as to the Union power "to raise" the finances required for the allotted subjects, pointing out that "whether these powers should be powers of direct taxation in the right of the Union or merely powers to levy contributions from the Provinces is a question of great importance on which the statement is silent."[14] He advocated direct taxation and referred, in support of his recommendations, to the experience of the "loose confederacy" under the Articles of Confederation. He quoted an appropriate passage from Farrand's *The Framing of the Constitution*, to explain the difficulties experienced by the confederacy in obtaining from each state the share of its contribution, and concluded:

> It was to rectify these and other defects that the Philadelphia Convention was called. Under the Constitution framed by that Convention—which is substantially the present Constitution of the United States of America—Congress has been given power "to levy and collect taxes, duties, imposts and excises to pay the debts and provide for the common defense and general welfare of the United States; to borrow money on the credit of the United States; to coin money, regulate the value thereof and of foreign coin." Thus the right of direct taxation was substituted for the right of levying contributions.[15]

13. Shiva Rao, op. cit., vol. II, p. 691. 14. Ibid., p. 701. 15. Ibid., p. 703.

Ayyar, in his note submitted to the "Union Powers Committee" of the Assembly,[16] referred at length to the "necessary and proper" clause in Article 1, Section 8, of the United States Constitution and quoted the words of Chief Justice John Marshall from *McCulloch* v. *Maryland*,[17] and the legal tender cases[18] in support of the doctrine of incidental powers. He then pointed out:

> In the judgments of the Supreme Court, apart from the expression "implied powers," there is also authority for inferring inherent and resulting powers. The expression "inherent powers" has been used with respect to a matter of national interest such as no particular State is competent to deal with. There have been doubts expressed as to this aspect of the Union power but a resulting power is one implied from a group of enumerated powers instead of from a single express power. Instances of this are found on p. 221 of Wills' *Constitutional Law*. On the question of inherent, implied and resulting powers, see *Willoughby*, Vol. I, 993-94: "Legal Tender cases, eminent domain, expelling aliens, acquisition and cessation of territory."[19]

In conclusion, he recommended that "the most prudent course will be to draft a clause on the lines of recent American decisions."[20] This recommendation was considered, along with several others, by a joint meeting of the Union Powers and Union Constitution committees of the Assembly in its meeting on July 2, 1947, and "it was agreed . . . to consider the necessity of having a provision on the lines of Article 1, Section 8, Clause (18) of the U.S.A. Constitution."[21]

Actually, however, neither the "necessary and proper" clause nor any variant of it ever found a place in the Constitution, because the entire situation changed in early June 1947, when the Congress Party agreed to the partition of the country into the two Dominions of India and Pakistan and the British Government announced its decision to effect the partition. The Constituent Assembly at New Delhi was now absolutely free to allot to the Centre or to the states any powers it liked.[22] Accordingly, the Committee on Union Powers, with the con-

16. Ibid., p. 714. 17. 4 Wheaton, 316.

18. *Latham* v. *United States* and *Deming* v. *United States*, 12 Wallace, 529.

19. Shiva Rao, op. cit. (n. 11 above), vol. II, p. 717.

20. Ibid., p. 718. 21. Ibid., p. 772.

22. Accordingly, Pandit Jawahar Lal Nehru, Chairman of the Union Powers Committee, forwarding the report of his committee to the President of the Constituent Assembly, wrote: "Now that the partition is a settled fact, we are unanimously of the view that it would be injurious to the interests of the country to provide for a weak central authority which would be incapable of ensuring peace, or coordinating vital matters of common concern and of speaking effectively for the whole country in the international sphere. . . . We have accordingly come to the conclusion—a conclusion which was also reached by the Union Constitution Committee—that the soundest framework for our Constitution is a Federation, with a strong Centre" (ibid., p. 777).

currence of the Union Constitution Committee, presented a modified report to the Constituent Assembly based on the premise that "the soundest framework of our Constitution was a Federation with a strong Centre." The federal ideal was still practically indispensable for luring the princely states, which, now liberated from the leash of "British paramountcy," were, in theory at least, free not to join any Dominion or to join either of them.[23]

The Concept of a Strong Centre

By October 1947 Rau had prepared a constitution draft to serve as the basic working document for the Drafting Committee set up by the Assembly under the chairmanship of Dr. B. R. Ambedkar.[24] This draft was mainly based on the reports of the various committees appointed by the Assembly at one of its earliest meetings and the decisions taken by the Assembly itself on those reports.[25] It was a thoroughgoing document comprising two hundred and forty clauses and twelve schedules. It was thoughtfully prepared, with marginal references indicating corresponding provisions in the other constitutions of the world. Except for the clauses concerning civil liberties or "fundamental rights," with which we shall deal separately, very few of these marginal notes refer to provisions of the United States Constitution. The obvious reason for this was that the need to take the Muslim League along had disappeared, and there was great freedom of choice in the matter of distribution of authority between the Centre and the states. The idea of a strong Centre was answered fairly well by the scheme of distribution available in the Government of India Act of 1935, which could be further improved by making suitable alterations. Therefore, the task was thereafter viewed by all concerned as one of adapting the existing framework to the new aspirations rather than one of writing on a clean slate.

23. In the Constituent Assembly, this report was "not discussed in full, and the Assembly considered only the first 37 items of the Federal List. Further consideration of the report was held over and, in fact, was never taken up again" (ibid., p. 776).

24. The Drafting Committee was appointed by the Constituent Assembly on August 29, 1947, under the Chairmanship of Dr. B. R. Ambedkar (a graduate of Columbia University, from where he obtained his doctoral degree, and the most important leader of the backward communities, including the "untouchables"). Before the appointment of this Committee, the Assembly had already received and considered the reports of its various committees earlier appointed, among which was the Advisory Committee on Fundamental Rights and Minorities, appointed on January 24, 1947, on a motion by Pandit Govind Ballabh Pant.

25. This draft is also called the first draft of the Constitution. But the "Draft Constitution" was a different document, prepared by the Drafting Committee under Ambedkar's chairmanship and submitted by Ambedkar to the President of the Constituent Assembly in February 1948. The Assembly began consideration of the Draft Constitution on November 4, 1948. The Constitution was finally passed in its present form on November 26, 1949.

Even so, at least one important, though thus far little used, provision of the Constitution of India in the sphere of distribution of powers between the Union and the states has been the product of direct contemporary United States inspiration. It is the provision in Article 249 of the Constitution which enables the Parliament of the Union to legislate on any matter which is placed in the exclusive state list; only the Rajya Sabha (upper house of Parliament) must have earlier passed a resolution supported by "not less than two-thirds of the members present and voting" declaring that "it is necessary or expedient in the national interest" that Parliament should make laws with respect to that matter. Incidentally, it is on the basis of one of those provisions that it may be said that the Constitution of India is not federal in character.[26]

The inspiration came during Rau's visit to the United States between October 26 and December 2, 1947, immediately after completing his draft Constitution for the Assembly. In his report to the President of the Constituent Assembly, Rau noted that as a result of the discussions during the visit abroad he had already proposed two important amendments to the draft, one of which was

> designed to secure that when the national interest requires that a certain matter, ordinarily falling in the exclusively provincial sphere, should be dealt with on a national basis, the Centre should have power to legislate on it on that basis.[27]

Those with whom he had discussions in Washington included "the Chief Justice of the Supreme Court, ex-Chief Justice Hughes and Justices Frankfurter, Burton, and Murphy."[28] At another place, Rau observes:

> On November 20 and 21, I saw Dr. Jessup [Professor of International Law], Professor Mirkine [Constitutional Consultant to the United Nations], Dr. Hamburger [Secretary General, *United Nations Year Book on Human Rights*], and Professor Dowling [Professor of Constitutional Law, Columbia University]. I had detailed discussions with each of them. Both Dr. Jessup and Prof. Dowling regard as very important the amendment giving power to the Centre to legislate on a subject which is normally provincial if it has come to be of national importance.[29]

26. The present writer considers the Constitution of India to be a "non-federal" Constitution. See P. K. Tripathi, "Federalism: Reality and the Myth," *Journal of the Bar Council of India*, 3, no. 3 (August 1974): 251-277. Thus far no other writer has agreed.

27. Shiva Rao, op. cit. (n. 11 above), vol. III, p. 218.

28. Ibid., p. 217.

29. Ibid., pp. 221-222. Rau was so greatly impressed with the need for vesting this power in the Centre envisaged in the draft he had prepared that on November 11, 1947, while he was still busy in consultations with American politicians, judges, and academicians in Washington, he despatched an air letter to New Delhi recommending a few amendments to accommodate this and other ideas. Explaining the object of the amendment on this point, he wrote: "The essence of the matter is that where legislation is called for on a national basis, the Central legislature should have power to enact it without

Apart from the distribution of legislative powers, there were a couple of other important matters on which Rau found the discussions with eminent Americans very instructive. Emulating the Irish Constitution, Rau's draft had provided for "Directive Principles of State Policy."[30] These were not to be judicially enforceable. In his air letter from Washington on November 11, 1947,[31] Rau suggested that the Constitution should expressly provide that no law made in discharge of the Directive Principles of State Policy should be considered void merely on the ground that it contravenes a fundamental right. Explaining his purpose he said:

> As a result of the discussions in Washington and Ottawa, I propose the following amendments: The object of these [two] amendments is to make it clear that in a conflict between the rights conferred by Chapter 2, which are, for the most part, rights of the individual, and the principles of policy set forth in Chapter 3, which are intended for the welfare of the State as a whole, the general welfare should prevail over the individual right. Otherwise, it would be meaningless to say, as Clause 10 does say, that these principles of policy are fundamental and that it is the duty of the State to give effect to them in its laws. In the Constitution of the United States of America, there are no express Directive Principles of State Policy, but the courts have developed what is equivalent thereof, namely, the doctrine of "Police Powers" which has been defined as the power "to prescribe regulations to promote the health, peace, morals, and the good order of the people, and to legislate so as to increase the industry of the State, develop its resources, and add to its wealth and prosperity." In the exercise of this power, the State may make laws for the general welfare which would otherwise be inconsistent with the American Bill of Rights. The courts in India might have been able to develop a similar doctrine but for the language of Clause 9 of the draft Constitution. Hence the amendments proposed.[32]

From no less persons than Justice Frankfurter and Judge Learned Hand a willing Rau received his baptism of skepticism for the doctrine

---

amending the Constitution. Such legislation may be needed not only in such spheres as education, cooperative farming, or public health, but also in a matter which is coming to be regarded as one of the national and, indeed, almost international importance, namely, safeguarding the civil rights of all citizens: e.g., removing the social disabilities of Harijans. . . . The report of the President's Committee just published in the U.S.A. recommends that the National Government of the United States must take the lead in safeguarding the civil rights of all Americans and that Congress must enact the necessary legislation" (ibid., p. 227).

30. These were recommended by the Advisory Committee, in its report to the Constituent Assembly, and were already approved by the Assembly along with the rest of its recommendations. Rau's draft, as was already noted, was based on this groundwork already accomplished.

31. See n. 29 above.

32. Shiva Rao, op. cit. (n. 11 above), vol. III, p. 226. What are referred to as Chapters 2 and 3 are, in the Constitution, Parts III and IV, respectively; Clause 10 in the letter corresponds to Article 37 of the Constitution, and Clause 9 corresponds to Article 13.

of judicial review. In his report to the President of the Assembly, he said:

> Indeed, Justice Frankfurter considered that the power of judicial review implied in the due process clause, of which there is a qualified version in Clause 16 of our draft Constitution, was not only undemocratic (because it gave a few judges a power of vetoing legislation enacted by the representatives of the nation) but also threw an unfair burden on the judiciary; and Justice Learned Hand considered that it will be better to have all fundamental rights as moral precepts than as legal fetters in the Constitution.[33]

Rau's meeting with President Harry Truman was also very interesting. The President commended to him the United States provision for an indissoluble Senate one-third of whose members retire every two years. Rau was able to reply, "We had, in fact, copied this provision in the Indian Constitution." Further on, Rau's report says:

> I then mentioned that we had specially noted the step taken by him in December 1946, in appointing a committee on civil rights—particularly the civil rights of the underprivileged classes. The committee's report had just been published and has proved how valuable was a periodic investigation of this kind and accordingly we had inserted in the Indian Constitution an express provision empowering the President to appoint, from time to time, a commission to investigate the position of the backward classes. I added that we had gone further and had actually anticipated one of the recommendations of the President's Committee. The committee had recommended that there should be a special section in the Department of Justice, both at the Centre and in the States, to protect the civil rights guaranteed by the Constitution. We have provided in the Indian Constitution for the appointment of Special Officers for minorities, both at the Centre and in the provinces for a similar purpose.[34]

The provision in Rau's draft regarding the appointment of a commission to investigate the position of the backward classes finds expression in Article 340 of the Constitution of India. This article authorizes the President of India to appoint a commission "to investigate the conditions of socially and educationally backward classes within the territory of India and the difficulties under which they labour and to make recommendations as to the steps that should be taken by the Union or any State to remove such difficulties and to improve their condition." The provision in his draft regarding the appointment of "Special Officers for minorities both at the Centre and in the provinces" for the protection of civil rights guaranteed in the Constitution was also

33. Ibid., p. 218. Clause 16 of his draft, referred to in the passage quoted, was to this effect: "No person shall be deprived of his life or personal liberty without due process of law, nor shall any person be denied equality before the law within the territories of the Federation."

34. Ibid., p. 221.

slightly modified in the course of subsequent debates at the various stages. Finally, the Constitution provided for the appointment of such Special Officer only by the Centre and not by the states. The Special Officer under the Constitution is only meant for the Scheduled Castes, the Scheduled Tribes, the backward classes, and the Anglo-Indian community, and not for all "minorities." It is his duty "to investigate all matters relating to the safeguards provided for" those groups "under this Constitution and report to the President upon the working of those safeguards at such intervals as the President may direct." The President must place all such reports before each house of Parliament.

The "strong Centre" concept had become a part of the unquestionable credo of the Drafting Committee headed by Ambedkar. But even for this, support if not inspiration was found from no other than the United States Constitution. In his historic speech in the Constituent Assembly on November 4, 1948, while moving the Draft Constitution for the consideration of the Assembly, Ambedkar alluded to the criticism that the Centre envisaged by the draft was "too strong," and observed:

> However much you may deny powers to the Centre, it is difficult to prevent the Centre from becoming too strong. Conditions in the modern world are such that centralization of powers is inevitable. One has only to consider the growth of the Federal Government in the U.S.A. which, notwithstanding the very limited powers given to it by the Constitution, has outgrown its former self and has over-shadowed and eclipsed the State Governments. The same conditions are sure to operate on the Government of India and nothing that one can do will help to prevent it from becoming strong.[35]

In fact, if the attention given to the United States Constitution in this important speech is any measure of its influence on the Draft, and ultimately on the Constitution of India, that influence has been truly immense. A major portion of this speech—occupying eighteen pages in Shiva Rao's monumental work[36]—deals with detailed and comparative references to the provisions in the Draft and the corresponding provision under the United States Constitution. After stating the preliminaries, Ambedkar comes straight to the question of the form of government envisaged by the Draft. He explains that although the head of the Union is called the President, the presidential form of government in the United States has not been adopted. He then states elaborately the differences that exist between the two forms in regard to the nature of the executive and its relations with the legislature. He explains briefly why the American form of government was not adopted and the British form was preferred. From this he moves on to the next theme—the

35. Ibid., vol. IV, p. 433. 36. Ibid., pp. 419-436.

choice of the federal form of constitution—with its concomitant of double polity adopted in the Draft, and says:

> This dual polity under the proposed Constitution will consist of the Union at the Centre and the States at the periphery, each endowed with sovereign powers to be exercised in the field assigned to them respectively in the Constitution. This dual polity resembles the American Constitution. The American polity is also a dual polity, one of it is known as the Federal Government and the other States which correspond respectively to the Union Government and the State Governments of the Draft Constitution. Under the American Constitution the Federal Government is not a mere league of the States nor are the States administrative units or agencies of the Federal Government. In the same way, the Indian Constitution proposed in the Draft Constitution is not a league of States nor are the States administrative units or agencies of the Union Government. Here, however, the similarities between the Indian and the American Constitutions come to an end. The differences that distinguish them are more fundamental and glaring than the similarities between the two.[37]

Ambedkar then explained some of the important features in the proposed Indian Constitution—the strong Centre-oriented features—which made it different from the United States. These included features like the absence of double citizenship and of separate state constitutions in India.

"So far I have drawn attention to the differences between the American Federation and the proposed Indian Federation," he said, after making these comparisons. "But there are some other special features of the proposed Indian Federation which mark it off not only from the American Federation but from all other federations." In this connection, he mentioned the provision for the declaration of emergency which enables the Union to exercise unrestrained legislative and executive authority overriding the authority of the states. "Such a power of converting itself into a unitary State no federation possesses. This is one point of difference between the Federation proposed in the Draft Constitution and all other federations we know of."[38] He then went on to explain some other distinguishing features of the Draft Constitution which freed it from "rigidity" and "legalism"—the "two weaknesses from which federation is alleged to suffer."[39]

Thus it will be seen that even in seeking to avoid the presidential form of government and strict federalism, the two very important features of the United States Constitution, the framers of the Constitution of India have been very largely influenced and guided by the constitutional experience of the United States. Naturally, however, the influence and guidance are most pronounced and direct in yet another

37. Ibid., p. 422. 38. Ibid., p. 424. 39. Ibid., p. 424.

area, namely, that of civil liberties, or "fundamental rights," as the Indian document calls them.

Fundamental Rights: Direct and Massive Borrowing

Although, in his speech moving the Draft Constitution in the Assembly, Ambedkar emphasized the departure from the United States Constitution in regard to federalism, he had just the opposite to say in regard to civil liberties. This "most criticized part of the Draft Constitution" was assailed during the period from February to October 1948—when it was circulated widely throughout the country to elicit criticism and opinion from the general public—mostly on the ground that the rights were "riddled with so many exceptions that the exceptions have eaten up the rights altogether." The critics generally referred to the Bill of Rights in the United States Constitution and complained that while "the fundamental rights in the American Bill of Rights are real because they are not subject to limitations or exceptions," those in the Draft proposed by Ambedkar are "a kind of deception." To dispel this misconception, he said,

> . . . it is wrong to say that fundamental rights in America are absolute. The difference between the position under the American Constitution and the Draft Constitution is one of form and not of substance. That the fundamental rights in America are not absolute rights is beyond dispute. In support of every exception to the fundamental rights set out in the Draft Constitution, one can refer to at least one judgment of the United States Supreme Court. It would be sufficient to quote one such judgment of the Supreme Court in justification of the limitations on the rights of free speech contained in Article 13 of the Draft Constitution. In *Gitlow* v. *New York*, in which the issue was the constitutionality of the New York "criminal anarchy" law which purported to punish utterances calculated to bring about violent change, the Supreme Court said: It is a fundamental principle, long established, that the freedom of speech and of the press, which is secured by the Constitution, does not confer an absolute right to speak or publish, without responsibility, whatever one may choose, or an unrestricted and unbridled license that gives immunity for every possible use of language and prevents the punishment of those who abuse this freedom.

It is, therefore, wrong to say that the fundamental rights in America are absolute while those in the Draft Constitution are not.[40]

The right to freedom of speech, mentioned by Ambedkar to illustrate his point, was stated in Article 13 of the Draft in these terms:[41]

> (1) Subject to the other provisions of this Article, all citizens shall have the right (a) to freedom of speech and expression. . . .
>
> (2) Nothing in sub-clause (a) of clause (1) of this article shall affect

40. Ibid., p. 431.
41. The corresponding article in the Constitution is Article 19.

the operation of any existing law, or prevent the State from making any law, relating to libel, slander, defamation, sedition or any other matter which offends against decency or morality or undermines the authority or foundation of the State.[42]

In the final version of the Constitution, there was some reorganization of the subjects on which laws restricting free speech were to be constitutionally permissive. They read, "libel, slander, defamation, contempt of court or any other matter which offends against decency or morality or which undermines the security of, or tends to overthrow, the State." The significant change was that "sedition" had been deleted, and undermining the "authority" of the State was also dropped. "Undermining the security of the State" or "tendency to overthrow the State" were the new tests substituted. *Dennis* v. *United States*[43] had not then been decided; but, Ambedkar's phrase "tendency to overthrow the State" came perhaps fairly close to anticipating the majority view of the United States Supreme Court in that case. The available United States precedents on this aspect of free speech, of course, included *Gitlow* v. *New York*,[44] and the text of Ambedkar's draft is reminiscent of the following sentence from the judgment of Mr. Justice Sandford in that case: "And, for yet more imperative reasons, a State may punish utterances *endangering the foundations* of organized governments and threatening its *overthrow* by unlawful means" (emphasis supplied).[45] There can be no doubt that Ambedkar had in his mind decisions like *Bridges* v. *California*,[46] *Times Mirror Co.* v. *Superior Court of California*,[47] the *Pennekamp Case*,[48] and *Craig* v. *Henry*[49] when he included "contempt of court" as one of the matters concerning which laws restrictive of free speech were to be permitted. On libel, slander, and defamation, he must have had cases like *Near* v. *Minnesota*[50] before him. The *Kingsley Pictures Case*[51] had, of course, not been decided by then, but the Minnesota Session Law involved in *Near* v. *Minnesota* did prohibit and punish "obscene, lewd and lascivious" publications. Thus, as far as the free speech provision in his draft was concerned, Ambedkar was probably justified in making the claim that, in support of every exception to the right, one can refer to at least one judgment of the United States Supreme Court. Ambedkar further observed:

42. This article, as will be seen later, was the subject of a very heated and enlightened debate in the Assembly resulting in several changes in the text, the most important of which was the introduction of the justiciable element represented by the word "reasonable" qualifying all permissive legislative restrictions.

43. 341 U.S. 494 (1951). 44. 268 U.S. 652 (1925).

45. Ibid. 46. 314 U.S. 252 (1941).

47. Ibid. 48. *Pennekemp* v. *Florida*, 328 U.S. 331 (1946).

49. 331 U.S. 367 (1947). 50. 283 U.S. 697 (1931).

51. *Kingsley International Pictures Corporation* v. *Regents*, 360 U.S. 684 (1959).

> What the Draft Constitution has done is that instead of formulating fundamental rights in absolute terms and depending upon our Supreme Court to come to the rescue of Parliament by inventing the doctrine of police power, it permits the State directly to impose limitations upon the fundamental rights. There is really no difference in the result. What one does directly the other does indirectly. In both cases, the fundamental rights are not absolute.[52]

What Ambedkar did not seem to have realized, however, was that by enumerating the interests for the protection of which restrictive legislation is permissible he imported a rigidity from which the judicially developed doctrine of police powers did not suffer. Furthermore, his draft did not indicate how far a law will be permitted to go in restraining free speech in protecting the countervailing public interest, say, in security of the State. These shortcomings, coupled with the rather rigid or literalistic view of the text adopted by the courts, made an early amendment of this clause unavoidable. The amendment,[53] however, did not discard the enumeration of the protected public interests, and the rigidity has, therefore, persisted to this day. But that is a different matter.[54]

Ambedkar was by no means the only person to lean heavily on the United States Constitution for drafting the fundamental rights. In the earlier stages, before the appointment of the Drafting Committee under Ambedkar's chairmanship, others, and particularly Ayyar and Munshi, played very important roles.

The commitment of the Indian leadership to justiciable fundamental rights went as far back, at least, as the year 1924 when the National Convention presided over by Sir Tej Behadur Sapru prepared the Commonwealth of India Bill.[55] This Bill was actually introduced in the British House of Commons by Mr. George Lansbury, a leading member of the Labour Party, and had its first reading in the House in December 1925, but could not be pursued owing to the defeat of the Labour Government. It contained a "declaration of rights." The rights were enumerated under seven heads, and included the right freely to profess and practice religion, the right to free expression, and the right to equality. It was not expressly stated that these were to be justiciable. But the Supreme Court was to be the final interpreter of the Constitution, and it was unlikely that the United States precedents would not be

52. Shiva Rao, op. cit. (n. 11 above), vol. IV, p. 432.

53. The First Amendment, 1951.

54. On the circumstances compelling this amendment, and on its limitations, see P. K. Tripathi, *Spotlights on Constitutional Interpretation* (Bombay: N. M. Tripathi Pvt. Ltd., 1972), chap. 13 (titled "India's Experiment in Freedom of Speech, etc."), p. 255.

55. Shiva Rao, op. cit. (n. 11 above), vol. I, pp. 43-50 (Document No. 11).

emulated. The next milestone in constitution-making was the report of the Motilal Nehru Committee set up by the All Parties Conference held in February 1928.[56] The report, known as the Nehru report, had wide acceptance and support in the country and was hailed as a proof of the ability of Indians to sink their differences and to rule themselves under their own constitution. The Nehru Report provided for a separate section dedicated to "fundamental rights." Here again, there was no express mention of judicial review of legislation for the enforcement of the rights; but it is obvious that most of them were intended to be justiciable.

The Government of India Act of 1935 provided for non-discrimination[57] and for compensation for property compulsorily acquired for public purpose.[58] The non-discrimination provision was practically nullified by an exception saving discriminatory action sanctioned by the Governor in a province or by the Governor-General at the Centre. Naturally, therefore, it never presented any occasion for judicial review of discriminatory legislation or even executive action. The right to compensation was understood not to extend to situations where legislation modified and diminished the rights of landowners for the benefit of their tenants.[59] In other words, the right was merely to be available when there was a direct transfer of ownership of property from the proprietor to the government, and not in a variety of other situations understood in the United States to involve the "taking" of property without direct acquisition.

The Cabinet Mission Plan announced by the Viceroy of India on May 16, 1946, which set into motion the processes leading to the setting up of the Constituent Assembly, had in a special paragraph "recommended" the setting up of an "Advisory Committee on the rights of citizens, minorities and tribal and excluded areas," to report to the Union Constituent Assembly "upon the list of Fundamental Rights" and upon certain other matters concerning the protection of minorities and administration of tribal areas. Accordingly, the Advisory Committee was set up on January 24, 1947. At its first meeting, held on February 27, 1947, the Committee, presided over by Sardar Patel, elected five sub-committees, including one on "Fundamental Rights" and another on "Minorities." The provisions concerning fundamental rights in the Draft Constitution presented to the Assembly in February 1948, were mainly the product of the fundamental rights sub-committee approved by the Advisory Committee. It was this sub-committee on fundamental rights which borrowed heavily from the experience of the United States.

56. Ibid., p. 58 (Document No. 16). 57. Section 298. 58. Section 299.
59. See *Thakur Jagannath Baksh Singh* v. *United Provinces*, A.I.R. 1943 F.C. 29.

Constitutional guarantee of justiciable fundamental rights had by that time become a matter of national aspiration, to which the partition of India made really no difference. It was not only a question of protecting the rights of minorities; there were several other vital interests and values to be secured, for example, the right to travel, reside, and settle in any part of the country, or the right—even of the majority community—to practice religion or to be treated with fairness and without arbitrary discrimination. The setting up of separate sub-committees for fundamental rights and minorities will itself bear testimony that the fundamental rights were viewed in a broader perspective than mere guarantees for the interests of the minorities.

Hardly any foreign experience other than that of the United States was available in the realm of fundamental rights. The Australian Constitution had a single fundamental right which could not be taken away or abridged by legislation, namely, the right to free exercise of religion.[60] That right was itself drafted on the model of its counterpart in the United States Constitution, and the Australian case law on the subject added hardly anything fresh or important. The Canadian Constitution had no such rights. The Irish Constitution, which was relied upon for the incorporation of some non-justiciable duties of the State—the Directive Principles of State Policy—had also little guidance to offer in regard to justiciable fundamental rights inasmuch as the rights guaranteed therein were all subject to law. The remaining constitutions in the world either had no guaranteed rights, or had rights which were not justiciable, or had hardly any length of tradition or experience to encourage emulation. No wonder, therefore, that in the sub-committee on fundamental rights three leading members, Munshi, Ambedkar, and Ayyar, each a lawyer of high standing, leaned very heavily on the United States Constitution for preparing the draft of the fundamental rights.

The preliminary question whether to plump for fundamental rights enforceable by the judiciary, or to opt for rights which might be subject to the overriding power of the legislature, was disposed of without much difficulty. The minutes of the very first meeting of the sub-committee record that, after a short discussion, "it was agreed that before the bill of rights was drawn up, the sub-committee should have a clear idea about the points to be concentrated upon." The chairman then invited the members to express their opinions, and Ayyar was the first to speak. The minute reads:

> Alluding to the Charter of fundamental rights and guarantees embodied in the Irish and American Constitutions, Sir Alladi Krishnaswamy Ayyar

60. Section 116 of the Commonwealth of Australia Act, 1900.

pointed out that citizens' rights to be embodied in a Constitution should consist of guarantees enforceable in courts of law, and it was no use laying down precepts which remained unenforceable or ineffective. The Supreme Court of the United States, whenever its power is invoked under the Fourteenth Amendment to the Constitution, prevents a State from depriving any person of life, liberty or property otherwise than by due process of law. Sir Alladi advised the sub-committee to take the United States as model for the protection of the basic rights of the citizens.[61]

Munshi, agreeing with Ayyar, said that the justiciable rights must be worked out first, and later some non-justiciable rights may also be considered. He emphasized, in regard to the justiciable rights, that the constitution must provide for writs to be issued by the courts.[62]

Ambedkar agreed with Munshi. He also "informed the sub-committee that he had prepared a long list of fundamental rights which he proposed to lay before the sub-committee."[63]

Ambedkar's promised memorandum was submitted to the sub-committee on March 24, 1947. The influence of the United States Constitution was writ large on the face of this memorandum. The preamble to the memorandum began with the words "We the people" and referred to the Indian Union as the "United States of India."[64] Article II, Section I, of the "memorandum and draft" said, "The Constitution of the United States of India shall recognize the following fundamental rights of citizenship,"[65] and then follows a list of rights which include, *inter alia*, the following:

1. All persons born or naturalized within its territories are citizens of the United States of India and of the State wherein they reside. Any privilege or disability arising out of rank, birth, person, family, religion or religious usage and custom is abolished.

2. No State shall make or enforce any law or custom which shall abridge the privileges or immunities of citizens; nor shall any State deprive any person of life, liberty and property without due process of law; nor deny to any person within its jurisdiction equal protection of law.

10. The right of the people to be secure in their persons, houses, papers and effects against unreasonable searches and seizures, shall not be violated, and no warrants shall issue, but upon probable cause, supported by oath or affirmation, and particularly describing the place to be searched, and the persons or things to be seized.

12. No law shall be made abridging the freedom of speech, of the press, of association and of assembly except for consideration of public order and morality.

13. No Bill of attainder or *ex post facto* law shall be passed.

14. The State shall guarantee to every Indian citizen liberty of con-

61. Shiva Rao, op. cit. (n. 11 above), vol. II, p. 115. 62. Ibid.
63. Ibid. 64. Ibid., p. 84. 65. Ibid., pp. 85-86.

science and the free exercise of his religion, including the right to profess, to preach and to convert within limits compatible with public order and morality.

16. No person shall incur any penalties of any kind whatsoever by reason of his caste, creed or religion nor shall any person be permitted to refuse to fulfill any obligation of citizenship on the ground of caste, creed or religion.[66]

Nor did Ambedkar confine his borrowing to the text of the United States Constitution. He was aware of the difficulty felt in the United States in enforcing the Civil Rights Act of 1875 on the ground that Congress could not legislate in the field of civil rights, and so long as a state abstained from taking positive action supporting segregation the courts could not intervene to prevent social discrimination by private action. He, therefore, provided in his draft for specific fundamental rights dealing with the problem:

4. Whoever denies to any person, except for reasons by law applicable to persons of all classes and regardless of their social status, the full enjoyment of any of the accommodations, advantages, facilities, privileges or inns, educational institutions, roads, paths, streets, tanks, wells and other watering places, public conveyances on land, air or water, theatres or other places of public amusement, resort or convenience where they are dedicated to or maintained or licensed for the use of the public, shall be guilty of an offense.

5. All citizens shall have equal access to all institutions, conveniences and amenities maintained by or for the public.

6. No citizen shall be disqualified to hold any public office or exercise any trade or calling by reason of his or her religion, caste, creed, sex or social status.[67]

Being himself a member and leader of the discriminated classes he wanted to take no chances in regard to this matter. In Section II of the same Article, under "remedies against invasion of fundamental rights," he sought to provide a second string to the bow by providing:

That the authority of the Legislature and the Executive of the Union as well as of every State throughout India shall be subject to the following limitations:

It shall not be competent for any Legislature or Executive in India to pass a law or issue an order, rule or regulation so as to violate the following rights of the subjects of the State:

(1) To make and enforce contracts, to sue, be parties, and give evidence, to inherit, purchase, lease, sell, hold and convey real and personal property;

(2) to be eligible for entry into the civil and military employ and to all educational institutions except for such conditions and limitations as may be necessary to provide for the due and adequate representation of all classes of the subjects of the State;

66. Ibid., p. 86 et seq. 67. Ibid.

(3) to be entitled to the full and equal enjoyment of the accommodations, advantages, facilities, educational institutions, privileges of inns, rivers, streams, wells, tanks, roads, paths, streets, public conveyances on land, air and water, theatres and other places of public resort or amusement except for such conditions and limitations applicable alike to all subjects of every race, class, caste, colour or creed.[68]

In the "explanatory notes" appended to the memorandum he acknowledges that the "provisions of Clause 2 are borrowed from the Civil Rights Protection Acts, 1866, and of March 1, 1875, passed by the Congress of the United States of America to protect the Negroes against unequal treatment."[69]

In the section relating to remedies, Ambedkar's draft suggests, on the United States pattern, that the "United States of India shall provide (1) that the judicial powers of India shall be vested in a Supreme Court," and that the "right to apply for a writ shall not be abridged or suspended unless when in cases of rebellion or invasion the public safety may require it."[70] He also borrowed from the Thirteenth, Fourteenth, and Fifteenth Amendments to provide that the "Union Legislature shall make laws to give effect to such provisions as require legislation for that purpose and to prescribe punishments for those acts which are declared to be offenses."[71]

Among the other members who submitted separate drafts for the consideration of the sub-committee was Munshi, whose draft was finally accepted by the sub-committee, on March 24, 1947, as the basis for discussion "in conjunction with other drafts."[72] Munshi, on the whole, took the substance of the provisions in the United States Constitution and, unlike Ambedkar, avoided the literal text. Yet, even in Munshi's draft, the text of the United States Constitution could be easily recognized. Here is a sampling:

Article III, Section (10):

No person shall be denied equal protection of the laws within the territories of the Union.

Article V, Section (4):

No person shall be deprived of his life, liberty or property without due process of law.

Article VII, Section (3):

Every form of slavery or traffic in human beings or compulsory labour other than public service equally incumbent upon all or as part of the punishment pronounced by a court of law is abolished and if such form of traffic or labour is enforced it shall be punishable by the law of the Union.

68. Ibid., pp. 88-89. 69. Ibid., p. 98.

70. Ibid., p. 88. Article II, Section II, Clause 1, sub-clauses (1) and (4).

71. Ibid., p. 88. Article II, Section I (21). 72. Ibid., p. 116.

> Article X, Section (3):
>
> No soldier shall, in time of peace, be quartered in any house, without the consent of the owner and in time of war except in a manner prescribed by law.
>
> Article X, Section (4):
>
> Expropriation for public reasons shall only be permitted upon conditions determined by law and in return for just and adequate consideration determined according to principles previously laid down by it.
>
> Article XII, Section (2):
>
> No person shall be tried for the same offense more than once and he shall not be compelled in any criminal case to be a witness against himself; nor shall the burden of proving his innocence be thrown on him.
>
> Article XII, Section (3):
>
> No person shall be subjected to prolonged detention preceding trial, to excessive bail, or unreasonable refusal thereof or to inhuman and cruel punishment or be denied adequate safeguards and procedure.
>
> Article XII, Section (6):
>
> Full faith and credit shall be given throughout the territories of the Union to the public acts, records and judicial proceedings of the Union and every unit thereof, and the manner in which such acts, records and proceedings shall be proved and the effect thereof determined shall be prescribed by the law of the Union.[73]

Besides these provisions, which bore obvious textual resemblances to the corresponding provisions in the United States Constitution, there were many others in the drafts presented to the sub-committee by Munshi, Ambedkar, and others which corresponded to the substance of one provision or another in the United States Bill of Rights. In fact, almost every important fundamental right which was included in these drafts and which finally became a part of the Constitution of India has its counterpart in the United States Bill of Rights. In most cases the text is deliberately altered because the true import of the guarantee as it now obtains in the United States after about one hundred and sixty years of judicial application will be—or so it was thought—more truly captured by an altered text. The case of the guarantee of free speech is one in point. As Ambedkar explained in the Constituent Assembly, an absolute statement of guarantee of free speech in the Constitution of India would have created more uncertainty than a statement qualified by those exceptions which have been judicially recognized in the United States over the long years.

In some cases, the text was also altered because Indian experience, aspirations, and policies were just different. The provision for freedom of religion illustrates this genre. India, with her memories of *Sati* and her awareness of a host of anachronistic social customs sheltered behind religion could not afford to leave all "practice" of religion

73. Ibid., pp. 75-79.

immune from legislative reform. Nor could she afford to forget the history of communal riots engineered by the obscurantist and antisocial elements by indulging, in the name of religion, in practices offending the sentiments of other communities. The Indian Constitution, therefore, guaranteed the freedom "to profess, practice and propagate religion," but, unlike in the United States, expressly subjected it to laws of health, morality, and public order; and expressly provided that the regulatory and restrictive power of the law will reach all "economic, financial, political or other secular activity which may be associated with religious practice," and the law may bring about "social welfare and reform" or throw open "Hindu religious institutions of a public character to all classes and sections of Hindus."[74]

In yet another category of cases, the texts are different because the social format of the problem as it obtained in the United States in the late eighteenth century was different from that in India in the middle of the present century, although the essential nature of the problem as well as the basic human issues involved are nearly the same. The Thirteenth Amendment to the United States Constitution provided against slavery and involuntary servitude and empowered Congress to enforce the injunction by legislation. In India the problem took the form of "untouchability," and the Indian Constitution appropriately provides that "untouchability is abolished, and its practice in any form is forbidden. The enforcement of any disability arising out of 'untouchability' shall be an offense punishable in accordance with law."[75] Another article deals with the problem of involuntary labour: "Traffic in human beings and *begar* and other similar forms of forced labour are prohibited and any contravention of this provision shall be an offense punishable in accordance with law."[76] Indeed, Munshi's draft, as we have already seen, spoke of abolishing "every form of slavery," and Professor K. T. Shah's draft also said, "Slavery of any kind is forbidden. No rights which would amount to property of any kind in human beings, or enslavement of one individual by another, or by groups or corporations, shall be recognized."[77] Consequently, in Clause 15 (1) of the report of the subcommittee on fundamental rights, "slavery" was one of the four social evils prohibited. However, when this Clause came up for discussion in the Advisory Committee, Mr. Rajagopalachari promptly protested:

> May I suggest that we need not adopt the laws of America as enacted at the time of slavery. What is intended is that forced labour and any

74. Constitution of India, Article 25. 75. Ibid., Article 17. 76. Article 23.
77. Shiva Rao, op. cit. (n. 11 above), vol. II, p. 53 (fundamental right, 39).

> form of involuntary servitude except as a punishment for crime whereof party shall have been duly convicted are prohibited, etc.[78]

And with this the "slavery" provision was dropped without ado.

It is neither necessary nor practicable to trace the development of every provision, or even several provisions, in Munshi's or Ambedkar's draft through the various stages of discussion in the sub-committee, in the Advisory Committee, and then in the Constituent Assembly itself through the last stage when it does or does not find a place in the Constitution. However, a review of the progress of the due process clause through the various stages of this journey will be not only illustrative but also, it is hoped, interesting and even rewarding.

Due Process: Resisted and Abandoned

In Munshi's draft, which was picked up by the sub-committee on fundamental rights as the principal or working draft, two provisions were significant from the point of the "due process" guarantee. These were to be found in sub-sections (1) and (4) of Article V, the Article itself being titled "Rights to Freedom."[79]

The "Rights to Freedom" enumerated in sub-clause (1) included the rights of free expression, free association, free assembly, and such other rights. In their progress from Munshi's draft to the Draft Constitution on which the Constituent Assembly commenced debate on November 4, 1948, these rights to freedom underwent great changes in style and content. But their essence remained the same. In the Draft Constitution, these rights found a place in Article 13. The rights were stated in bare terms in sub-clauses (a) to (g) of clause (1) of the Article, and in clauses (2) to (6) of the same Article provisos were incorporated permitting the State to impose restrictions on each of the rights for the protection of specified social objects like security of the State, public order, or safeguarding the interests of aboriginal tribes or of the general public. The Article did not say that these restrictions must be "reasonable" or "proper" or "due"; and this omission, as we shall see, was severely objected to during the debate in the Assembly. But for the present we return to the deliberations on Munshi's draft in the sub-committee on fundamental rights.

The other provision referred to above was in sub-clause (4) of Article V of Munshi's draft to the effect: "No person shall be deprived of his life, liberty or property without due process of law." It was this—the due process clause—which was subjected to very keen discussion and tough resistance at practically every stage of its journey to the Draft Constitution, before the Constituent Assembly.

It may perhaps be surmised at this stage that Munshi, in all

78. Ibid., p. 255. 79. Ibid., p. 75.

probability, took his "due process" clause from the Fifth and not from the Fourteenth Amendment to the United States Constitution. This is already indicated by the fact that he did not regard "liberty" in the clause to comprehend the right of free speech, association, and the like, which he separately mentioned in sub-section (1) of his Article V. The surmise is further strengthened by the separate provision elsewhere in his draft (in his Article X) for "just and adequate consideration" for private property expropriated for "public reasons." The epithet "just" seems to be obviously borrowed from the Fifth Amendment, because there is no provision at all for compensation in the Fourteenth; and even in Section 299 of the Government of India Act, 1935, whose influence is equally manifest in Munshi's Article X, mention is made only of "compensation" for the property acquired, and not of "just and adequate consideration."

Be that as it may, in the sub-committee itself Munshi's "due process" guarantee for "life, liberty and property" was subjected to the criticism that it will defeat the ineluctable tenancy reforms contemplated in several states. It had to be put to a vote in the sub-committee, but survived by five votes to two.[80] Yet another effort was made, at the sub-committee stage only, to dislodge or qualify heavily the "due process" guarantee in Munshi's draft. In a note circulated by him "on the effect of some of the proposed clauses," Rau pointed out that the "due process" clause has spawned a great deal of litigation in the United States; it had led to a great deal of uncertainty regarding the standards of constitutional behaviour and would, if adopted in India, pose a threat to the validity of social welfare legislation concerning tenancy reform, price control, regulation of wages, and the working conditions of labour. His note then referred to the decision of the United States Supreme Court in *Louisville Joint Stock Land Bank* v. *Radford*,[81] in which the Court declared unconstitutional a congressional law scaling down mortgage debts with a view to protecting the interests of the farmers, and went on to say:

> It should be noted that the Fifth Amendment of the U.S.A. Constitution contains the "due process" clause and also another clause which provides that private property shall not be taken for public use without just compensation. Our draft contains both these clauses (see Clauses 11 and 27). It must be admitted that the clauses are a safeguard against predatory legislation; but they may also stand in the way of beneficent social legislation.[82]

Rau recommended to the sub-committee that a new clause should be added to its report mitigating the effect of the "due process" and the

80. Ibid., p. 122. 81. 295 U.S. 555 (1935).
82. Shiva Rao, op. cit. (n. 11 above), vol. II, p. 151.

"just compensation" clauses by empowering the State "to limit by law the rights guaranteed" by these clauses "wherever the exigencies of the common good may require." But the sub-committee rejected this suggestion also by a majority vote.[83]

In the Advisory Committee, however, B. N. Rau's skepticism was shared by three very important men, each of whom had rich administrative experience. They were Mr. Goving Ballabh Pant, Chief Minister of Uttar Pradesh, Mr. C. Rajagopalachari, former Chief Minister of Madras, and Mr. K. M. Panikkar, Dewan (Chief Minister) of the princely state of Travancore. During deliberations in the Committee, Pant wanted to know whether the "due process" clause would render it unconstitutional for persons to be detained, for short periods, without trial, or for landlords to be disabled from ejecting or evicting their tenants from urban houses and rural lands. And when he was informed that there was a possibility of the clause having such consequences, he expressed his strong opposition to it. He said:

> It comes to this. The future of this country is to be determined not by the collective wisdom of the representatives of the people, but by the fiats of those elevated to the judiciary. If this is the case, then I strongly oppose it. The words "due process of law" should be altered. The language should be fool-proof so that every judge may be expected to give the same sort of ruling. We should not put in words which give rise to controversies.[84]

Finally, the Committee accepted the suggestion made by Panikkar that "property" be taken out of the phrase "life, liberty and property" in the "due process" clause suggested by Munshi.[85] Munshi wisely yielded, saying, "I agree with this formula. We shall deal with property separately." The clause was, therefore, adopted in the truncated form, extending the "due process" guarantee only to "life and liberty." But Pant was not satisfied, because "liberty" could, in the first place, frustrate detention without trial, and, secondly, it could even defeat social legislation like tenancy reform, price-control, or legislation for the welfare of the poor, such as debt relief or amelioration of the working conditions of labour. He wanted the phrase "due process" to be out. He only said: "I do not agree, but I keep quiet."[86]

The matter, of course, did not rest there. Rau, who shared Pant's apprehensions about the protean concept of "liberty," continued to work at it. He persuaded the Drafting Committee to agree to qualify "liberty" by the word "personal."[87] It was thought that so qualified, "liberty" could not be construed broadly to comprehend things like freedom of contract or even the right to free speech. Such of these rights

83. Ibid., p. 166. 84. Ibid., p. 243. 85. Ibid., p. 245.
86. Ibid., p. 247. 87. Ibid., vol. III, pp. 199 and 328.

as were considered worthy of constitutional protection had already been secured separately. It was believed, perhaps, that "personal liberty" would mean no more than freedom from incarceration, and "due process" protection to "liberty" in this limited and qualified sense would only mean fair trial.

It was at this stage that Rau made his visit to the United States and learned from Justices Frankfurter and Learned Hand that the "power of judicial review implied in the 'due process' clause of which there was a qualified version in Clause 16 of our Draft Constitution was not only undemocratic . . . but also threw an unfair burden on the judiciary." The upshot of it was that he persuaded the Drafting Committee to remove the expression "due process" altogether from the draft to be placed before the Constituent Assembly. Article 15 of that draft was simply without the expression "due process." It read: "No person shall be deprived of his life or personal liberty except according to procedure established by law." A footnote explained that the expression "except according to procedure established by law," substituting the words "without due process of law" was more specific and was taken from Article XXXI of the Japanese Constitution.[88]

Thus the attempt to incorporate the "due process" clause from the United States Constitution seemed to have completely failed even before the Constituent Assembly began considering the Draft Constitution prepared by its Drafting Committee, and the expression "due process" found no mention anywhere in the Draft Constitution.

Due Process: Strong but Disguised Comeback

It was noted earlier that Article 13 of the Draft Constitution incorporated the seven freedoms, beginning with the freedom of speech, in clause (1), and the restrictions permitted to be placed on each of these freedoms for various purposes, such as the security of the State, public order, and the like, were stated in clauses (2) to (6) of the same article.[89]

88. Ibid., p. 523.

89. Clause (1), enumerating the seven freedoms, was in these terms: (1) Subject to the other provisions of this article, all citizens shall have the right (a) to freedom of speech and expression; (b) to assemble peaceably and without arms; (c) to form associations or unions; (d) to move freely throughout the territory of India; (e) to reside and settle in any part of the territory of India: (f) to acquire, hold, and dispose of property; and (g) to practice any profession, or to carry on any occupation, trade or business.

A sampling of the qualifying clauses from (2) to (6) may be given: "(2) Nothing in sub-clause (a) of Clause (1) of this article shall affect the operation of any existing law of prevent the State from making any law, relating to libel, slander, defamation, sedition or any other matter which offends against decency or morality or undermines the authority or foundation of the State. . . . (4) Nothing in sub-clause (c) of the said clause shall affect the operation of any existing law or prevent the State from making any law, imposing, in the interests of the general public, restrictions on the exercise of the right conferred by the said sub-clause (ibid., p. 522)."

In the United States these freedoms have been judicially "incorporated" in the concept of liberty guaranteed by the "due process" clause in the Fourteenth Amendment. However, the provision of Article 13 of the Draft Constitution fell short of the "due process" standards primarily for the reason that no standard of judicial review was prescribed for the restrictions to be imposed by the State on these freedoms. This was noticed by a large number of members in the Constituent Assembly, and a spate of amendments was moved to rectify the error. Explaining the deficiency, Sardar Hukum Singh observed:

> Now who is to judge whether any measure adopted or legislation enacted is "in the interest of the general public" or in the interest of public order, or whether it relates to "any matter which undermines the authority or foundation of the State?" The sphere of the Supreme Court will be very limited. The only question before it would be whether the legislation concerned is "in the interest of public order." Only the *bona fides* of the legislation will be the main point for decision by the Court and when once it is found by the Court that the Government honestly believed that the legislation was needed "in the interest of the public order," there would be nothing more left for its interference.[90]

Hukum Singh pointed out that "in other countries like America, it is for the Supreme Court to judge the matter, keeping in view all the circumstances," and asked for the deletion of the qualifying clauses altogether. Mr. Damodar Swarup Seth referred to Ambedkar's explanation that the qualifying clauses corresponded to the police powers judicially evolved by the Supreme Court in the United States and said that "the limitations embodied in the Draft Constitution are far wider than those provided in the United States."[91]

But perhaps the most pertinent criticism and the best suggestion came from Pt. Thakur Das Bhargava. He endorsed the criticism made by the earlier speakers and observed that the provision of sub-clauses (2) to (6) would be satisfied as soon as a legislature claimed that it was satisfied or it honestly believed that the restrictions on the freedom were necessary for the purposes mentioned in those clauses. He, therefore, suggested that the word "reasonable" should be inserted in each of the clauses to qualify the permissible "restrictions." He said:

> Sir, one speaker was asking where the soul in the lifeless Article 13 was? I am putting the soul there. If you put the word "reasonable" there, the court will have to say whether a particular Act is in the interests of the public and, secondly, whether the restrictions imposed by the legislature are reasonable, proper and necessary in the circumstances of the case. The courts will have to go into the question and it will not be the legislature and the executive who could play with the fundamental

90. C.A.D., vol. VII, p. 733 (C.A.D. stands for Constituent Assembly Debates).
91. Ibid., p. 713.

> rights of the people. It is the courts who will have the final say. Therefore, my submission is that we must put in these words "reasonable" or "proper" or "necessary," or whatever good word the House likes. I understand that Dr. Ambedkar is agreeable to the word "reasonable." Otherwise, Article 13 is a nullity. It is not fully justiciable now and the courts will not be able to say whether the restrictions are necessary or reasonable.[92]

Ultimately, Ambedkar accepted, amongst others, the amendment moved by Bhargava,[93] and the restrictions permitted on the various freedoms in Article 13 became justiciable.

Did the several members of the Constituent Assembly who advocated and won the cause of liberty by introducing the element of justiciability in regard to the seven freedoms in Article 13, beginning with the freedom of speech, realize that they were striving for the adoption of the "due process" doctrine so far as those freedoms were concerned? It may be safely assumed that they did not have any scholarly or technical knowledge of the doctrines of "due process" and "police powers." They might not have been aware, for instance, that in the Constitution of the United States the due process guarantee for "life, liberty and property" figures at two different places, namely, in the Fifth as well as in the Fourteenth Amendment. They might not have been familiar with the doctrine of selective incorporation of the Bill of Rights into the Fourteenth Amendment through a progressively widening construction of the word "liberty." Mr. Mahboob Ali Baig, for instance, while speaking of the distinction between leaving the determination of constitutionality to the judiciary, on the one hand, and to the legislature, on the other, said:

> This distinction was recognized by the framers of the American Constitution in that famous Fourteenth Amendment which clearly laid down that no Congress can make any law to prejudice the freedom of speech, the freedom of association and the freedom of the press. This was in 1791, and if the American citizen transgressed the limits and endangered the State, the judiciary would judge him and not the legislature or the executive.[94]

Yet, their sense of direction was perfect. They knew that the freedoms enumerated in the Thirteenth Article were meaningful only if legislation seeking to restrain them was justiciable on the ground of propriety or reasonableness or some other standard of assessment of desirability. They were also at least vaguely aware that in the United

92. Ibid., pp. 739-740.

93. Ibid., p. 741. For some reason, not quite apparent, the word "reasonable" was not inserted in Clause (2) of Article 19 relating to freedom of speech and expression. However, that was done a year and a half later, in June 1951, by the First Amendment to the Constitution.

94. Ibid., p. 728.

States the Constitution has carried out the experiment of authorizing the judges to apply the standards, and the results there obtained encourage emulation. And they all knew that the "due process" clause was the key to the enforcement of judicially supervised standards. Some among them, like Bhargava, were certainly more knowledgeable and were able to see that the same standards can be enforced by using either the expression "due process" or the expression "reasonable." In either case, the standards are determined and the lines of demarcation between freedom and permissible restraint are drawn by the judges.

The next battle for judicial standards was fought over Article 15 of the Draft Constitution. It was this Article which originally started with a full-fledged enunciation of the guarantee of "due process" against deprivation of "life, liberty or property." It was subsequently reduced to "due process" guarantee for "life and personal liberty." And, finally, "due process" was eliminated and the Article only guaranteed that no person shall be deprived of his "life or personal liberty except according to procedure established by law." Bhargava and like-minded members moved amendments seeking to restore the "due process" guarantee.

Bhargava himself moved that the Article should read: "No person shall be deprived of his life or personal liberty without due process of law." In his speech explaining and supporting his amendment, Bhargava said:

> The house has already accepted the word "reasonable" in Article 13. At least seventy percent of the Acts which can involve personal liberty have now come under the jurisdiction of the courts, and the courts are competent to pronounce an opinion on such laws, whether they are reasonable or not. The House is now estopped from adopting another principle. In regard to personal liberty and life, the question is much more important. So far as the questions of life and personal liberty are concerned, they must also be under the category of subjects which are within the jurisdiction of the courts.[95]

The debate on the amendment to restore "due process" in the text of Article 15 was, perhaps, one of the most assiduous debates in the Assembly. Those who supported the amendment and those who favoured the status quo argued their cases with great zest, and opinion in the House seemed to sway from one side to another, each time a speech was made. The consideration of the amendment was postponed for a week at the request of Ambedkar, the Chairman of the Drafting Committee. And, finally, Ambedkar announced that he was himself unable to decide whether to accept the amendment or not. He left the matter to the decision of the House with these words: "It is rather a case where a

95. Ibid., p. 847. 96. Ibid., p. 1001.

man has to sail between Charybdis and Scylla and I, therefore, would not say anything. I would leave it to the House to decide in any way it likes."[96]

When put to a vote, the amendment was rejected by the House. But the matter could not rest there. It was realized by the members of the Drafting Committee itself that Article 15, as it stood, gave no guarantee of a "reasonable" or "proper" or "due" procedure in matters of life and personal liberty. In particular, it gave no guarantee of a fair trial with aid of counsel in a duly established court of law. At the final state of the deliberations of the Assembly, therefore, Ambedkar himself moved an amendment introducing a new Article, 15A, to guarantee every person accused of an offense a fair trial and the right, pending the trial, not to be detained without the order of a magistrate. Introducing this new article, Ambedkar referred to the great dissatisfaction expressed in the House and outside when the amendments seeking to introduce the "due process" guarantee for "life and personal liberty" were negatived, and observed:

> We are, therefore, now, by introducing Article 15A, making, if I may say so, compensation for what was done then in passing Article 15. In other words, we are providing for the substance of the law of "due process" by the introduction of Article 15A.[97]

Towards the end of the debate on the new article, Ambedkar again said:

> Ever since that Article (Article 15) was adopted, I and my friends had been trying in some way to restore the content of due procedure with its fundamentals without using the words "due process." I should have thought that the Members who are interested in the liberty of the individual would be more than satisfied for being able to have the prospect before them of the provisions contained in Article 15A.[98]

The new Article was, of course, approved by the House with certain minor amendments.

Due Process: Courts Fail to Recognize

It is evident from the debates in the Constituent Assembly that the framers of the Constitution of India consciously adopted the doctrines of "due process" and "police powers." True, they did not adopt the expressions "due process" and "police powers." They also did not use the famous phrase "life, liberty and property." The exigencies of their own circumstances led them to provide for the seven freedoms in a separate article, and the compulsions of social milieu persuaded them to accept departures from the textual and substantive details of the United States Constitution. Yet, they basically stuck to the core of "due

97. C.A.D., vol. IX, p. 1497. 98. Ibid., p. 1556.

process," which is that the principal rights of speech, religion, association, property, and so forth should be secure against arbitrary deprivation or encroachment by the executive as well as the legislature through the operation of judicial review on the broad ground of reasonability or propriety of all governmental action, and that fair trial with the help of legal counsel should rule out arbitrary arrest, detention, or bodily injury.

In fact, no constitution which secures liberties by providing for judicial review of executive and legislative action on the basis of judicially supervised standards of reasonableness can simply succeed in avoiding the doctrines of "due processs" and "police powers." Because, as Bhargava and other members of the Constituent Assembly rightly understood, "due process" is none other than the test of "reasonableness" applied by the judiciary in assessing the quality of the legislative measures affecting the liberty of the individual. And what is police power but the other side of the same coin? To define the boundary of an island is no different from defining the boundary of the sea that surrounds it. A statement of how far the State will be permitted to encroach upon the liberty of the individual is identical with the statement of how far a citizen can enjoy his liberty without encroachment from the State, although the one is characterized as a statement of police powers and the other of liberty protected by due process. Consequently, when the Constitution of India provided for the various freedoms in clause (1) of Article 19 and laid down the judicially supervised limits of permissible restraint in clauses (2) to (6) of the same Article, it provided for due process as well as police powers. The reasonable restrictions permitted in those clauses are none other than the contours of the police powers permitted by the Constitution of India in regard to the liberties mentioned in the main part of the Article. Similarly, Article 22, which secures the right to fair trial, and Article 20, forbidding double jeopardy, *ex post facto* penal laws, and self-incrimination, constitute part of the same scheme of demarcating the line dividing liberty and permissible restraint, or defining individual rights protected by due process and corresponding police powers of the State.

It follows, therefore, that notwithstanding the differences of detail —which might in some instances be of no inconsiderable significance— there is a basic identity of values and of the means and methods of achieving them among all the countries where civil liberties or fundamental rights are secured by judicial review. Consequently, institutional experiences of one country, particularly those concerning the judiciary and its functional relationship with the other two branches of government, must have relevance and value for all others. Since the United States has had the longest experience, extending over two centuries in this field where India is one of the latest to arrive, the experience of the former can illuminate vistas in the path of the latter. In the early years of the working of the Constitution of India, the United States precedents were cited before the Supreme Court and were received with natural readiness. Gradually, however, their use has almost disappeared, and the keenness to maintain touch with the constitutional developments in the United States has generally palled.

One reason for this decline of interest in United States jurisprudence has been the belief prevalent among Indian lawyers that the Constitution of India has rejected the "due process" doctrine.[99] This, we have noted, is evidently incorrect with regard to "liberty" as well as "property." Even "personal liberty" in the narrowest sense of freedom from imprisonment has been secured against arbitrary deprivation by the laying down of requirements of fair trial in Articles 20 and 22.[100]

99. This belief is grounded in certain observations in the Supreme Court opinions in the very first case that came up before the Court, namely, *A. K. Gopalan* v. *State of Madras* (A.I.R. 1950 S.C. 27). Chief Justice Kania observed: "A perusal of the report of the drafting committee to which our attention was drawn shows clearly that the Constituent Assembly had before it the American Article and the expression "due process of law" but they deliberately dropped the use of that expression from our Constitution. . . . If the Indian Constitution wanted to preserve to every person the protection given by the due process clause of the American Constitution there was nothing to prevent the Assembly from adopting the phrase, or if they wanted to limit the same to procedure only, to adopt that expression with only the word 'procedure' prefixed to 'law.'"

Mr. Justice B. K. Mukherjee (later he became Chief Justice) held: "In the first place it is clear that the framers of the Indian Constitution did not desire to introduce into our system the elements of uncertainty, vagueness and changeability that have grown round the 'due process' doctrine in America. . . . The uncertainty and elasticity are in the doctrine itself which is a sort of hidden mine, the contents of which nobody knows and it is merely revealed from time to time to the judicial conscience of the Judges. . . . In the Indian Constitution, the word 'due' has been deliberately omitted and this shows clearly that the Constitution makers of India had no intention of introducing the American doctrine" (p. 102).

Mr. Justice S. R. Das (later he became Chief Justice) observed: "That doctrine (due process) can only thrive and work where the legislature is subordinate to the judiciary in the sense that the latter can sit in judgment over and review all acts of the Legislature. Such a doctrine can have no application to a field where the Legislature is supreme. That is why the doctrine of 'due process of law' is quite different in England where Parliament is supreme. . . . In the main, subject to the limitation I have mentioned, our Constitution has preferred the supremacy of the Legislature to that of the judiciary. The English principle of due process of law is, therefore, more in accord with our Constitution than the American doctrine which has been evolved for serving quite a different system. . . .In the next place, it is common knowledge that our Constitution makers deliberately declined to adopt the uncertain and shifting American doctrine of due process of law. . . . Finally, it would be incongruous to import the doctrine of due process of law without its palliative, the doctrine of police powers. It is impossible to read the last mentioned doctrine into Article 21" (pp. 117-118).

100. Obviously the learned judges missed the true significance of these two articles as importing the essence of fair trial in the Constitution. As Ambedkar said, Article 22 (his Article 15A) was to make amends or compensate for what was denied by weeding out the expression "due process" from Article 21 (Article 15 of the Draft Constitution).

"Liberty" in the broader sense as inclusive of the freedoms of speech, and so forth, has been secured in Article 19. In spite of the fact that Rau and Pant succeeded in withdrawing "property" from "due process" protection, this right was also ultimately protected by sub-clause (f) of Clause (1) of Article 19 which guaranteed the right to "acquire, hold and dispose of property" subject only to "reasonable restrictions" like the other rights in that article.

Another reason which made the doctrines of police powers and due process unpopular among the Indian lawyers was the failure of some early judges to perceive and recognize the police power in regard to the right of property in Clause (5) of Article 19.[101] The confusion caused by their unsuccessful explorations proved inhibitive.[102] Lastly, perhaps the most important reason for the cooling down of the Indian lawyer's interest in the constitutional jurisprudence of the United States is his lack of acquaintance with it. Almost all the judges of the Supreme Court and the lawyers who argue before them have, from the very beginning, been persons familiar with the principles of English constitutional law but not with those of the United States Constitution. And, as Indian precedents fill up the interstices of constitutional law even the initial need to consult and explore unfamiliar foreign constitutions seems gradually to wear down.

This is not to suggest that United States precedents on specific issues should be regularly followed or even considered in India. That is neither possible nor at all desirable. Indian courts must build, as they have indeed been doing, their own *corpus juris* based on the text and social background of the Constitution of India. This text, as we have seen, makes significant departures from the United States Constitution

101. In *Charanjit Lal* v. *Union of India* (A.I.R. 1951 S.C. 41), State of *West Bengal* v. *Subodh Gopal* (A.I.R. 1954 S.C. 92), and *Dwarkadas Shrinivas* v. *Sholapur Spinning and Weaving Mills* (A.I.R. 1954 S.C. 119), Mr. Justice S. R. Das steadily took the view that the police power in regard to the right of property is not to be found in Article 19 which—after guaranteeing the right to acquire, hold, and dispose of property—permitted the State to impose reasonable restrictions on the right for the social objectives mentioned in Clause (6) of the Article. Instead, the learned Judge held that the doctrine of police powers in regard to property was to be found in Clause (1) of Article 31 which said, "No person shall be deprived of his property save by authority of law." This led him to two indefensible conclusions: first, that Article 19 has no relevance when the property is altogether lost to the owner, because then only Article 31 (1) is available; and second, that when "total deprivation" occurs as a result of law without actual "acquisition" by the State, there is no check of "reasonability" on the legislation, whereas that check is available if there is no "total deprivation" but only slight encroachment. For criticism and constructive suggestion, see P. K. Tripathi, op. cit. (n. 4 above), chapter 5 generally, and especially pp. 241 and 249.

102. Thus, for instance, Seervai, in his *Constitutional Law of India* (N. M. Tripathi, Bombay, 1967), has criticized Mr. Justice Das, not for his failure to locate the doctrine of police powers in Article 19 (5), but for applying the doctrine at all (pp. 526-527). Seervai is criticized by the present writer; see P. K. Tripathi, op. cit. (n. 54 above), p. 329 et seq.

and makes its own innovations. It is meant to function in Indian conditions and to guide the destinies of the people of India compatibly with their genius. The Indian courts need not even care to think in terms of the United States doctrines like police powers and due process. In this regard the framers of the Constitution of India have themselves given the lead by abandoning the use of those expressions. Nevertheless, since both constitutions seek to uphold the somewhat incompatible principles of democracy and judicial review, there is bound to be a basic similarity of tensions, experiences, and perceptions, especially in situations where this institutional incompatibility threatens to erupt into situations of crisis. In such matters the mature experience of the United States is bound to have great relevance for India, and insulation from that experience may prove needlessly expensive.

One such matter where the United States experience must be emulated if the integrity of judicial review is to be seriously viewed as a cherished value concerns the age of retirement of the judges of the Supreme Court and the High Courts—the courts endowed with the exercise of that enormous and delicate power. Independence of the judges of any court, and especially of these courts, cannot be left merely to the faith in the individuals appointed as judges, although that faith remains a factor of considerable significance. The proved wisdom of the Act of Settlement, 1701, and of the United States Constitution which secures a life tenure for the federal judges cannot be brushed aside by superficial observations that the judges in India already have a longer and more secure tenure than the civil servants, or that Indian conditions of climate and expectation of life are different.[103] Unless judges of these courts are given a tenure up to the age of at least seventy years, and a pension thereafter equal to their emoluments while in office, it will be unfair to expect that they will not, immediately after retirement, seek employment either from the government or from private companies—both powerful and wealthy clients before them while on the bench. Is it very difficult to perceive the danger to the system from such a situation? Is the danger too remote?[104]

What is noted about the age of retirement also holds equally good for their ridiculously low emoluments. Their salaries had been fixed more than a quarter of a century ago, and were not handsome even then. Since then, however, the decline in the buying power of the rupee has rendered the salaries almost ridiculous. Is a decent salary for a

103. Under the Constitution of India, a judge of the Supreme Court is retired at the age of sixty-five and that of a High Court at the age of sixty-two. Before that time they can be removed only through the process of impeachment as in the United States. The pension after retirement is paltry. Most judges like to get work after retirement.

104. In India nobody seems to bother.

judge expected to devote all his energies and thoughts to the enunciation and application of the principles of the Constitution a price too high?

In his report to the President of the Constituent Assembly after his return from the United States, Rau had said:

> Again, Justice Frankfurter was very emphatic that any jurisdiction exercisable by the Supreme Court should be exercised by the full Court. His view is that the highest Court of appeal in the land should not sit in divisions. Every Judge, except, of course, such Judges as may be disqualified by personal interest or otherwise from hearing particular cases, should share the responsibility for every decision of the Court.[105]

It is difficult to see why this principle was not incorporated in the Constitution. As things stand, all the judges seldom sit together. And the possibility of a Chief Justice constituting benches altogether arbitrarily cannot be ruled out. Especially, some of the ablest judges may never get the chance to contribute their best to constitutional interpretation. This has an obvious bearing on the independence of the Supreme Court judge.

There is yet another matter in regard to which United States experience can be extremely valuable and has been unwisely ignored. The anti-majoritarian element implicit in the doctrine of judicial review, initially highlighted by Jefferson and Thayer, has been well recognized. That recognition never led to the abandoning of judicial review, but it did underscore the need for caution and restraint in its exercise. If ever such caution and restraint are ignored, the democratic will can hope to assert itself by the difficult but not altogether impracticable process of constitutional amendment. As Dean Rostow rightly observed:

> Where judges are carrying out the function of constitutional review, the final responsibility of the people is appropriately guaranteed by the provisions for amending the Constitution itself, and by the benign influence of time, which changes the personnel of the courts.[106]

But can the judges obstruct the people from discharging this "final responsibility" by striking down constitutional amendments themselves? Surely, if the Constitution itself confers that power in express and unmistakable terms, it has to be exercised. It may, perhaps, in that event, have to be exercised even more cautiously and sparingly than the power to review ordinary legislation; but that is a different matter. Yet, how express and unmistakable must those terms be? Can the power be said to be conferred when there is no mention of it in the text of the Constitution? Can it be read in the following text?

105. Shiva Rao, op. cit. (n. 11 above), vol. III, p. 219.

106. Eugene V. Rostow, "The Democratic Character of Judicial Review," *66 Harvard Law Review* 193 (1952-53): 195.

PART XX
AMENDMENT OF THE CONSTITUTION

368. *Procedure for amendment of the Constitution*

An amendment of this Constitution may be initiated only by the introduction of a Bill for the purpose in either House of Parliament, and when the Bill is passed in each House by a majority of the total membership of that House and by a majority of not less than two-thirds of the members of that House present and voting, it shall be presented to the President for his assent and upon such assent being given to the Bill, the Constitution shall stand amended in accordance with the terms of the Bill:

Provided that if such amendment seeks to make any change in—

(a) Article 53, Article 55, Article 73, Article 162 or Article 241, or

(b) Chapter IV of Part V, Chapter V of Part VI, or Chapter I of Part XI, or

(c) any of the Lists in the Seventh Schedule, or

(d) the representation of States in Parliament, or

(e) the provision of this article,

the amendment shall also require to be ratified by the Legislatures of not less than one-half of the States by resolutions to that effect passed by those Legislatures before the Bill making provision for such amendment is presented to the President for assent.

I take the liberty of quoting the entire Part XX of the Constitution of India here because there comes a time when sophisticated argument must yield place to each one's seeing it for himself. I respectfully take the view that the Article does not empower the Court to strike down constitutional amendments on substantive grounds, in such explicit terms at least without which the power of judicial review ought not to be extended to constitutional amendments. The Supreme Court of India, in fact, held, as early as in the year 1951, that the "Constituent power" of Parliament in Article 368 cannot be subjected to judicial review on the ground that it offends the fundamental rights.[107] However, in 1967, by a majority of six against five in the Golak Nath case,[108] the Supreme Court reversed that decision and held that constitutional amendment was subject to the guarantee of fundamental rights in the same way as ordinary legislation. This doctrine rested mainly on the theory that there was no difference between ordinary law and the Constitution, or, more realistically, on the inability of Government lawyers to articulate the distinction between the two. Subsequently, the present writer articulated that distinction in his first Telang Memorial lecture at the Bombay University in 1971.[109] Consequently, in 1973, in the Kesavananda Bharati case, the Supreme Court almost unanimously

107. *Shankari Prasad* v. *Union of India* (A.I.R. 1967 S.C. 458).

108. *I. C. Golak Nath* v. *State of Punjab* (A.I.R. 1967 S.C. 1643).

109. P. K. Tripathi, op. cit. (n. 4 above), chapter 1, "Golak Nath: A Critique," p. 17.

overruled Golak Nath;[110] but at the same time what is claimed to be a majority of the thirteen-judge bench has laid down that the "basic structure and framework of the Constitution" cannot be altered or impaired by a constitutional amendment under Article 368. That position, again, as on earlier occasions, is sought to be reversed by a constitutional amendment;[111] and the validity of the amendment will itself depend upon the soundness of the "basic structure" ruling given by the Supreme Court which it seeks to reverse!

That the power to strike down a constitutional amendment on the ground that it affects or injures the "basic structure" of the Constitution flows from the text of Article 368 is, with due respect, at best a "benevolent illusion" of the type referred to by the late Professor Alexander Bickel in the context of Justice Black's insistence that the text of the First Amendment is absolute.[112] Such illusions help people to imagine that they rule themselves. To quote Bickel's thoughtful words:

> But it is very dangerous. To begin with, the illusion is a two-edged sword, which can be turned very sharply against the Court. . . . What is even more ominous, the illusion may even engulf its maker and breed, and it has occasionally done, free ranging "activist" government by the judiciary. Such government is incompatible on principle with democratic institutions, and in practice it will not be tolerated. This way lie crises such as the Court-packing fight of 1937, in which the Court, if it persists, must ultimately be the loser. The truth is that the illusion of judicial impotence and automation may, when fostered, be first acquired by the people and last, with the accompanying feel of omnipotence, by the judges themselves. But it is also first lost by the people and last by the judges. One day the judges may abandon it too late.[113]

In Bickel's words, again, no court, like the Supreme Courts of the United States and India, should "tell itself or the world that it draws decisions from a text that is incapable of yielding them. That obscures the actual process of decision, for the country, and for the judges themselves, if they fall in with the illusion."[114] That also ignores the ground rule that "the integrity of the Court's principled process should remain unimpaired, since the Court does not involve itself in compromises and expedient actions."[115]

Nothing can furnish a more convincing vindication than recent events in India of Thayer's view, endorsed by Bickel, that judicial review "may, in a larger sense, have a tendency over time seriously to

110. *Kesavanarda Bharati* v. *State of Kerala* (A.I.R. 1973 S.C. 1461).

111. The Constitution (Forty-second Amendment) Act, 1976.

112. Alexander M. Bickel, *The Least Dangerous Branch* (Indianapolis: Bobbs-Merrill, 1962), p. 92.

113. Ibid., pp. 92-93. 114. Ibid., pp. 96-97. 115. Ibid., p. 95.

weaken the democratic process." Throughout the years when Mr. Nehru was Prime Minister the opposition parties in the Parliament were divided and weak. The fundamental right to get compensation for property acquired by the State for public purpose was construed throughout the period somewhat in favour of the individual, and Parliament passed a series of constitutional amendments, to undo, as it were, the damage caused by judicial interpretation to the provisions of Article 31 of the Constitution.[116] The people looked upon the Court rather than the opposition parties for the vindication of the fundamental right, and the opposition remained weak, apologetic, and ineffective. Then, after Nehru's death the Court gave, in 1967, the wrong decision in Golak Nath, attempting to deny Parliament the power to abridge a fundamental right by constitutional amendment. It was followed, in 1970, by the decisions in the Bank Nationalisation case, which invalidated a Central Act acquiring the business and assets of the fourteen biggest Banking Companies in India,[117] and the Privy Purse case,[118] which invalidated the Presidential Order terminating the pensions and other privileges of the erstwhile princes. Both these judgments could be criticized for departing from the strict constructionist views of the relevant constitutional provisions and excessive concern for the property rights of the individual. In fact, they both derived their strength from Golak Nath, which stood behind them to assure that the fundamental right to property as construed by the Supreme Court would remain beyond the reach of Parliament's power of amendment. Thus judicial activism aiming to create new fundamental rights for the citizen had reached its zenith. It was at this stage towards the end of 1970 that Prime Minister Mrs. Gandhi snapped the decision to hold the elections to Parliament a year earlier than due, with the proclaimed objective of obtaining the electorate's approval for her economic programmes and expropriatory legislation. Mrs. Gandhi's party was returned to power with a stunning majority of more than two-thirds in Parliament, and the opposition was completely routed. That proved beyond doubt that judicial protection to fundamental rights had blunted the edge of democratic protest.

Then came the declaration of emergency in June 1975, followed by several arrests and occasional complaints of harsh treatment of jailed politicians. But this time, in *Additional District Magistrate, Jabalpur* v. *Shivkant Shukla*,[119] the Supreme Court refused to issue *habeas corpus* during the period when a Presidential Order under Article 359 of the Constitution had suspended the enforcement of the fundamental rights

116. See n. 4 above. 117. *R. C. Cooper* v. *Union of India* (n. 4 above).
118. *Madhay Rao Scindia* v. *Union of India* (A.I.R. 1971 S.C. 530).
119. A.I.R. 1976 S.C. 1207.

of equal protection (Article 14), personal liberty (Article 21), and fair trial (Article 22). Yet, no sooner did the Court step aside than the Thayer doctrine began to operate in the reverse, as it were, and the democratic forces began to rally around the fundamental rights of the individual. The upshot of it all was that the opposition, which had laid divided and ineffective and spurned by the electorate ever since the commencement of the Constitution, was united and galvanized into a single party, under the name of the Janata Party, and in an unprecedented response from the people secured an absolute majority in the House of People, or the lower house of Parliament, relegating the Congress Party for the first time in the history of the Constitution to the opposition benches.[120] The Congress Party lost practically all the seats to the House from the nine North-Indian states supposed to be the bulwark of its strength;[121] and Prime Minister Indira Gandhi was herself defeated in her constituency by a convincing margin of over fifty thousand votes. One is tempted to say, in retrospect, that the philosophy of judicial restraint and tolerance of the democratic processes commended itself to the Supreme Court several years too late. It may not be too rash to surmise, too, that if the Court had once again persisted in assuming to itself the mantle of the Constitution makers, as in Golak Nath and other cases, and if it persuaded itself to bypass the barrier of the constitutional inhibition in Article 359 to enforce the fundamental right by issuing the writ in the recent *habeas corpus* cases, the democratic process would not have sprung into action as it did. Anyone in India who cared to acquaint himself with the United States experience and with the thinking of American jurists on these matters would have known that the surest way to destroy fundamental rights is to try to protect them Golak Nath style by stretching and bending the text of the Constitution to the frustration of the democratically expressed will of the people—that there are no shortcuts to the hard way of winning the support of the electorate for drubbing the governmental policies one does not like. Also, it is hoped that Americans who care to know about events in India will find satisfying confirmation of their own experience on this crucial aspect of the working of their great institutions.

120. In the elections held in March 1977, the Congress Party secured only 151 seats in a House of 542.

121. These are the states of Uttar Pradesh, Bihar, West Bengal, Orissa, Madhya Pradesh, Rajasthan, Punjab, Haryana, and Himachal Pradesh.

V

Indonesia

Editorial Note

Fifth largest in population among the world's nations, with a population approaching 140 million, Indonesia's land area is nonetheless scattered out over a 4,000-mile archipelago of nearly 14,000 islands. One of these, Java (including here two small adjacent islands for statistical convenience), though only 7 percent of Indonesia's land area, houses four hundred volcanoes, more than two-thirds of the citizenry, and, every year, an additional one and a half million new people on the job market. Enriched and exacerbated by languages, dialects, and ethnic groups numbering in the many hundreds, Indonesia's social and political fabric is possibly unparalleled in diversity and complexity.

Exultant anticipation of dramatic advance upon the liberation from Dutch political shackles in 1949 stumbled painfully upon Cold War rocks, imposed and ill-fitted Western "problem-solving" mechanisms, the detritus of innumerable decades of Dutch exploitation and neglect, and recrudescent traditional conflicts. Sporadic forays toward independent development initiatives fell repeatedly afoul the vicious cycle of rich nation/poor nation disparities. Today, by standard measure of income from such exports as oil, timber, tin, copper, nickel, bauxite, coffee, and rubber, Indonesia—it is claimed—has made ten- to

Note: Chief Justice Seno-Adji's paper was adapted for this symposium by Lawrence W. Beer, with the author's permission. All footnotes in this chapter have been added by the Editor and Daniel S. Lev.

twenty-five-fold brobdingnagian leaps forward toward a better life. One counters that the average Indonesian remains by far the poorest Asian in the Association of Southeast Asian Nations, has had no schooling, and grows perhaps less literate. And oil, the biggest bubble of sophisticated early seventies enterprise, representing some three-fourths of Indonesia's annual increment of hard dollars and cents in the bank, imploded overnight in 1975. It now represents a lead balloon of debt, which despite Western rescue operations will encumber Indonesia for years to come and which challenged the most basic premises of current governmental policy. But Indonesia is rebounding.

The paraphernalia of constitutional democracy are maintained and occasionally elaborated or simplified, but pressures of exigency—and protection of incumbency—at times expanded the militarization of actual governmental functioning. Parliamentary bodies and political parties are faint shadows of their former stature, yet even at their height were derivative, faintly foreign, uncomfortable creations in their Indonesian incarnation. And the brutal reality may be that the survival of these institutions is irrelevant before the immediate, material challenge to alleviate the enduring problems of everyday survival.

No less complex is Indonesia's legal order, which has undergone considerable evolution since the revolution of 1945-1950. The formal base of Indonesian law is the colonial version of Dutch civil law, and the Indonesian legal system remains fundamentally within the civil law *Rechtsstaat* tradition. The colonial institutional heritage, which consisted of distinct court systems for various population groups, underwent a drastic revision that began during the Japanese occupation of 1942-1945. At that time the civil courts were unified into a single, three-instance hierarchy, now consisting of first instance courts (*pengadilan negeri*) at the district level, appellate courts (*pengadilan tinggi*) generally at the provincial level, and a supreme court of cassation (*Mahkamah Agung*) in Jakarta. Customary courts were eliminated by 1960. Alongside the civil judiciary, however, there remains a nationwide system of Islamic courts, organized under the Ministry of Religon, as well as a system of military justice under the Ministry of Defense. Administrative courts are provided for in the Basic Law on Judicial Organization of 1971, but have not yet been established. The Supreme Court has no substantial review powers, though there have been lively debates over the issue in Indonesia's recent legal history.

Indonesia's substantive law awaits major revision. The procedural code (H.I.R.) inherited from the colony remains in force, as does the criminal code (K.U.H.P.). The civil and commercial codes have been amended considerably in fact by the operation of new statutes, but there is yet to be a successful attempt at drafting wholly new codes. In one area of substantive law, however—family law, particularly with respect to inheritance—the Supreme Court itself has been a major force for innovation.

Indonesia's turbulent political history is reflected in its constitutional evolution. The first constitution in 1945 provided for strong executive leadership, but was set aside in favour of a parliamentary order in the constitution of 1950, which replaced a short-lived federal constitution. The 1950 constitution was provisional, however, pending debates over a new constitution in the Constituent Assembly elected in 1955. These debates did not progress very far before the Constituent Assembly was permanently adjourned by President Sukarno in 1959. In July of that year the 1945 constitution was restored and remains in effect.

DANIEL S. LEV
ROGER K. PAGET

An Indonesian Perspective on the American Constitutional Influence

Oemar Seno Adji
Chief Justice, Supreme Court of Indonesia

Indonesia's Constitutional History

While discussing the principles and elements of the Indonesian State, one of Indonesia's founding fathers stated that in framing our Constitution he took the Constitution of the United States of America as a basic source for comparison. The resultant Constitution of 1945 naturally differs from the U.S. Constitution in many respects; but one can also find parallelism and similarities in both spirit and structure. Was this merely coincidence, or did the U.S. Constitution have a perceptible influence on the Indonesian Constitution of 1945? We know that the Dutch constitutional influence was not the basic source. But these matters should be looked at in the context of the constitutional history of Indonesia.

Indonesia was under Dutch colonial control for centuries prior to World War II, when it was occupied by the Japanese. In the waning days of that war in 1945, Indonesian nationalists proclaimed Independence and promulgated what is called "the Constitution of the Proclamation State." However, the Dutch still controlled large areas of the country, and years of struggle and negotiation passed before all of Indonesia was free of colonial control.[1] In 1949 a provisional constitution of the United States of Indonesia was developed; but the federal structure of this constitution was ill-suited to the needs of a nation composed of many thousands of islands, and so this system remained in effect only from January to August 1950. At that point, in 1950, the Provisional Constitution of the Unitary State was promulgated. This 1950 document, like the 1945 Constitution, provided for a unitary and parliamentary system of government. But the 1945 Constitution differs from both the 1949 and 1950 constitutions in that it established a presidential cabinet system of a non-parliamentary character, under

1. On the history of Indonesia's nationalist movement, see George McT. Kahin, *Nationalism and Revolution in Indonesia* (Ithaca: Cornell University Press, 1952).

which the President is both the chief executive and the head of state, as is the President of the United States.[2]

In 1959 a movement emerged demanding a return to the 1945 Constitution. This movement succeeded, and since that time the 1945 Constitution has been in force in Indonesia.

Underlying all the constitutions of Indonesia and binding the State together has been an unchanging State ideology, a string of unity, the *Pancasila* (Five Principles, or pillars) of Indonesian society: (1) belief in God; (2) a humanism which is just and civilized; (3) the unity of Indonesia; (4) democracy guided by prudence through consultation and representation; and (5) social justice for the whole Indonesian people.[3] The Preamble to the Constitution of 1945 states, among other things:

> . . . that to be independent is indeed the right of every nation and therefore every kind of colonialism in the world shall be abolished, because it is in discord with humanity and justice. And the struggle for independence already has arrived at the blessed moment, that brings Indonesia in happiness and safety to the gate of freedom, united, sovereign, just and prosperous.
>
> With the blessing of God, the Almighty and by the urge of noble desire for an independent national existence, the Indonesian people therefore hereby declares its independence. Pursuant to this declaration, in order to establish an Indonesian Government, which protects the whole Indonesian nation and the whole Indonesian fatherland, to promote the public welfare, to educate the nation, and to participate in the implementation of a world order based on independence, eternal peace and social justice, the independence of the Indonesian nation is established under a Constitution of the Republic of Indonesia and embodied in the structure of the Republic of Indonesia in accordance with popular sovereignty and [the Pancasila].

It can be said that this Pancasila ideology stands unchangeable, by whatever legal means, whether the Constitution establishes a federal system or a unitary system, and whether the government is or is not parliamentary.

The Five Principles of the Pancasila were formulated in the

2. A translation of the 1950 constitution can be found in R. Supomo, *The Provisional Constitution of the Republic of Indonesia*, trans. Garth N. Jones (Ithaca: CMIP, 1964). A translation of the 1945 constitution can be found in Daniel S. Lev, *The Transition to Guided Democracy* (Ithaca: CMIP, 1966). Formal features of the federal structure are discussed in A. Arthur Schiller, *The Formation of Federal Indonesia 1945-1949* (Hague and Bandung: van Hoeve, 1955). Comparative discussions and analyses of Indonesia's three constitutions are available in A. K. Pringgodigo, *The Office of President in Indonesia as Defined in the Three Constitutions in Theory and Practice*, trans. Alexander Brotherton (Ithaca: CMIP, 1957); and J. A. C. Mackie, "Indonesian Constitutions, 1945-60," in R. N. Spann, *Constitutionalism in Asia* (Bombay: Asia Publishing House, 1963).

3. The Pancasila originated in a speech by the late President Sukarno, on June 1, 1945, during discussions of a committee whose function it was to prepare for independence as the Japanese occupation drew to an end. See Kahin, op. cit., pp. 122ff.

Preamble of the 1945 (and current) Constitution, which also includes a declaration of independence by the Indonesian people. A comment of one of the framers of our Constitution, Professor Mr. Mohd. Yamin, calls to mind the drafting of the Constitution of the United States of America:[4]

> Before me is the structure of the Republic of the United States of America, which time and again has been used as an example for several constitutions in the world, for this is the oldest constitution existing in the world and contains three elements: (1) the Declaration of Rights in the city of Philadelphia (1774); (2) the Declaration of Independence of July 4, 1776; (3) finally, the Constitution of the United States of America (1787).

The Indonesian declaration of independence in the preamble of its Constitution reminds one of the U.S. Declaration of Independence, which categorically states, in the following well-known formulation, "that all men are created equal; that they are endowed by their Creator with certain unalienable rights . . ." and "to secure these rights, governments are instituted among men, deriving their just powers from the consent of the governed." The U.S. Constitution, embodying the principles of the Declaration, is the true beginning of modern documentary constitutionalism, and shares much in spirit with the Indonesian Constitution.

The President, the Parliament, and the People's Consultative Assembly

Indonesia's system is one of presidential government, in which the President is not responsible to Parliament as under a parliamentary structure. State Ministers are answerable to the President, not to the legislature. The legislature, like the U.S. Congress and unlike a parliamentary system, does not have the power to remove an elected President; but Indonesia differs from the United States in that it does not have such a legal institution as "impeachment." Instead, Indonesia has a system of presidential responsibility to the People's Consultative Assembly, and the President cannot dissolve either this body of 920 members or the Parliament. The elucidation of the 1945 Constitution (the so-called "Proclamation Constitution") refers to the People's Consultative Assembly as the supreme holder of State power (*Die gesamte Staatsgewalt liegt allein bei der Majelis*) and, from the people's standpoint, a personification of the whole Indonesian people (*Vertretungsorgan des Willens des Staatsvolkes*). The People's Consultative Assembly consists of all members of Parliament (460 persons) and an

4. Yamin, *Naskah Persiapan Undang-Undang Dasar 1945* (Documents on the Preparation of the 1945 Constitution. Jakarta: Yayasan Prapanca, 1959), vol. I, p. 229.

equal number of representatives drawn from regional groups and functional groups.[5] The People's Consultative Assembly defines the broad outlines of State policy, and elects the President and Vice-President by majority vote. If the President is seen to deviate from the Constitution and basic State policy, the Parliament can convene an extraordinary meeting of the People's Consultative Assembly, and the People's Consultative Assembly can remove him from office. This happened during the late 1960s in the case of the late President Sukarno.

The Indonesian Constitution and Forms of Law

The American Declaration of Independence goes side by side with the United States Constitution as a constitutional document; similarly, the Indonesian declaration of independence found in the Preamble is historically inseparable from the 1945 Constitution. A constitution embodies not only legal rules but also non-legal rules which express the spirit of the constitution, a *geistlichen Hintergrund*, and the atmosphere surrounding the text of the constitution. For Indonesian constitution-makers, the U.S. Constitution was a "documentary forerunner," and Rousseau's Social Contract was a "literary forerunner" contributing to the constitutional spirit of Indonesia.

The election of 1971 constituted the present Parliament, and the People's Consultative Assembly, which elected President Suharto and his Vice-President, duly specified the outline of State Policy.[6] Provisions for periodic general elections are not laid down in the 1945 Constitution, but are stipulated in an organic Law (*loi organique*) of the Constitution. A word about the relationships between the Constitution, State Policy, and various forms of laws is in order.

The Constitution serves as the highest form of law and the basis and sources of all subordinate legal provisions of the State, such as Resolutions of the People's Consultative Assembly, Laws, Government Regulations such as Substitutional Laws, Government Regulations, Presidential Decrees, and other implementing regulations such as a Minister's Regulations.

The Constitution of Indonesia, under Article 37, can be amended under the following conditions: two-thirds of the members of the

5. Functional groups include, for example, students, women, intellectuals, labor, etc.

6. General (now President) Suharto successfully crushed the attempted coup of September 30, 1965. He thereafter assumed authority for maintaining order and in 1967 was designated acting President by the Provisional People's Consultative Assembly. He was made President in 1968 and reelected in 1973, when the Assembly also elected the Sultan of Yogyakarta as Vice-President. Presidential elections are held every five years.

People's Consultative Assembly must be present during discussions of amendment, and at least two-thirds of those present during the discussions must approve an amendment. Thus, we have a "rigid constitution." As a matter of legal policy, there has been little tendency to alter or amend the 1945 Constitution since its reinstatement. Moreover, Indonesian jurists consider the Pancasila found in the Preamble unalterable by legal process.

The 1945 Constitution is very brief, containing only thirty-seven Articles. This Constitution provides for the establishment of the basic State organs, such as the Executive—the President, Vice-President, and State Ministers—the People's Consultative Assembly, the Parliament, the Supreme Court, the Supreme Advisory Council, and the Supreme Auditing Office. But the organization, tasks, competence, and composition of these institutions are left to the *lois organiques* for further specification. The Basic Police Law, the Basic Law on Public Prosecutors, the Basic Law of the Judiciary, the Law on General Elections, the Laws on the Composition and Powers of the Parliament and the People's Consultative Assembly, the Laws on the Supreme Advisory Council, and the Laws on the Supreme Auditing Office are examples of such legislation.

A Resolution of the People's Consultative Assembly is of a higher legal order than a Law. A Law may be seen as executing not only the Constitution but also Resolutions of the People's Consultative Assembly. Resolutions of the People's Consultative Assembly present policy outlines to be implemented either by legislation or, in executive matters, by presidential decree. Thus, for example, a Resolution of the People's Consultative Assembly in the 1960s (No. 11/1966, 1968) requires that general elections be held that are direct, public, independent, and secret; and that the drawing up of the necessary pursuant laws be completed within the period of time specified by the Resolution of the Assembly. At the same time, a Resolution of the People's Consultative Assembly ordered the Government jointly with the Parliament to issue laws simplifying and regulating party organizations and functional organizations.

Indeed, based on the above-mentioned Resolution of the Assembly, the Law on General Elections, the Law concerning Members of the People's Consultative Assembly and Representative Bodies, the Laws on the Composition and Powers of the People's Consultative Assembly, the Parliament, and the Regional Representative Councils were subsequently issued. Furthermore, based upon said laws, the General Election of 1971 took place and the legislative bodies were established.

The brevity of the Indonesian Constitution of 1945 calls to mind a statement made by K. C. Wheare when replying to the question "What should a Constitution contain?" His answer was very brief: "The very minimum, and that minimum to be rules of Law"; and at another point he summed up by saying, "One essential characteristic of the ideally best form of Constitution is that it should be as short as possible."[7] Such a perspective accords with the spirit of the "Framers of the Constitution of Indonesia," who limited themselves to establishing the Basic Rules in the Constitution and assigned implementation thereof to Resolutions of the People's Consultative Assembly. The Assembly in turn entrusts to the Government the task of their execution, in executive matters, and to the Parliament the role of legislation (*Gesetzgebung*). This charge to implement Resolutions is mandatory.

"Rechtsstaat" Indonesia and Separation of Powers

The Indonesian State is a *Rechtsstaat*, not a *Machtstaat*, a constitutional system, not an absolutist State. Textually, the Constitution of 1945 contains no explicit provision calling for a Rechtsstaat, nor is any further information on the subject offered in the Note of Explanation of the 1945 Constitution.

However, the Indonesian conception of Rechtsstaat, as outlined in jurisprudence and duly adopted by the government, contains three special characteristics. These have arisen from comparisons made between the principles of "Rule of Law" (in a sense broader than that of A. V. Dicey)[8] and "Socialist Legality," as follows:

1. Recognition and protection of fundamental rights, embodying equality in the political field, in law, and in the social, economic, cultural and educational fields.
2. Legality, in the sense of law in all its forms.
3. An independent judiciary, which is impartial and free from the influence of any other power or force.

As discussed earlier, the State ideology on which the Indonesian Rechtsstaat is founded is the Pancasila (Five Principles). There is similarity here with the principles of all "Rule of Law" states, including the United States of America, particularly as those principles have been broadly outlined by the International Commission of Jurists. The International Commission of Jurists focuses on both the dignity of men and their diversity, but not so as to prejudice the three above-mentioned special characteristics of Indonesian constitutionalism.

In the Indonesian scheme of "separation of powers," there are five powers, not three as in the U.S. Constitution: the Executive, the

7. K. C. Wheare, *Modern Constitutions* (London: Oxford University Press, 1966, 2nd ed.), pp. 33-34.

8. A. V. Dicey, *Introduction to the Study of the Law of the Constitution* (London: Macmillan, 1961, 10th ed.), p. 183.

Legislative, and the Judicial powers, the Supreme Advisory Council, and the Supreme Auditing Office. These powers are separate. However, as C. F. Strong notes, the business of constitutional government is so complex that it is difficult to define the area of each department in such a manner as to leave each independent and supreme in its allotted sphere.[9] As an example, let us look briefly at the status of the Indonesian judiciary.

With respect to the courts of the Unitary Indonesian State, an independent judiciary is one essential element of Indonesian constitutionalism. Article 24 of the Constitution stipulates that judicial power shall be vested in the Supreme Court and such subordinate courts as may be established by law, and that the organization and competence of those courts shall be provided by law. A high point and crowning achievement in judicial development came with the Basic Law of the Judiciary in 1970.[10] Courts of four different jurisdictions are established: Ordinary Courts of general jurisdiction, Religious Courts, Military Courts, and Administrative Courts. The Supreme Court, at the pinnacle, holds exclusive jurisdiction over cases in cassation. The courts are independent and free in carrying out their functions. But following civil law traditions, rather than American common law tradition, the Supreme Court does not have the power of judicial review over acts of the executive or legislative branches of government, though it may review regulations that are pursuant to legislative acts. Laws may be interpreted, but not reviewed as in American judicial practice.

Indonesia does not have a body like the Conseil Constitutionelle of France, which can rule on the constitutionality of organic laws before their promulgation and on regulations of the parliamentary assemblies before they are first applied. Neither is there found in Indonesia what is called the *Bundesverfassungs-gericht*, or Constitutional Court, as in West Germany, which has the competence to exercise judicial review of the laws, and whose own position must be made to accord with that of the Supreme Court, the highest tribunal.

In judicial decision-making, we rely upon a combination of code law (in the civil law tradition), legislation, and jurisprudence more than upon case law or precedent. However, Indonesian courts also follow adat law (customary law) and enforce it in private disputes; this reminds us of the common law and the law of equity. In this respect, our approach to adat law in the courts places us in a unique intermediate position between civil law courts and common law courts. As Professor ter Haar has noted, the codification and court system under Indonesian

9. C. F. Strong, *Modern Political Constitutions* (London: Sidgwick and Jackson, 1958, 5th ed.), pp. 255-256.

10. Law 14/1970, *Lembaran Negara* (State Gazette) no. 74, elucidation no. 2951.

statutory law is akin to the civil law system of Continental Europe, but Indonesia's unwritten law resembles more the common law system and the law of equity.[11]

Fundamental Rights in Indonesian Constitutionalism

Finally, the Indonesian Constitution, like that of the United States, guarantees the freedom of opinion, expression, and religion, and provides for equality before the law. (Article 27 provides that all citizens are equal before the law and in government and shall without exception respect the law and the government.) But as with the history of United States "separate but equal" doctrine until 1954, our history, society, and politics have conditioned the meaning of these principles in Indonesia.

It is interesting to us that while our Basic Press Law upholds the notion of "a free and responsible press," as recommended by the American Commission on the Freedom of the Press chaired by Robert Hutchins, the press in the United States takes a more libertarian view of its functions. Furthermore, there are guarantees of press freedom in both the U.S. Constitution (First Amendment) and the U.S.S.R. Constitution (Article 25), but principles and performance are in fact quite different in the two countries. Our press has observed at close hand both authoritarian and libertarian conceptions in practice, and Indonesia's law and journalists favor stress on the idea of the social responsibility of the press, a free *and* responsible press.

As mentioned earlier, belief in God is a basic principle of our constitutional State, and freedom of religion is guaranteed. Our historical experience leads us to a more positive affirmation of God than is accepted by the American constitutional notion of freedom of religion.[12] There does not exist in Indonesia a "wall of separation of Church and State," rigidly dogmatic in character and without flexibility, such as that found in the rulings of the United States Supreme Court and the Criminal Code of the U.S.S.R. Neither is there in Indonesia a "separation" (*Trennung*) that glorifies the separation (*vom Staat und Kirche*) in such a way as to encourage anti-God and anti-religious conceptions and laws, as in the U.S.S.R. Such a spirit would

11. Of works available in English on Indonesia adat law the most prominent is B. ter Haar, *Adat Law in Indonesia* (New York: IPR, 1948), a translation from the Dutch by E. Adamson Hoebel and A. Arthur Schiller.

12. Indonesia is predominantly an Islamic country, with perhaps 90 percent of the population professing to be Muslims, but with varying degrees of devoutness. Hinduism, Catholicism, and Protestantism also have substantial followings and are recognized by the Ministry of Religion, whose fundamental responsibilities, however, have mainly to do with Islam. The political party system has traditionally been organized in part around religious symbols, and religious conflict has been endemic.

be contrary to that found in the legal life of Indonesia. Indonesia accepts the principle of "non-preferential treatment" of all religions existing in Indonesia, but does not recognize the unity of State and Church (*Einheit von Staat und Kirche*). There is neither separation nor unity of Church and State; the secular and the spiritual are distinguishable, but they flow together.

In conclusion then, along with the historical influence noted above of the Declaration of Independence and the constitution of the United States, I can say there are both similarities and differences in the Indonesian and U.S. Constitutions deriving from the historical and political development and the aspirations and ideologies of our two states.

VI

Japan

Editorial Note

Japan is an ancient Northeast Asian country composed of the four main islands of Hokkaidō, Honshū, Shikoku, and Kyūshū, and thousands of small islands. In its premodern history, Japan was usually isolated from substantial external contacts, but is now actively trading with virtually all the nations of the world. No noteworthy in-migration of foreign peoples has occurred in recorded Japanese history, apart from the forced immigration of Koreans for war labor purposes before 1945. For many centuries the Japanese people have been remarkable for their racial, ethnic, linguistic, and cultural homogeneity. Since her defeat in World War II (1945) Japan has been pacifist, in principle, preference, and international practice, while becoming the world's third-ranking economic power and a leader in science, technology, education, and the arts. Japan and the United States carry on the largest overseas trade in human history.

Japan is a bit smaller than California, and only 15 percent of the land area can be farmed. About 80 percent of the 113 million people on the islands live in urban environments. Japan is extraordinarily dependent on imports of food, industrial raw materials, and energy resources. Her economy is oriented toward mass consumption and the export of sophisticated manufactured goods.

Note: Footnotes have been added by Ronald G. Brown, who adapted Professor Ukai's paper for this symposium. Professor Ukai then edited the chapter and notes.

For almost a century, except during an interlude of firm-handed military rule (ca. 1930-1945) and foreign expansion, Japan has chosen to establish its system of law upon a constitutional form of government. Since the forced opening of Japan to Western commerce and influence in the 1850s, foreign categories have shaped the form, but not necessarily the content, of the legal system. Partly because of the changes to dominance of German legal influence in the late nineteenth century and of American legal impact after 1945, Japan has experienced two constitutions whose texts are fundamentally different in their visions of national policy.

The first modern constitution, adopted in February 1889, came after nearly two and a half centuries in which a fairly strong central government (Tokugawa), presiding over hundreds of feudal domains, felt no need to set forth national ideals in a constitutional document. Although Tokugawa law, feudal house law, and local customary law constituted a sophisticated legal system, the only premodern constitution-like document in Japanese history was the seventeen articles drafted by Prince Shōtoku in A.D. 604 which exhorted the nation to respect the Emperor and to follow certain moral principles. In the Constitution of the Empire of Japan (1889), the Emperor Meiji was "restored" (*Meiji ishin*) formally to his proper place as the nation's real, not merely ritual sovereign. So it was said, but others continued to rule Japan in the Emperor's name. The institutional forms were based, in part, on the studies of officials and law students who had traveled to Germany, France, and the United States. Legally protected opportunities for popular participation under the constitutional scheme were rather narrow, but its major characteristics won approbation from leading European and American legal scholars.

If the first constitution was foreign inspired, the second constitution may be said to have been foreign induced. Within five months after the end of World War II, various constitutional revisions suggested by the Japanese government to the American Occupation authorities were rejected. However, after only one more month of Occupation-supervised constitution-writing, a document was produced which established far-reaching protections of equality, freedom, and political participation. The Constitution of Japan (*Nihonkoku Kempō*) became effective, without major changes, about a year later in the spring of 1947.

Certain features of the 1889 Constitution may still be found in the 1947 Constitution. The Emperor remains, but as a "symbol of the unity of the people." Both documents provide guarantees of freedom of expression, but the Meiji Constitution contains more restrictive qualifying clauses. Significantly, neither constitution was instituted on popular demand; rather, the 1889 Constitution was an imperial gift, while that of 1947 was approved by the Diet and the Occupation authorities.

The present Constitution enumerates the basic rights of the people in thirty-one articles (Chapter III). It expressly provides for rights of univeral adult suffrage (Article 15), education for all (Article 26), freedom to travel (Article 22), and collective bargaining (Article 28), rights which in the United States, by comparison, have only been recognized as the result of judicial interpretation, laws, or constitutional amendment—not in the original Constitution itself. Other provisions in Japan's Constitution have yet to be adopted in the United States or widely accepted elsewhere. For example, Article 9 is unique in expressly renouncing war as a right or an instrument of national policy; and in other countries, provisions like Article 24, which upholds the "equality of the sexes," are still in dispute.

In Japan, as elsewhere, gaps exist between constitutional rights in the text and in actual practice. Nevertheless, there is little influential talk of rewriting or scrapping the present Constitution. In fact, it is remarkable that despite heavy doses of foreign influence, neither constitution was or has been changed by amendment.

If the direction of Japanese constitutional law is to change toward a restriction or strengthening of individual rights, the evolution most likely will come about through interpretations by an independent judiciary. Judges are constitutionally independent in administration and decision-making under the Supreme Court, but are bound by the Constitution (Article 76). The courts, in tandem with other forces in Japan's political and economic life, will decide whether the Constitution will continue as a living and maturing document or will become but a dead letter whose precepts have outlived their historical usefulness.

August 1977

RONALD G. BROWN

The Significance of the Reception of American Constitutional Institutions and Ideas in Japan

Nobushige Ukai
Professor of Public Law, Senshu University

Japan's Modern Constitutional History

Commodore Perry's visit to Japan in 1853 was the fanfare to the opening of a nation which had been closed to most outside influences, especially that of modern Western civilization, for more than two hundred years. The issue of the opening of Japan resulted in a split of its leadership between two factions. One side supported the idea to open the country to foreign influence. The other continued to believe in the divine nature of Japan and strongly advocated the slogan "Respect the Emperor and repel the barbarians!"[1]

In several instances, the threat of military force was necessary to convince the more militant, anti-Western, feudal lords who controlled Japan prior to Perry's visit. However, in one of history's little ironies, those who earlier were so insistent on resisting the encroachment of the West were the first to turn toward the adoption of Western-like institutions with admiration and to eagerly receive all the blessings that such a society might provide.

The aim of the Meiji Restoration in 1867 was to restore the formal powers of government to the Emperor, who was only a symbolic figurehead under the prior feudal system. Nevertheless, much day-to-day political power remained in the hands of *samurai* leaders from two prominent clans (Satsuma and Chōshū) who served as the Emperor's advisors. Immediately, they adopted an American type of organizational system in their government, which attempted to incorporate the spirit of democracy by institutionalizing the election of government officials.[2] Later, when a Western type of electoral system of legislature

1. W. G. Beasley, *The Modern History of Japan* (New York: Praeger Publishers, 1963), pp. 85-87.

2. Ibid., p. 132. The organization of the Meiji era government, established January

was adopted, squabbles among political parties and government efforts to dictate voting behavior were notorious.

In 1889, the year before the first elections for the lower house of the Japanese parliament were carried out, a written constitution was promulgated by the Emperor as the "Constitution of the Empire of Japan." Based on the monarchy-focused constitutions of Germany and Austria in that period, the document was drafted by a group of bureaucrats, led by Prince Hirobumi Ito, who believed both in imperial sovereignty and in authoritarian administration.[3] It was this vision of government which established a pseudo-constitutional monarchy that led, after a series of assassinations and revolts, to the takeover of the government by the militarists in the 1930s, ultimately a deplorable war, and then the subsequent surrender in 1945.

The text for Japan's modern-day Constitution was drafted by staff members of General Douglas MacArthur, the Supreme Commander for the Allied Powers (SCAP), and then, in effect, given to the Japanese. It was officially promulgated in 1946 and became fully effective in May 1947. The new Constitution is generally a mixture of American and British constitutions; its scope is quite unlike the basic emphasis of the Meiji Constitution, since it embodies the principle of popular sovereignty.[4]

In adjusting to the postwar Constitution, Japan clearly has evolved political and legal institutions which at times accelerate Western constitutional tendencies while in great part retaining the vitality of the indigenous forces of the Japanese social context. We can briefly consider examples of this phenomenon. First, if we look at the political scene, we can find that the General Headquarters of SCAP in 1945 encouraged Japan to adopt the American model of a strong legislature

---

3, 1868, revolved around "three offices" (*sanshoku*): (1) a General Director, the post occupied by an imperial prince; (2) a group of Conferees, consisting of court nobles and some *daimyō*, the feudal lords in the earlier period; and (3) a group of Councilors, including many young *samurai*, the military leaders.

3. For a comparative analysis of pre-1945 and present-day Japanese constitutionalism, see "Introduction," H. Itoh and L. W. Beer, *The Constitutional Case Law of Japan* (Seattle: University of Washington Press, 1978). See also Nobutaka Ike, *Beginnings of Political Democracy in Japan* (New York: Greenwood Press, 1969), pp. 171-180, 188-191; Kenzo Takayanagi, "A Century of Innovation: The Development of Japanese Law, 1868-1961," in Arthur T. Von Mehren (ed.), *Law in Japan: The Legal Order in a Changing Society* (Cambridge: Harvard University Press, 1963); and Yosiyuki Noda, *Introduction to Japanese Law*, translated from French by A. H. Angelo (University of Tokyo Press, 1976). An English translation of the Meiji Constitution can be found in Hideo Tanaka, assisted by M. D. H. Smith, *The Japanese Legal System* (University of Tokyo Press, 1976), p. 16.

4. The Emperor is regarded as the symbolic leader of the State, but his position is derived from the will of the people. The Constitution of Japan (1947), art. 1 (hereafter cited as Constitution).

like the U.S. Congress. But although the present Japanese system is a combination of the British parliamentary government and the American theories of separation of powers between executive and legislature, the daily operations of government are controlled by a strong Cabinet.

In a similar way, the Japanese legal system also has selectively adopted Western ideas. Supposedly, the Occupation in 1945 was initiated upon Japan's so-called unconditional surrender. But, actually, the legal terms were not strictly unconditional. The conditions in the Potsdam Declaration and the basic principles in the postwar Constitution itself established that the Japanese government should henceforth faithfully observe fundamental freedoms, such as freedom of religion, thought, and the press. With its many centuries of tradition of strong government, Japan was not prepared for this sudden burst of freedoms. But because of the importance of these rights the Supreme Court's job of interpreting such fundamental freedoms in the Japanese context has taken on added significance.

In both the political and the legal sphere, the example of the United States has been instructive for comparative purposes. In the United States, Cabinet members do not initiate bills directly in the Congress. Similarly, in Japan, there is a theory that the Cabinet lacks power to initiate bills in the Diet, the two-house Japanese parliament (consisting of a House of Representatives and a House of Councilors). This theory, however, is quite different from the Meiji Constitution, which expressly provided for "government bills" on the principle that legislative power was in the hands of the Emperor with the consent of the Diet.[5] Furthermore, there was a clear provision in the law of the Diet that "government bills" would be considered prior to deliberation of any individually sponsored bills.[6] In practice, the present situation has changed so that both the Cabinet and the Diet have legislative bureaus which help prepare bills for consideration. As in Britain, however, there may be little real difference between a "government bill" and a "member's bill" of the majority party since the majority party controls the Cabinet.[7]

Judicial Review in Japan

In regard to judicial powers, we can make further useful comparisons with the United States to illustrate. In the United States, the doctrine of judicial review by which the Supreme Court has the power to review legislative actions was announced by the Court itself in *Marbury* v.

5. The Constitution of the Empire of Japan, 1889, Art. 38.
6. The Diet Law (*Kokkai hō*) of 1890, Art. 26.
7. Concerning delicate intra- as well as inter-party politics, see Hans Baerwald, *Japan's Parliament* (London: Cambridge University Press, 1975), pp. 82-102.

Madison,[8] rather than explicitly stipulated in the U.S. Constitution. By contrast, the postwar Japanese Constitution expressly sets forth the power of judicial review of acts of the Diet as well as review of administrative rules and official acts.[9] Probably because the doctrine is so clearly stated in the Japanese Constitution, the Supreme Court has been extremely careful in declaring laws invalid. Prior to 1976, for example, the Japanese Supreme Court had not followed the lead of the U.S. Supreme Court in *Baker* v. *Carr*,[10] in which the judicially imposed barrier of "political questions" was removed to permit review of legislative reapportionment cases. On April 14, 1976, the Japanese Supreme Court found that the apportionment provisions of the Election Law were unconstitutional,[11] since they were contrary to the principle of political equality guaranteed by Article 14 of the Constitution.[12]

Up to this point, I have commented generally on the development of political and legal institutions that were adopted along with the postwar Japanese Constitution. Beyond this initial discussion, however, it is also instructive to consider the evolution in interpretations of the Constitution as practiced by the lawyers and judges in Japan. In particular, I feel that this is a good time to reconsider the legacy of the Occupation in the light of fundamental concepts of political liberty in the United States.

In 1949, the United States Cultural Mission, composed of five distinguished American professors (including Professor Edwin O. Reischauer), visited Japan. In its subsequent report, the scholarly panel touched upon the importance of securing a greater degree of freedom in Japan. They felt that, because of Japan's past record of direct government interference in universities, it was necessary to take extraordinary precautions to insure the continuing intellectual freedom of scholars.[13]

In a country like Japan, which has a long history of absolute government control and strict limitations on basic civil rights, a much larger degree of freedom should be recognized by the courts, perhaps

8. 1 Cranch 137 (1803). Concerning judicial review in Japan generally, see John M. Maki, *Court and Constitution in Japan* (Seattle: University of Washington Press, 1964), pp. 306-348 passim; and Tanaka, op. cit. (note 3 above), pp. 686-694.

9. Constitution, Art. 81.

10. 369 U.S. 186 (1962). Concerning "political questions" in Japan generally, see Dan F. Henderson (ed.), *The Constitution of Japan: Its First Twenty Years, 1947-67* (Seattle: University of Washington Press, 1968), pp. 125, 145, 165.

11. *Kurokawa* v. *Chiba Prefecture Election Supervision Commission, Hanrei Jihō* (No. 808) 24 (Sup. Ct., G. B., April 14, 1976).

12. Constitution, art. 14 (1): "All of the people are equal under the law and there shall be no discrimination in political, economic or social relations because of race, creed, sex, social status or family origin." See also the discussion in the text at note 35.

13. Civil Information and Education Section, Supreme Commander for the Allied Powers, Report of the U.S. Cultural Science Mission to Japan, January 1949, pp. 101-6.

more even than in the United States. In a country that does not have a tradition of basic freedoms, the people cannot be expected to exercise their rights to the fullest extent immediately. In Japan, even the slightest limitation on these freedoms may cause the people to back away from asserting their rights, thus creating a much greater restrictive effect than is actually applied by the courts. This kind of effect is what the United States Cultural Mission was referring to in its report. It is in this area that the influence of the United States experience can play a vital role.

During its first thirty years, the postwar Japanese Supreme Court has decided in only two cases that laws were unconstitutional after it was claimed that basic rights were infringed. The often stated judicial pretext for this exceptionally careful attitude is that the Diet should be the sole authority to decide the extent of legislative acts.

In the first instance in which a law or a State action was found unconstitutional the case centered on a provision in the Customs Law that permitted confiscation of goods and ships which were owned by third parties and used in illegal customs activities. The Court ruled that such confiscation could occur only when the third party had prior knowledge that the goods were used illegally.[14] The Court concluded that without notice and a hearing the provision in Article 31 of the Constitution for due process of law had been violated. In 1963, the Diet passed an additional law which now provides for detailed procedures, including notice and a hearing, before confiscation is permitted of property held by a third party in customs cases.[15]

The second case concerned a defendant who was raped by her father, bore several children, and was coerced into continuing the irregular relationship even after she had a chance to start a normal, married life. She was convicted of murdering her father under the "patricide provision" of the Japanese Criminal Code, which calls for a more severe penalty in cases of patricide than in other cases of murder or manslaughter.[16] In 1950, the Court had rendered a decision in a similar case, declaring that the "patricide provision" was constitutional

14. *Nakamura et al.* v. *Japan, 11 Keishu* (No. 16) 1593 (Sup. Ct., G. B., November 28, 1962). An English translation of this decision can be found in Itoh and Beer, op. cit., Case 7. See also Nobushige Ukai and Nathaniel L. Nathanson, "Protection of Property Rights and Due Process of Law in the Japanese Constitution," in Henderson, op. cit., pp. 248-250.

15. Emergency Measure on Confiscation Procedure as to Third Party Possession in Criminal Matters (*Keiji jiken ni okeru daisansha shoyubutsu no bosshu tetsuzuki ni kansuru ōkyu sochi hō*), Law No. 138 of 1963.

16. Article 199 of the Criminal Code specifies that the penalty in murder cases can range from a minimum sentence of three years in prison to a maximum sentence of death. However, in patricide cases, which are governed by Article 200, only the alternative sentences of life imprisonment or death can be given by the judge.

on the grounds that the distinction between patricide and other forms of homicide was reasonable, and therefore differently assigned penalties did not impair the "equality under the law" provision in Article 14 of the Constitution. In that decision, only two dissenting opinions were filed among the fifteen justices participating.[17] However, in 1973, given the facts as stated above, the Supreme Court reversed itself and found that another "patricide provision" was contrary to Article 14.[18] It is interesting that although the decision was nearly unanimous (except for one dissent based on precedent by Justice Takezo Shimoda, former ambassador to the United States), the rationale for the decision was divided into two points of view. Eight justices representing a clear majority on the court, led by Chief Justice Kazuto Ishida, reasoned that since the penalty for patricide was too heavy, it could not be deemed constitutional.[19] Six other justices, a progressive group headed by Justice Jirō Tanaka, argued that the "patricide provision" was per se unconstitutional because establishing separate treatments and applying unequal penalties according to family linear relationships was inherently a violation of Article 14. The concurring opinion stated that the "patricide provision" reflected an undemocratic tendency remaining from the Chinese codes and from the Tokugawa era of law, which was in effect just before the opening of Japan in the mid-nineteenth century —a tendency which could not be tolerated in a modern democratic nation such as Japan.

The effect of these two cases declaring laws unconstitutional is not clear. In theory, we can say either that the decisions result in the elimination of the offending unconstitutional provision from the text of the laws or that the decisions merely bind only further cases which appear before the courts. However, in my opinion, decisions of uncon-

17. *Japan* v. *Yamato*, 4 *Keishū* (No. 10) 2126 (Sup. Ct., G.B., October 25, 1950). See Maki, op. cit. (n. 8 above), pp. 129-155.

18. *Aizawa* v. *Japan*, 27 *Keishū* (No. 3) 256 (Sup. Ct., G.B., April 4, 1973). See John O. Haley, "Recent Developments—Constitutionality of Penalty Under Article 200 of the Penal Code for Killing of Lineal Ascendant," 6 *Law in Japan: An Annual* (1973), pp. 173-174. While the court in *Aizawa* found the patricide provision in Article 200 of the Penal Code unconstitutional, this decision did not upset the result in *Yamato* that the similar provision in Article 205 of the Code was constitutional. Therefore, in a later case brought under Article 205 (which establishes a comparatively severe penalty for accidental patricide), the Supreme Court declared that provision constitutional. *Matsui* v. *Japan*, 28 *Keishū* (No. 6) 329 (Sup. Ct., First Petty Bench, September 26, 1974).

19. If a defendant surrenders voluntarily, his sentence of life imprisonment, according to Articles 42 and 68 of the Criminal Code, is automatically mitigated to a seven-year term, and later, according to individual circumstances, under Articles 66, 71, and 68 of that Code, can be reduced further to a term of half of that period, i.e., only three and a half years. However, further mitigation of sentence, such as stay of execution, cannot be granted, since it is possible only when the assessed sentence is three years or less. Therefore, no such mitigation in penalty could apply to patricide cases, since only life imprisonment or death are alternative sentences.

stitutionality can be applied only to the actual parties affected by the decisions. Differences in opinion among the justices as to the precise ruling can be resolved by positive action by the Diet to clear up ambiguities. For instance, it is necessary for the Diet either to strike a provision from the code or to reduce penalties assigned to infractions under the law to meet judicial objections of unconstitutionality. Until the Diet acts, the possibility remains that the same question might again be brought before the Supreme Court.

With regard to legal theories about the effect of a law that is declared unconstitutional and with regard to other types of legal questions, the Japanese judicial system could learn a great deal from the constitutional experience of the United States. Today, in the Japanese courts, we can find arguments about basic theories of U.S. constitutional law, such as "void on its face," "void for vagueness," and "prior restraint," which can be used as the rationale to strike down or limit laws which, if enforced, would be unjustly applied against fundamental human rights. Leading U.S. cases which have shaped these theories are often cited by the courts, opposing attorneys, and scholars in both law and political science.[20] In such a climate, I think that the need for specific decisions by Japanese courts which guarantee fundamental civil rights is evident, and, furthermore, I believe that the Supreme Court can best assume this responsibility. But what form should this responsibility take? Using examples from individual cases, I should like to indicate two points which seem important for clarification about the areas into which the Supreme Court must move in order to guarantee basic civil rights.

The "Dual Standard" Principle and the "Public Welfare"

First of all, the Court must provide more clarifying distinctions between property rights and personal rights. A "dual standard" approach would apply different approaches to these two kinds of fundamental rights, since there are genuine differences between rights derived from a tangible or economic basis and those derived from an intangible or moral basis. Both of these ideas are tied to the concept of "public welfare," an expression developed in the American constitutional experience. In the United States, the battle in legal thinking was between lawyers who believed that the U.S. Constitution protected the freedom of contract and enabled unrestricted disposition of property, and the lawmakers who believed that principles of social rights implied in the

20. Among the commonly cited U.S. cases are *Shelton* v. *Tucker*, 364 U.S. 479 (1960), statute required membership reports, and *Aptheker* v. *Secretary of State*, 378 U.S. 500 (1964), passport statute found restrictive of right to travel.

same document required legislation to control big business in order to help the less fortunate in society. An intermediary position would argue that fundamental rights can be restricted if the public welfare demands it. However, in the sphere of personal civil liberties, no restrictions should be imposed. Such guarantees should be more or less absolute, as in the First Amendment to the U.S. Constitution. In actual practice, only the guarantees of economic rights should be limited by the phrase "public welfare."

In a general way, the Japanese Constitution appears to be sympathetic toward the "dual standard" principle. Based on the United States experience, the drafters of the Constitution were astute enough to place the "public welfare" limit on human rights in two separate articles. Article 22 guarantees the freedoms of residence and occupation, but only "to the extent that [they] do not interfere with the public welfare."[21] Article 29 guarantees the right to own or hold property, but only "in conformity with the public welfare." The insertion of the "public welfare" concept, especially in the light of the prior history in the United States of constitutional disputes about economic and social rights, was a wise precaution. On the other hand, the deletion of the words "due" and "property" in Article 31, which describes the freedoms of "life" and "liberty" that may not be taken away from a "person," clarifies the state of the law. This article makes it clear that restrictions on property should be considered separately from questions about due process of law, thus precluding Japan from the difficulties encountered in the United States when the Supreme Court declared that an early child labor law was unconstitutional.[22] In Japan, the presence of the "public welfare" language in Article 29 considerably strengthens the impact of Article 31. An alternative interpretation, perhaps more generally accepted, suggests that, although Article 31 guarantees "life"

21. General provisions concerning the "public welfare" are found in the Constitution, Arts. 12 and 13: "Article 12. The freedoms and rights guaranteed to the people by this Constitution shall be maintained by the constant endeavor of the people, who shall refrain from any abuse of these freedoms and rights and shall always be responsible for utilizing them for the public welfare. Article 13. All of the people shall be respected as individuals. Their right to life, liberty, and the pursuit of happiness shall, to the extent that it does not interfere with the public welfare, be the supreme consideration in legislation and in other governmental affairs." Concerning the public welfare clause in relation to civil liberties, see Lawrence W. Beer, "Freedom of Expression in Japan with Comparative Reference to the United States," in R. P. Claude (ed.), *Comparative Human Rights* (Baltimore: Johns Hopkins University Press, 1976), p. 99.

22. *Hammer* v. *Dagenhart*, 247 U.S. 251 (1918). After the U.S. Supreme Court struck down child labor legislation based on the power of Congress to regulate interstate commerce, the Congress attempted to circumvent the decision by regulations through the use of the congressional power to tax and at one time even considered a constitutional amendment. However, in *United States* v. *Darby*, 312 U.S. 100 (1941), the Court questioned the wisdom of the *Hammer* decision and upheld minimum wage provisions based on the commerce power.

and "liberty" but not "property," the rights of property are nevertheless an authentic part of liberty, since they are implicitly guaranteed. By this view, the guarantee of "due process of law" is nothing more than the all-encompassing "by the law of the land," which is found in the British tradition. The difficulty with this interpretation is whether it can be said that, even if the key word "property" is eliminated, the same "due process of law" guarantee still prevails. Despite the general acceptance of the view of implicit guarantees, I still believe that the drafters displayed wisdom and foresight in the selective insertion and exclusion of key words.

Whichever interpretation is accepted, one can still observe that the "dual standard" approach is maintained in constitutional litigation in Japan. However, since it is not always easy to identify whether a particular freedom should be classified as a property right or a personal right, various cases have brought about a mixture of results. For example, in a case involving the regulation of pharmaceuticals, the Supreme Court declared that a law restricting the minimum distance between two pharmacies was unconstitutional because it infringed upon the guarantee of freedom of occupation in Article 22 of the Constitution.[23] The Court reasoned that the distance requirement lacked a necessary and rational relationship to the purpose, which was to prevent the distribution of inferior medicines.[24] In a different case, a majority of the Court reached a contrary result, rejecting the claim that a basic freedom had been impaired. The majority decision sustained a penal provision[25] which regulated the distribution of books when the purpose was to control the expression of obscenity.[26] One indication that the results in these two cases are not easily reconcilable is the fact that some justices in the latter case filed strong dissents.

Japan's Supreme Court on Individual Rights and Liberties

A second area which requires clarification in discussing the future direction of the Japanese Supreme Court centers on the applicability of constitutional guarantees to relationships among private citizens. This area appears to be quite sensitive. Apparently, a theory that would directly apply such guarantees has little support. But some urgent

23. Pharmaceutical Law (*Yakuji hō*), Law No. 145 of 1960, Art. 6 (2), (4).

24. *K. K. Sumiyoshi* v. *Governor of Hiroshima Prefecture, Saibansho Jihō* (No. 665) (Sup. Ct., G. B., April 30, 1975). See also John O. Haley, "The Freedom to Choose an Occupation and the Constitutional Limits of Legislative Discretion," *Law in Japan: An Annual* 8 (1975), pp. 188-204, which includes a translation of the decision.

25. Criminal Code (*Keihō*), Law No. 45 of 1907, Art. 175.

26. *Ishii et al.* v. *Japan*, 10 *Keishū* (No. 23) 1239 (Sup. Ct., G.B., October 15, 1969). For a translation of the famous De Sade Decision, see H. Itoh and L. W. Beer, op. cit. (n. 3 above), Case 26.

problems, such as matters in which private discrimination is alleged, can be resolved by the indirect application of such guarantees. In particular, the use of the judicial principle of "state action" as conceived by the United States seems attractive to Japan in this respect.[27] The "state action" principle is based on the premise that private actions can be regulated to the extent that private agreements will be enforced through decisions by the courts. Essentially, the principle combines the best of both the direct and indirect application methods. The principle may not be as all encompassing as the direct approach, but at the same time it is stronger than the indirect approach. I can best explain my point of view by looking at some recent cases before the Japanese Supreme Court. These cases, in general, indicate the need for more judicial recognition of civil liberties. All three of the following cases deal with incidents arising from employment relationships.

For convenience, we can refer to the first of these examples as the Post Office Employees Case. The defendants, officers of the Post Office Employees Union, were given criminal penalties for urging workers at the Tokyo Central Post Office to participate in a union meeting during working hours. Their efforts resulted in thirty-seven postal employees leaving their working place. For our purposes here, the significance of the case is whether the rights of the convicted union leaders to assemble the work force should have been constitutionally protected by the Supreme Court.

Two legal provisions are relevant to the case. First of all, Article 28 of the Japanese Constitution guarantees the right of workers to organize and act collectively. However, a special provision in the law governing workers in the postal service provides a penalty for those who obstruct postal service activities.[28]

According to the Supreme Court decision, labor rights, although guaranteeed as fundamental human rights, are not absolute in character, but may be restricted within constitutional limits. A majority of the Court viewed the Constitution as requiring an equilibrium between property rights and labor rights. The approach is flexible and purpose oriented. In its view, the rational constitutional balance would apply restrictions on labor only within a "necessary minimum." Although acknowledging that public employees generally are denied the right to strike,[29] the majority reasoned that an obstruction caused by a strike,

27. In the United States, the "state action" principle was initially applied to deny the enforcement of racially restrictive covenants in a property sale agreement, *Shelley* v. *Kraemer* 334 U.S. 1 (1948). A narrower statement of the principle requires that the state must be involved "to some significant extent" before private conduct will be regulated, *Burton* v. *Wilmington Parking Authority*, 365 U.S. 715 (1961).

28. Postal Law (*Yūbin hō*), Law No. 165 of 1947, Art. 78.

29. Public Enterprise Labor Relations Law (*Kōkyō kigyōtaitō rōdō kankei hō*), Law No. 257 of 1948, Art. 17 (1).

even if illegal, would be justified if it was not accompanied by violence. Since the applicable laws did not provide explicitly for a criminal penalty in the case of an illegal strike, the punishment assessed against the defendants could not be sustained. Therefore, the Supreme Court reversed the lower court's decision which convicted the defendants, on the grounds that the only proper sanctions were discharge from employment or civil compensation, not a criminal penalty.[30]

By contrast, the minority view provides a rigid, harsh, and text-oriented approach which we can find repeated in later decisions. The minority, looking at the strict language of the relevant laws,[31] argued that, since the right to strike was prohibited in the Public Enterprise Labor Relations Law and a criminal penalty for obstructing the postal service was specified in the Postal Service Law, the two statutes read together left no room for denying the illegality of the defendants' actions.

The same patterns in judicial approach, alternating between flexibility and rigidity, can be seen in the series of decisions in the Sarufutsu case. The town of Sarufutsu, having a population of about 5,000 persons, lies on the extreme tip of Hokkaido, the large island in the northernmost part of Japan. The case, again involving a post office employee, dealt with a conviction under a provision of the National Public Employees Law which generally prohibits political activities of national government employees.[32] For putting up political posters in his spare time, the employee was convicted in the initial judicial proceeding in the summary court and fined 5,000 yen (now about $20).

In this instance, a more flexible approach to basic freedoms was based on the principle of the "least restrictive alternative," an American legal doctrine, which was submitted in a brief by Professor Nobuyoshi Ashibe of Tokyo University. The theory, which also is sometimes described in terms of the "less drastic means" or the "less offensive alternative," is designed to enable the court to choose a reasonable, less difficult course in applying the law in order to sidestep the particular problems of constitutional questions.[33] In this instance, the Sapporo High Court adopted the principle in order to declare the public service law unconstitutional only insofar "as applied" to the facts here.[34]

30. *Sotoyama* v. *Japan*, 8 *Keishū* (No. 20) 901 (Sup. Ct., G. B., October 26, 1966).

31. Ibid.

32. National Public Employees Law (*Kokka kōmuin hō*), Law No. 120 of 1947, Art. 102 (1). See also Lawrence W. Beer, "Recent Developments—Constitutionality of Restricting the Freedom of Expression of Public Employees," 8 *Law in Japan: An Annual* (1975), pp. 205-8.

33. The criteria by which the U.S. Supreme Court may choose to apply a "least restrictive alternative" rather than face a constitutional question directly appear in the concurring opinion of Justice Louis Brandeis in *Ashwander* v. *TVA*, 297 U.S. 288 (1936).

34. *Japan* v. *Ozawa, Hanrei Jihō* (No. 560) 30 (Sapporo High Court, June 24, 1969).

However, a newly emerging majority on the Supreme Court, which favored the rigid approach, led to a reversal of the High Court decision. The Court held that since government employees must be politically neutral in order to retain the trust of the public, prohibitions on certain political activities by government employees did not exceed the limits of reasonable, necessary, and unavoidable restrictions on freedom of expression under the Constitution.[35] As a result, the Court refused to loosen the restrictions on a basic freedom enjoyed by all other workers in Japan except public employees. Control in Japan over a government worker's political activities continues to be much stricter than in Western countries.

As a final example of recent Supreme Court cases dealing with civil liberties, we can consider the implications of the Mitsubishi Plastic Company case. In this instance, a graduate of Tōhoku University successfully passed a placement examination at the plastic company and was subsequently hired on a trial basis. At the end of the test period, however, he was denied permanent employment on the grounds that he had failed to disclose his political activities as a student. The Supreme Court ruled on the case as a matter of law, but remanded to the lower court on a question of fact-finding as to what the plaintiff employee had actually said in the placement interview and what he actually had done politically while a student.[36]

The precise question of law concerns whether a prospective employer may properly investigate a job applicant's creed or thought and then require the applicant to report these matters. A unanimous Supreme Court ruled that an enterprise, by denying employment on the basis of an applicant's thought or creed, does not necessarily act illegally. In reaching this conclusion, the Court cited a law which guarantees that laborers will not be discriminated against because of their creed,[37] but it narrowly read the provision as not applying to job applicants. Hence, an employer may freely choose his employees. Furthermore, the Court noted, a reserve clause which gives an employer the right to dismiss an employee after a trial period of evaluation and a background investigation is proper within reasonable limits.

A short while ago, an out-of-court settlement was reached in this case. The former employee was rehired, received the equivalent of thirteen years of back pay and additional consolation payments totaling

35. *Japan* v. *Ozawa*, 28 *Keishū* (No. 9) 393 (Sup. Ct., G.B., November 6, 1974).

36. *Takano* v. *Mitsubishi Jūshi K. K.*, 27 *Minshū* 1536 (Sup. Ct., G.B., Dec. 12, 1973). See "Recent Developments—Constitutional Law—Applicability of Civil Rights and Freedom of Thought Clauses to Conduct of Private Parties," 7 *Law in Japan: An Annual* 151 (1974). Constitution, "Art. 19. Freedom of thought and conscience shall not be violated."

37. Labor Standards Law (*Rōdō kijun hō*), Law No. 49 of 1947, Art. 3.

25 million yen (about $100,000), and also became entitled to all the rights and privileges of other employees at the Mitsubishi Plastic Company.

From these three cases which we have examined, I think it is evident that strong support for imposing restrictions on civil liberties still exists within the Japanese Supreme Court. In recent years, the trend toward the more rigid, restrictive approach has resulted mainly from the mandatory retirement of justices who favored the more flexible approach. There is a particular danger in the implications of the Mitsubishi case, since the ruling suggests that guarantees of equality and freedom of thought and conscience do not apply to relations between private persons. This problem can be analyzed by focusing on the Fourteenth Amendment in the U.S. Constitution in connection with racial discrimination problems. In the United States, discrimination in restaurants, theaters, and other similar places cannot be regarded as legal so long as the discriminatory acts are regarded as state action or as denying rights against discrimination in particular places guaranteed in such laws as the Civil Rights Act. However, in Japan we have the situation that the Constitution protects those who suffer under discrimination, but does not apply to citizen-to-citizen relationships.

If a private person believes in a certain religious sect, can he discharge an employee who does not believe in that religion? Can a newspaper published by a certain political party discharge an employee who is not loyal to the party? These questions can only be answered affirmatively in a legal context in which constitutional guarantees are not applied to cases between individuals. In such cases, as I mentioned earlier, I feel that it is proper for the American theory of "state action" to be applied.

Methods of Interpretation

What is basically important in comparative legal research is not to concentrate on a detailed scrutiny of legal terminology used in the text of the Constitution, a practice common in prewar Japan. Rather, the emphasis must be on learning and understanding the differences in historical backgrounds of the countries that are compared. Only then can we construct the proper infrastructure which can serve as the driving force in a remodeling of society based on structures that facilitate freedom and peace. To this writer, there appears to be a fundamental dichotomy between the new type of Japanese constitutional methodology based on the American approach and the older type based on the German approach. Yet, we cannot call either right or wrong, but must simply choose the method that suits the historical context of Japan. In my opinion, for the last quarter of this century, and possibly for generations to come, the American type of constitutional methodology and interpretation will best suit Japan.

Under the old and new constitutions in Japan, different styles of interpretation have become fashionable. Under the Meiji Constitution, there existed only two schools of interpretation, one oriented toward the Emperor and the other toward the Diet. All seventy-six articles in the Constitution were interpreted according to one of these views with the result that the prevailing tendency was toward an authoritarian approach.[38] Under the present Constitution, however, the interpretations are much more diversified. One interpretation becomes the guiding principle to settle particular cases only after many ramifications and contrasting views are discussed.

In conclusion, I believe that the constitutional experience of the United States can be an important model for Japan, since the Japanese Constitution itself is a direct result of the United States experience of more than two hundred years. Since we have not yet developed a self-oriented behavior pattern in the confusion of the postwar period, we Japanese have tried to organize a new society with the Constitution of Japan as its guiding star.

38. See Frank O. Miller, *Minōbe Tatsukichi—Interpreter of Constitutionalism in Japan* (Berkeley and Los Angeles: University of California Press, 1965), and Richard H. Minear, *Japanese Tradition and Western Law* (Cambridge: Harvard University Press, 1970).

VII

Malaysia

Editorial Note

Malaysia in its diversity and far-flung geographical profile bears some similarity to Indonesia. Yet special problems have followed from the fact that two groups perceived as ethnically alien to the region, Chinese and Indians, make up nearly half the population. Malaysia's twelve million people are preponderantly concentrated in peninsular Malaya, leaving Sarawak and Sabah geographically distant, sparse in population, and appreciably less advanced, in conventional civilizational terms, despite greater ethnic diversity.

Malaysia—formally proposed in 1961 to include peninsular Malaya, Singapore, and the northern Borneo territories of Sabah, Sarawak, and Brunei—came into existence in 1963, but without Brunei, which chose to remain separate. Like the several other federations brought into existence under British auspices during the same period, the creation of Malaysia entailed considerations of the dissolution of the empire, reduction of military obligations balanced by offsetting Western ally pressures to create viable states, and responsiveness to genuine nationalist aspirations. Although, compared with the other experiments in federationism, Malaysia boasts the distinction of survival, this has been accomplished only with considerable, ongoing costs.

The brittle fabric of contorted constitutional quid pro quo de-

Editor's Note: Concerning the author, see J. Victor Morais, *A Man of His Time: Lord President Tan Sri M. Suffian* (Kuala Lumpur: Percetakan Perdana Sdn. Bhd., 1974).

signed to appease the diverse territorial, ethnic, language, resource, religious, and other interests first splintered in 1965, with potentially ugly racial and territorial conflict resulting in the severance of Singapore, which became a separate, independent nation.

Some years of showcase democracy then transpired, until 1969 when racialism in peninsular Malaya erupted at a pitch of violence with serious socio-political consequences in terms of the growth of security forces and structured provisions for racial favoritism. And the Bornean components, on a different plane altogether, chafe at what some feel is a new form of colonial tutelage.

Still, Malaysia's complex party structure has endured in relative success, helped by a healthy economic base, diversified in recent years through aggressive programs to attract foreign investment and to develop an industrial base. Staple exports such as rubber, palm oil, tin, copper, and timber are increasingly augmented by sectors of urban high-technology production. While Malaysia's $2,000 per capita gross national product lags markedly behind Singapore, the fundamental resources base affords more stable long-term economic security.

The heritage of English law in both Malaysia and Singapore remains very influential, the links with the formal tradition having suffered no major breaks through political revolution or domestic upheaval. The strength of these links is manifest still in the Malaysian provision for appeal from the Supreme Court to the British Privy Council, a connection strongly favored by many lawyers. Similarly, until recently, most lawyers in Malaysia and Singapore were trained in England. Law training was begun at the University of Singapore in 1957, and the first law faculty in Malaysia was opened in the early 1970s.

In both countries there are unified civil judiciaries, whose Supreme Courts exercise both original and appellate jurisdictions. In Malaysia Islamic courts are organized in each constituent state, and in Singapore also provision is made for Islamic justice for the minority Malay population. The legal professions of Malaysia and Singapore are well developed and growing.

Substantive law in Malaysia and Singapore has evolved also from principles rooted in English common law tradition. In Malaysia, however, as in Indonesia, local customary (adat) law has always received considerable attention as a special area of national law.

DANIEL S. LEV

May 1978 ROGER K. PAGET

The Malaysian Constitution and the United States Constitution

Tun Mohamed Suffian bin Hashim
Lord President of Malaysia

First, a few words about Malaysia. The country is to the south of Vietnam about two hours away by jet and is in two parts: Peninsular Malaysia on the Asian mainland and, across the South China Sea, two states, Sabah and Sarawak, sometimes referred to collectively as East Malaysia. Malaysia is about the same size as California and its population is approximately ten million.

Malaysia is a federation of thirteen states headed by His Majesty the Yang Dipertuan Agung (King). The Federation has fourteen legislatures and fourteen governments: one for the Federation and one for each of the thirteen states. Each of the nine Malay states is headed by a hereditary Sultan, and each of the other four states by a Governor federally appointed.

The Federation first came into existence in 1895, and in 1946 was enlarged to embrace all the states in the Malay peninsula. On August 31, 1957, it was granted independence by the British, who had ruled for 125 years. (Previously we had been ruled for 125 years by the Portuguese, who conquered us in 1511, a few years after Columbus had reached America and thought he was in the East Indies, and thereafter by the Dutch for 150 years.) In 1963 the Federation, then named the Federation of Malaya, was further enlarged and renamed Malaysia when Singapore and the two states in Borneo (Sabah and Sarawak) joined it on being granted independence by the British. (Singapore left Malaysia in 1965.)

Malaysia is a parliamentary democracy and has held general elections every five years as prescribed by the Constitution: in 1959, 1964, 1969, and 1974. The Malaysian King acts in accordance with the advice of the federal Cabinet, and each Sultan and Governor in accordance with the advice of the state Cabinet. Legislative and executive power is divided between the federal government on the one hand and each of the state governments on the other by a written constitution.

This constitution (promulgated on August 31, 1957) as amended is known as the Malaysian Constitution and applies not only to the federal government but also to all state governments. At the same time each state has its own written constitution, applying only to that state.

In what way has the Malaysian Constitution been influenced by the United States Constitution?

At the outset I should say that I learned my law in England, where the law schools hardly touched on the U.S. Constitution, probably for fear that Malaysians and others from the Empire might follow the bad example set by the organizers of the Boston Tea Party, and so I should admit that my knowledge of the United States Constitution is rather meagre. I should further and frankly admit that the Malaysian Constitution has been little influenced by the U.S. Constitution, at least directly, except for the incorporation of concepts that are universal and are found in the constitutions of many countries, such as the separation of powers between the three branches of government, the supremacy of the constitution, the rule of law, the independence of the judiciary and of the bar, the outlawing of discrimination, the guarantee of fundamental liberties, and the like. Our Constitution has been little influenced by the U.S. Constitution because, unlike the Philippines and Japan, we have had little political and legal contact with the United States. Our main legal links have been with Britain, India, and Australia.[1] (At one time we were governed by the British from Calcutta.) The Malaysian Constitution is modelled on the Indian Constitution.[2] It bears many similarities to that Constitution and the Constitutions of many Commonwealth countries that were granted independence after World War II as the British dismantled their Empire. (It would have borne many more similarities to the United States Constitution, if Americans had not two hundred years ago jumped the gun and taken the law into their own hands by unilaterally declaring their independence.)

Here I shall discuss the main similarities and the main differences between the Malaysian and United States constitutions.

The main similarities are these: (1) Both constitutions are written. (2) The United States and Malaysia both operate on the principle of supremacy of the constitution and judicial review of legislative and executive acts. (3) Both constitutions guarantee fundamental liberties,

1. Ed. note: Ahmad Bin Mohd. Ibrahim, *Toward a History of Law in Malaysia and Singapore* (Singapore: Stamford College Press, 1970).

2. Ed. Note: For analysis, see the author's *An Introduction to the Constitution of Malaysia*, 2nd ed. (Kuala Lumpur: Ibrahim Bin Johari, P. K. Govt. Printer, 1976); Tun Mohamed Suffian, H. P. Lee, and F. A. Trindade (eds.), *The Development of the Constitution of Malaysia in Its First Twenty Years: 1957-1977* (Selangor, Malaysia: Oxford University Press, 1978); and L. A. Sheridan and H. E. Groves, *The Constitution of Malaysia* (Dobbs Ferry, N.Y.: Oceana Publications, 1967).

which are, in the main, enforceable. (4) Both constitutions provide for nations operating on the federal principle and provide for distribution of power between federal and state organs. (5) Both federal legislatures are bicameral.

The main differences are these: (1) The nature of the two constitutions is different. (2) The systems of government are different (parliamentary system versus presidential system). (3) Approaches to and contents of fundamental liberties are different. (4) Methods of implementing the federal principle are different. (5) The Malaysian Constitution expressly allows derogation from certain fundamental liberties. (6) Citizenship provisions differ. (7) Certain features of the Malaysian Constitution are not found in the U.S. Constitution. Examples are the position of our King (the Yang Dipertuan Agung), the position of rulers, and the position of religion. Islam is a religion of the Federation, but freedom of religion is guaranteed.

With regard to main similarity (1), though both are written, the nature and approach of the two constitutions differ. The United States Constitution is a short one, containing only seven articles in the original text, and twenty-six subsequent amendments. It includes only essential and fundamental provisions, which are written in general terms, leaving other provisions to be worked out by legislation. The Malaysian Constitution (like the Indian) is more elaborate and detailed; many provisions which could have been left to legislation are included in the Constitution. The Malaysian Constitution has Articles 1 to 181, but the actual number of articles is more than 181 because many amendments (19) have since 1957 introduced new articles which are referred to as, for example, 16A, 43A, 43B, and also there are thirteen schedules. (The United States Constitution, too, might have been a long and complex document if it had not been drafted two hundred years ago by a small elite serving a small population with not too many lawyers.)

The Malaysian Constitution was drafted in 1956-57 by an independent five-member Royal Commission headed by the late Lord Reid, a distinguished Judge of the House of Lords, and consisting of Professor Ivor Jennings, a retired Governor-General of Australia, a retired Chief Justice of the Allahabad High Court, and a Judge of the High Court of Pakistan. At the last minute a Canadian member could not participate. This Commission spent a year in the country traveling everywhere, listening to the views of every political party, every organization, and any individual who wished to make representations. Its draft was published for further public discussion, debated, and, with amendments to accommodate all conflicting interests, became our Constitution when it was confirmed as law by the federal and state legislatures. (In this way our constitution-makers secured public and social support for our supreme law.)

A second main similarity is that both our countries follow the system of constitutional supremacy and judicial review of unconstitutional legislative and executive acts. As the Malaysian Constitution is the supreme law of the land, the Malaysian government is a limited government. Although the King enjoys legal immunity, he is sworn to uphold the Constitution, and if any of his official acts is unconstitutional or unlawful, the minister through whom he acts may be called to account in the courts. Similarly, the power of ministers and other public officials is limited by the Constitution, and so is that of Parliament, which may make law only on subjects specified in the Constitution and provided that it is not contrary to the Constitution. To adjudicate on the constitutionality or validity of executive and legislative acts, the Malaysian Constitution establishes an independent judiciary whose members may not be removed from office before the compulsory retirement age of sixty-five, except on the recommendation of a committee of five judges, whose salary and conditions of service cannot be altered to their disadvantage, and who are *entitled* to a pension. (The rest of the public service retire at fifty-five and are only eligible for a pension.)

Though it is true that neither the Malaysian nor the United States government enjoys plenary powers to do what it likes, yet there are some differences in our systems. The first difference is that the United States Constitution does not expressly say that laws which conflict with the Constitution are invalid and can be so declared by the courts: that basic principle had to be established by the courts. (What the United States Constitution states in Article VI, Section 2, is that "this Constitution and the Laws of the United States which shall be made in pursuance thereof . . . shall be the supreme law of the land.") The Malaysian Constitution, on the other hand, makes this concept explicit: Article 162 (6) provides that any pre-independence law that is inconsistent with the Constitution has to be construed so as to bring it into accord with the Constitution, and Article 4 provides that any post-independence law that is so inconsistent is to the extent of the inconsistency void.

The United States Constitution itself does not restrict judicial review; any restrictions are imposed by the courts themselves, by doctrine such as *locus standi*, or by the doctrine of avoiding constitutional questions, and so forth. The Malaysian Constitution, however, contains express provisions limiting the extent of judicial review.[3] For instance, Article 4 (3) says that the validity of any law made by the

3. Ed. note: For judicial precedents, see S. Jayakumar, *Constitutional Law Cases from Malaysia and Singapore*, 2nd ed. (Singapore: Malayan Law Journal Pte. Ltd., 1976); for current developments, see *The Malayan Law Journal* (1302 Shenton House, Shenton Way, Singapore 1).

legislature cannot be questioned on the ground that it is outside the power of the legislature concerned except in three types of proceedings: (a) in proceedings for a declaration that the law is invalid on the ground that it is outside the power of the legislature; or (b) if the law is made by the federal legislature, in proceedings between the Federation and one or more states; or (c) if the law was made by a state legislature, in proceedings between the Federation and that state. Article 4 (4) further provides that proceedings of type (a) shall not be commenced without leave of a judge of the Federal Court (the highest court in the land) and that the Federation shall be entitled to be a party to any such proceedings, and so shall any state that would or might be a party to proceedings brought for the same purpose under types (b) and (c).

With regard to main similarity (3), though both constitutions guarantee fundamental liberties which are in the main enforceable, our approach and the contents of our provisions are different from those of the United States. The United States Constitution (so I understand) enshrines fundamental liberties without restrictions and qualifications; the U.S. courts take on the task of determining what kinds of restrictions are permissible in the interest of society as a whole. The Malaysian Constitution, on the other hand (like the Indian), expressly provides that certain fundamental liberties are qualified (not absolute) and may be diminished.

For example, Clause (2) of Article 9 provides that every Malaysian citizen has the right to move freely throughout and to reside anywhere within the Federation, but at the same time it provides that this right is subject to any law relating to security, public health, public order, or the punishment of offenders.

Another example is Article 10, which provides that every citizen has the right to freedom of speech and expression, but that Parliament may by law restrict this right in the interest of security, friendly relations with foreign states, public order or morality, and so forth.

Other examples of the different contents of our provision for fundamental liberties are (a) equal protection, (b) due process of law, (c) right to counsel, and (d) citizenship. In the U.S. Constitution the *equal protection* concept is not elaborated, and the courts have to determine what is and what is not in violation of equal protection. But in the Malaysian Constitution, while certain types of discrimination are prohibited, yet exceptions are allowed. For example, Article 8 (2) provides that there shall be no discrimination against citizens on the grounds only of religion, race, descent, or place of birth in any law or in the appointment to any office or employment under a public authority or in the administration of any law relating to the acquisition, holding, or disposition of property or the establishing or carrying on of any trade, business, profession, vocation, or employment. At the same time it provides that this prohibition is subject to exceptions authorized by the Constitution: for example, Clause (5) of the Article provides that this Article does not invalidate or prohibit, among other things, any provision relating to personal law, and Article 153 expressly provides for favoured treatment of Malays and natives of Borneo.

The U.S. Constitution contains the *due process* concept whereby no person shall be deprived of life, liberty, or property "without due process of law." This concept has been evolved by the U.S. courts in such a way that the law must not be arbitrary or capricious, and the law itself may have to conform to rules of natural justice. In Malaysia we have Article 5 (1), which provides that no person shall be deprived of life or personal liberty "save in accordance with law," and Article 13, which provides that no person shall be deprived of property "save in accordance with law." At first glance these two Articles seem similar to the due process concept. But the Malaysian courts have interpreted "law" to mean enacted law, and therefore, first, Articles 5 and 13 impose restrictions only on the executive and not on the legislature, and, second, there is no scope for including rules of natural justice in "law."[4]

In the United States Constitution the Sixth Amendment provides inter alia that "in all criminal prosecutions the accused shall enjoy the right . . . to have the assistance of counsel for his defense." The U.S. courts have interpreted this and other provisions in recent years to mean that the *right to counsel* commences from the moment of arrest and that the accused is entitled to counsel from that moment. In Malaysia, on the other hand, the corresponding Article 5 (3) provides: "Where a person is arrested he shall be informed as soon as may be of the grounds of his arrest and shall be allowed to consult and be defended by a legal practitioner of his choice." The courts have interpreted this to mean that although the right to counsel commences from arrest, the right cannot be exercised immediately, as a balance has to be struck between that right and the duty of the police to protect the public from wrongdoers by apprehending them and collecting whatever evidence exists against them.[5] Also, in Malaysia there is no suggestion that a person on a criminal charge is entitled to counsel at public expense, though persons on a capital charge are as a matter of course assigned counsel by the courts at the public expense. (A legal aid scheme under the control of the Attorney-General is still in its infancy.)

4. *Comptroller General of Inland Revenue* v. *N.P.* (1973) 1 M.L.J. 165; and *Arumugam Pillai* v. *Government of Malaysia* (1975) 2 M.L.J. 29.

5. *Ooi Ah Phua* v. *Officer-in-Charge, Criminal Investigation, Kedah/ Perlis* (1975) 2 M.L.J. 198.

Concerning *citizenship*, the United States Constitution provides simply that "All persons born or naturalized in the United States, and subject to the jurisdiction thereof, are citizens of the United States and of the State wherein they reside" (Fourteenth Amendment). So the United States has only two categories of citizens: those born in the United States and subject to its jurisdiction, and those who have been naturalized. In Malaysia the Constitution provides for four categories of citizenship: by operation of law, by registration, by naturalization, and by incorporation of territory. Also, not everybody born in Malaysia is a citizen: one is so only if he was born on and after independence (August 31, 1957) and before October 1962; if he was born after September 1962, but before September 16, 1963, he is a citizen only if one of his parents was at the time of his birth either a citizen or a permanent resident, or if he was not born a citizen of any other country; and if he was born on or after September 16, 1963, he is a citizen only if one of his parents was at the time of the birth either a citizen or a permanent resident.

As for main similarity (4) (both the United States and Malaysia operate on the federal principle and provide for distribution of power between federal and state organs), in the United States the Constitution spells out what powers "are delegated" to the centre "nor prohibited" to states and provides that anything not so delegated to the centre nor prohibited to the states is reserved to the states respectively or to the people. The Malaysian Constitution, on the other hand, follows the Indian Constitution in providing for a federal list, a state list, and a concurrent list, which spell out in great detail federal subjects, state subjects, and concurrent subjects with respect to which the federation, the states, and both the federation and states, respectively, have legislative and executive power, and further in providing in Article 77 that residual power on subjects not in the lists shall be vested in states. (Malaysia is a small country, and consequently the Constitution deliberately provides for a strong central government: thus subjects like the police and education, which in the United States are state subjects, are federal in Malaysia.)

With respect to main similarity (5) (both the United States and Malaysia have bicameral legislatures), in the United States members of the Senate are elected directly by the people of each state, whereas in Malaysia each state legislature elects two senators, and in addition the federal government also has power to appoint thirty-two senators. Also, the Malaysian Senate has less power than the lower house (the House of Representatives); our Senate can at best delay but not veto legislation (except for constitutional amendments), while in the United

States the Senate's approval is essential. In both countries members of the lower house are elected directly by the people.

Apart from the differences mentioned above, the most significant difference relates to the system of government. The United States follows the presidential system. The American President is elected independently from legislators; he is not a member of the legislature and not answerable to it (he is responsible to the people), nor can the legislature throw him out on a vote of no confidence as in the United Kingdom, India, and Malaysia (but he may be dismissed by impeachment). Furthermore, since the President is not a member of the legislature, his party may not be the one in control of either house or both. Also, in the American system only the President and Vice-President are elected. Cabinet members are not elected, and indeed they must not be members of the legislature, and they may be (and have been) appointed by the President even from amongst members of the party in opposition to his. Prime Ministers envy the President his ability to appoint to his Cabinet individuals of paramount ability from outside of politics.

In Malaysia, because we follow the United Kingdom system of parliamentary government, the head of state (the King) is distinct from the head of government (the Prime Minister). The Prime Minister must be a member of the legislature, and his choice of Ministers is limited to persons who are willing enough to stand the rough and tumble of politics to run for Parliament, not necessarily a good qualification for high office. The Prime Minister's party or coalition is in the majority in the legislature, and he and his Ministers are responsible to the people, not directly but indirectly to their representatives in Parliament; his party or coalition must give up office if they cease to enjoy the confidence of the majority in the legislature. Our King, like the British Queen and the Indian President, must act on Cabinet advice and has no significant discretionary power.

Other main differences may be described thus:

Malaysia, as was already stated, is a federation of thirteen states, nine of which are headed by a hereditary Sultan and four of which are headed by a Governor. There is a Conference of Rulers, established by the Constitution, in which Sultans and Governors are members; every year this Conference meets three or four times, with the King and Prime Minister present, to discuss and decide policies of national importance.

The King of Malaysia is unique. Although he is elected, only a Sultan may stand. He is a hereditary Sultan, and yet he holds the office of King for a fixed term of five years. He is elected by the Conference of Rulers, yet Governors who are members of the Conference cannot participate in this election. While King he ceases to function as Sultan, and before coming to Kuala Lumpur he appoints a Regent to exercise his functions in his home state. The Constitution contains elaborate rules regarding his election, but for the purpose of this discussion suffice it to say that generally he is elected by seniority. (Some senior Sultans decline to stand because the King is very much a prisoner of palace and protocol.)

As for religion, while the American founding fathers, smarting under the religious persecution of seventeenth- and eighteenth-century Europe (when Christians were burning each other, all in the name of God), forbade the establishment of any religion, the Malaysian Constitution expressly provides that Islam shall be the religion of the Federation. But this does not mean that there is no religious freedom, for the Constitution further provides that other religions may be practiced in peace and harmony in any part of the Federation. Because of her geographical position at the crossroads of Asia, Malaysia has for centuries been exposed to the influence of Arabia, India, China, and Europe, and this has contributed to the spirit of religious and cultural toleration that animates her people.

Personal Reflections

Our Constitution has been amended too many times, in my opinion (nineteen times. It is amendable by Parliament; if two-thirds of the total members of each house approve, no ratification by states is necessary). This is regrettable, for a constitution should be regarded as sacrosanct and should not be amended often; but it is also understandable because our Constitution is long and contains many matters that should be left to ordinary legislation. It is now too late to shorten it.

The trend of amendments is to further strengthen an already strong central government. This is inevitable in a small country the size of ours, but care should be taken not to destroy state autonomy altogether.

Our Constitution mentions the rights of citizens, but not their duties to the country—and to their fellow-citizens—and this is a pity. Rights should be balanced by duties, and this should be made clear in the Constitution.

The Constitution mentions equality before law. It should also mention other forms of equality—such as economic, social, and cultural equality. The government and Malaysian leaders are aware, however, that without these other forms of equality there cannot be social justice, and that without social justice the country will fall prey to the Communist menace. Hence, vigorous efforts are being made to implement successive Five-Year Development Plans so as to increase the size of the national cake and everybody's share of it.

The Constitution secures and is a symbol of our political independence. Malaysians should also strive for economic independence and for a fair price for her produce compared with imported manufactures. For instance, in my youth the price of 1,330 pounds of rubber (Malaysia is the world's greatest producer of natural rubber) bought a car (the cheapest); today we have to sell six to seven times that much rubber to buy the cheapest car. In international trade there must be interdependence, but at the same time newly independent countries should not remain at the mercy of well-established trading nations.

Malaysia's Constitution and system of parliamentary democratic government have survived for twenty years. During our limited experience we have found that the contents of a constitution are important, but more important is the spirit of the men at the top whose duty it is to carry out its provisions. Do they believe in the system? Were they honest when they swore to uphold the Constitution and to uphold the rule of law? Do they believe in the independence of the judiciary and the value of a strong bar, incorruptible and fearless? If they do, then the Constitution is viable and there is hope and a future for the country. But if they are rogues or charlatans, determined only to satisfy their own personal and family ambitions, regardless of the wider interest of the nation, then the country will head toward the abyss—no matter how long and hard its founding fathers laboured to write the most nearly perfect Constitution in the world. So far Malaysia has been fortunate in having good men at the helm to guide her destiny.

VIII

The Philippines

Editorial Note

The Republic of the Philippines comprises an archipelago five hundred miles off the southeast coast of Asia. It includes seven thousand islands, of which several hundred exceed one square mile in area, and eleven account for 95 percent of both the nation's population of 45,000,000 and its land area of 116,000 square miles.

The Filipino people are of mainly Malay origin, with a considerable Chinese and a lesser Spanish infusion. Population is increasing at more than 3 percent per year. Nearly 85 percent of the people are Roman Catholic. Muslims account for 5 percent of the population and are dominant in the Sulu islands and parts of Mindanao. The Philippines has achieved relatively high standards of health and education, with life expectancy now close to sixty years, and a literacy rate over 80 percent. Most Filipinos speak one or more of seventy indigenous Malayo-Polynesian languages, many speak English as well, and a declining number also speak Spanish. Tagalog, the language of the Manila Region, and the basis of a national language known as Pilipino, has gained increasing currency throughout the country. English and Spanish are also recognized as official languages.

The Philippine economy is predominantly agricultural. Major crops include rice for domestic consumption, and sugar, coconut products, and bananas for export. Forestry and mining also contribute importantly to export earnings. Major trading partners are Japan and the United States. Despite official policies to encourage domestic ownership, the modern industrial sector remains dominated by American corporations. Gross national product per capita is estimated at $350.

At the beginning of the sixteenth century the Philippine Islands were inhabited principally by small Malay settlements along sea and lake coasts, with little organization of society above the village and clan level. In the southern islands, however, Islam was advancing rapidly, bringing larger and more complex social and political forms. After Magellan's "discovery" of the Philippines in 1521, Spain checked the Islamic advance and established a colonial regime that lasted until the Filipino revolution and American intervention at the end of the last century.

The Americans forcibly suppressed the revolutionary movement which the Filipinos had begun against Spain and continued against the United States. The new rulers soon reached an accommodation with the Filipino elite, and rapidly constituted a Filipino legislature, bureaucracy, and judiciary with considerable autonomy in internal affairs. The American colonial regime developed extensive public health and education systems. It did little, however, to develop a strong economy and a more equitable distribution of wealth and power. To the contrary, the American policy of free trade perpetuated an essentially colonial economy, which persists to this day.

In 1934, after long but amicable struggle on the part of the Filipino leadership, the United States Congress passed the Philippine Independence Act, providing for full independence in 1946 after a ten-year transitional period as a largely autonomous Commonwealth under American sovereignty. The following year the Filipino people voted acceptance of a Constitution drafted by the Philippine Constitutional Convention to establish both the transitional Commonwealth government and the independent Republic to be inaugurated in 1946. The Commonwealth period was interrupted by the Japanese occupation during World War II, but the Philippines attained independence as scheduled in 1946.

As an independent nation the Philippines achieved rapid recovery from the destruction of World War II, impressive standards of health and education, and until 1972, a democratic, though in significant aspects an ineffectual, government. Although heavily protective economic policies stimulated rapid growth of a complex of light import-substitution industries under Filipino entrepreneurship, those policies soon outlived their usefulness, and the economy stagnated. The government's effort to shift policy to promote labor-intensive export manufacturing met with only modest success. The crucial weakness of the government was its inability to implement fundamental reforms and to subordinate special interests to the public good in accordance with officially declared policies and standards. Land reform legislation was not carried out effectively. Welfare and social justice programs were overly ambitious in stated objectives and grossly deficient in the fiscal and political support required for implementation. Economic and political power remained concentrated in a few families. Political conflict among powerful factions became increasingly violent, and public order deteriorated.

In 1972, President Marcos declared martial law. This enabled him to manipulate a sitting Constitutional Convention to elicit a proposed new Constitution which would enable him to remain in office and, particularly in its transitional provisions, assure him of continuing power without interference by the legislature, the courts, the press, or necessity of election. In 1973, he proclaimed the new Constitution to be in effect by reason of approval in an informal plebiscite, which had been conducted in many areas by a show of hands under military supervision.

Indigenous Filipino law prior to Spanish rule was embedded in the norms, customs, and hierarchical patterns of a village society. The colonial regime established a formal legal system but never gained sufficient authority to give pervasive effect to formal law. By the end of the Spanish period, the Philippines enjoyed (or was afflicted by) a full array of codes and legal enactments, but these were of little effect in the day-to-day life of most people.

American rule brought an infusion of liberal political doctrine and constitutional law. When the struggle for independence shifted from armed revolution to legal and political channels, lawyers became prominent in politics and government, and they remain so today. The Philippines now has more lawyers per capita than most European nations.

The Constitution of 1935 incorporated fundamental principles of American constitutional law, such as separation of powers, judicial review of legislation, a bill of rights, and due process. The judiciary assumed an important role in the government and politics of the Commonwealth and the Republic. Although the lower courts were congested, slow, and often accused of favoritism and corruption, the Supreme Court enjoyed great respect and did not hesitate to nullify legislative and executive action. Politically prominent lawyers vigorously defended criminal defendants and political dissidents, and major political conflicts were translated into and resolved as legal disputes.

The Constitution of 1973 maintained most of the established Constitutional principles in form, but the President, invoking its transitional provisions and emergency powers, has been able to exercise power without regard to constitutional constraint. Although the judicial system was left intact by the declaration of martial law, jurisdiction of a number of politically sensitive cases was shifted to martial law tribunals. The Supreme Court has remained free from overt presidential manipulation, and it has heard cases presenting political issues of the most fundamental order. In a crucial case decided by a bare majority, with four justices dissenting, the Court declared the new Constitution to be in force and effect. To date, the Court has not decided an important case in direct opposition to the position of the President.

June 1978

JAMES L. MAGAVERN

The American Constitutional Impact on the Philippine Legal System

Enrique M. Fernando
Senior Associate Justice, Supreme Court of the Philippines

It is a privilege highly esteemed to have been invited to take part, even if in a modest capacity, in the Bicentennial celebration of the American Declaration of Independence. Rightfully has it been observed by Laski that the history of the United States "has changed the outlook of mankind wherever there has been power to reflect on the meaning of human affairs." As he stated further: "No state, until our own day, has done so much to make the idea of progress part of the mental make-up of man. No state, either, has done more to make freedom a dream which overcame the claims both of birth and of wealth."[1] De Tocqueville and Bryce, writing at earlier periods, were similarly laudatory.[2] There is considerable justification for the United States, then, to take legitimate pride in what has been accomplished these past two hundred years and to look forward with reasonable and cautious optimism to what may be achieved in the next century.

As an Asian coming from a nation which for almost half a century, from 1898 to 1946, was under American sovereignty, the author of this paper is a product of the American system of education then followed during that period. If the further consideration be borne in mind that the Philippines was under Spanish colonial rule for over three hundred years dating from 1565, it may be readily discernible why his thinking is colored by Western legal ideas. There was a time when there was a well-nigh automatic acceptance of their applicability to Philippine conditions. Fortunately, that time is no more. Since independence, there has been a greater sense of discrimination and a greater appreciation of the nation's Oriental heritage, even insofar as the ways of the law are concerned. The author, however, belongs to a generation that was not the beneficiary of such an approach. As a result, his study of the legal

1. Harold Laski, *The American Democracy* (New York: Viking, 1948) p. 3.
2. De Tocqueville, *Democracy in America* (1830); Bryce, *The American Commonwealth* (1888).

systems of neighboring Asiatic countries is rather meager. Nonetheless, an attempt will be made to refer briefly to comparable constitutional provisions in the charters of Southeast Asian states including India, Pakistan, and Sri Lanka, formerly Ceylon. Japan and South Korea will also receive some attention. The concentration though, for obvious reasons, will be on the legal system of the Philippines.

The American influence in Asian constitutional systems may be viewed from an abstract or conceptual level or in its more concrete or specific manifestations in terms of actual provisions or doctrines embodied in Asian charters. The former deals with constitutionalism as identified with a fundamental law, its supremacy being assured in the United States through the function of judicial review. The latter may refer to such broad categories as federalism, the presidential form of government, and the Bill of Rights. As, by and large, the first two have not recommended themselves for adoption in this part of the world,[3] necessarily, the major inquiry is centered on the extent to which fundamental rights and freedoms, as protected in the United States Constitution, have found their way in Asia. It may not be amiss, however, to speak of the depth of nationalistic fervor in the Asian scene and why, this factor notwithstanding, the United States Constitution served as a model.

Nationalism in Asia

Nationalism embodies the principle of self-determination—one nation, one state. It exemplifies the concept that a state is nothing but the juridical personification of the nation.[4] President Woodrow Wilson was its vigorous champion after World War I. His impassioned advocacy struck a responsive chord: it intensified the feeling of nationalism among peoples still smarting under foreign rule; it evoked their enthusiasm and stirred their hopes; it signified for them the end of colonialism—and it was high time, too. For those in Asia and Africa, the regret was that the blessing of such a gospel was not extended to them until after World War II. Then they had their day. Speaking of Asia alone, the Philippines gained her independence on July 4, 1946. In 1947, India, Pakistan, and Ceylon, now Sri Lanka, dissolved their ties with Great Britain. Burma followed early in 1948; so did Malaysia, but not until 1957. The Indonesians broke away from Dutch rule as early as 1945. The former French Indo-China now comprises Vietnam, Cambodia,

3. India and Malaysia are now the only two countries that have a federal structure. It was so with Pakistan until Bangladesh seceded in 1971. The presidential system is also in disfavor, except in Indonesia and Korea.

4. Cf. H. E. Cohen, *Recent Theories of Sovereignty* (Chicago: University of Chicago Press, 1937), p. 15.

and Laos, the first of them asserting her freedom in 1945 and the last two in 1949. Singapore left Malaysia in 1965, and Bangladesh seceded from Pakistan in 1971. Korea, occupied by the United States and Russian armed forces after World War II, was lost to Japan in 1945, at present there being the Democratic People's Republic in the north, and, in the south, the Republic of Korea.

At long last, a number of Asian peoples of diverse creeds and cultures, but with the common objective of freeing themselves from the grip of alien rule, assumed their independent status, full of hopes and aspirations for a better way of life. Adlai Stevenson, writing in 1954, could speak of millions of human beings from Africa to Indonesia, "emerging from foreign domination and fiercely demanding relief from hunger, pestilence, and oppression."[5] There was, and understandably so, the flowering of nationalism, as a means of attaining what he had so felicitously termed their "suddenly unattained aspirations."[6] Competent observers of the Asian scene, Orientals and Occidentals alike, are thus unanimous in their view of its potent influence at work. W. L. Holland could picture it "as a huge and often controlled source of energy."[7] Asiatic peoples, according to C. A. Buss, "usually cool and unemotional about political programs, become heated over nationalism."[8] As L. K. Rosinger stated, the "fires of nationalism" burn brightly, having been fed by the "poverty and discontent of masses of people" and "the deep Asian resentment at Western racial attitudes."[9] The same thought was echoed by Stevenson: "Nationalism is rampant. And the West, identified with the hated colonialism, is suspect."[10] G. E. Taylor, with specific reference to American foreign policy, was quite categorical: "Mutual confidence is hard to establish, for most of the countries of Southeast Asia have been colonies for varying lengths of time and their nationalist movements have a history of anti-West and often anti-capitalist feeling."[11]

There is pertinence to the query, therefore, of the effect of such dominant sentiment on the influence of American constitutional ways in the framing of the fundamental laws of each of these new states. The question does not admit of a uniform answer. The fires of nationalism burned just as brightly in the Philippines in the past as they do now, but

5. Adlai Stevenson, *Call to Greatness* (New York: Harper, 1954), p. 38.

6. Ibid., p. 43.

7. William L. Holland, ed., *Asian Nationalism and the West* (New York: Macmillan, 1953), p. 5.

8. Claude A. Buss, *The Arc of Crisis* (New York: Doubleday, 1961), p. 24.

9. Lawrence K. Rosinger et al. (eds.), *The State of Asia* (London: G. Allen, 1953), p.3.

10. *Call to Greatness*, p. 73.

11. George E. Taylor, *The Philippines and the United States* (New York: Praeger, 1964), p. 8.

with only one exception there has never been any period marked by deep resentment, much less bitter hostility, against the West. The last decade of the nineteenth century and the first few years of the twentieth century constitute the exception. For it was in 1896 that the full-scale rebellion by the Filipinos against Spain started, although for several years previous to that the separatist movement had been growing. From our standpoint it was a success: by 1898, the Spanish resistance was reduced to insignificance. It was the hope of the Filipinos that the United States in view of her tradition and her philosophy would be sympathetic to their cause. Such, unfortunately, was not the case; by the Treaty of Paris of 1898, the United States, having gone to war against Spain, acquired the Philippines by cession. The Filipinos had no choice but to continue the struggle against that country. As could have been expected, the superiority in arms and resources was too much to overcome. By 1904 at the latest, what was referred to by us as the Filipino-American War, and by Americans as the Philippine Insurrection, was at an end.

The policies adopted by the United States proved acceptable. Autonomy was promised, ultimately to lead to independence. Education and health received preferential attention. The civil service was efficient. While Protestant missionaries came to the Philippines, there was no interference with Catholicism. Indeed, civil and political rights were respected. With the acceptance of the democratic ways and institutions introduced by the United States, the rise of nationalism did not pose an obstacle to Philippine-American friendship. World War II gave further impetus to the cordiality that marked such relations. The Filipinos fought by the side of the Americans. After the surrender of Bataan and Corregidor, guerrillas continued to harass Japanese troops in the Philippines. They aided in the liberation of the Philippines by the American armed forces in 1945, ending the grim period of Japanese Occupation.[12] Then in 1946, the promised independence became a reality.

That was in accordance with the Philippine Independence Act enacted by the United States Congress in 1934. The recognition of Philippine political freedom was postponed until after a ten-year transition period under a Commonwealth status, the last stage from an American unincorporated territory to an independent existence. As was

12. As was noted in *Commissioner of Internal Revenue* v. *Guerrero*, L-20812, September 22, 1967, 21 Supreme Court Reports Annotated, hereinafter referred to as SCRA, 180, the role that the United States played in liberating the Philippines, considering that from 1942 to 1945 the Japanese army during the occupation period enforced repressive measures, severe in character, "elicited a vast reservoir of goodwill for the United States, one that has lasted to this day notwithstanding irritants that mar ever so often the relationship even among the most friendly of nations." At 188.

to be expected, there was a requirement that there be a constitution for such a regime. The understanding of the Philippine Constitutional Convention of 1934-35 was that the fundamental law to be drafted was not only for the Commonwealth but for the future Republic. With the training in self-government under American tutelage in the past three decades, it is easy to understand why such Constitution would embody certain basic features of that polity, such as the presidential form of government, the function of judicial review, and a bill of rights. It thus becomes even more evident why the upsurge of nationalism in the Philippines with its vehement cry for membership in the world community was certainly no bar to practices followed the years past. The United States Constitution, serving as a fit model, was ready-made for the purpose.

South Korea, now the Republic of Korea, is equally nationalistic, but having been spared from domination by a Western power, experienced no sense of dissatisfaction with the United States, to which, moreover, she is bound by ties of gratitude, as it was U.S. troops that played a decisive role in the bitter fratricidal conflict with the North. India, Pakistan, Burma, Sri Lanka, Malaysia, and Singapore, all former colonies of Britain—even if there were long pent-up grievances against the latter—appeared content with the introduction in their respective legal systems of the English common law, the merits of which they recognized. It is easily understandable, then, why for them there may be certain American constitutional concepts that could serve as models for possible inclusion in their respective charters. Indonesia, formerly a Dutch possession, was hardly an enthusiast as far as occidental culture is concerned. It does not mean, however, that the United States has nothing to offer as far as drafting a constitution is concerned. Considering recent events, it would be highly unrealistic to look for traces of American influence in the fundamental laws still in the making in Vietnam, Cambodia, and Laos.

The case of Japan is unique. She has been and is now fiercely nationalistic. For a long time she kept the West away from her shores, but from the Meiji era in the last third of the nineteenth century, she successfully made use of occidental institutions and practices suitable to her needs. Then came World War II, where she was among the vanquished. That was followed by the framing of her present Constitution, under Allied occupation with General Douglas MacArthur as the Supreme Commander. There is nothing surprising in her incorporating therein a large number of well-known American doctrines, especially where individual rights are involved. There is, in addition, the adoption of the concept of judicial review.

What may be impressed with more significance, however, is not so much the absence of any evidence indicative of displeasure with or resentment against the United States as a major Western power—this in the face of the brand of nationalism aroused in these new Asian states. It is the relative freedom possessed by them in the framing of their constitutions upon assuming their independent status. They could examine the contents of existing charters and determine which were suitable. They had, as it were, a wide counter from which to make their selection. To paraphrase Alexander Hamilton, they were given the opportunity to show their capability of establishing a good government from reflection and choice rather than depending solely on accident and force.[13] They could and did envision their constitutions as a vehicle, in the language of A. J. Zurcher, "to codify a rational and progressive political order [and] to discourage the abuse of political power."[14] Not only could they serve as symbols of political unity or as instruments of political discipline, they could also demonstrate political maturity. With such ideals in mind, certainly, the U.S. Constitution of 1787, as amended and as interpreted in landmark decisions, could very well serve as a fit model. That would be to reinforce faith in the possibility that what Jefferson called "the disease of liberty" may be spread in distant lands and far-off domains.

The influence of the United States, as was noted, could be shown by the incorporation, whether in express terms or by implication, of selected provisions or doctrines traceable to her Constitution. To be realistic, it may be on a purely verbal level, for the warning of the great jurist Oliver Wendell Holmes is ever timely. Constitutional provisions are not to be considered in the light of mathematical formulas having their essence in their form. They are organic living institutions, and their significance is vital, not formal.[15] As he so emphatically pointed out: "Constitutions are intended to preserve practical and substantial rights, not to maintain theories."[16] It would be to err on the side of undue optimism if the presence in the charters of these new Asian states of juridical formulations traceable to the U.S. Constitution were to be equated with the complete acceptance of what they signify for the American legal system. It does not admit of doubt, though, that by their inclusion there is at least manifest an intention not to ignore the meaning attached to them in the country of origin. There is likely to be that subtle weaving of what is native with what is foreign. It would be disappointing if the result is merely a canonization of accepted and

13. Cf. Alexander Hamilton, in *The Federalist* (Modern Library Edition, 1937), p. 3.

14. Arnold J. Zurcher, *Constitutions and Constitutional Trends Since World War II* (New York: New York University Press, 1951), p. 1.

15. Cf. *Gompers* v. *United States*, 233 U.S. 604, 610 (1914).

16. Cf. *Davis* v. *Mills*, 194 U.S. 451, 457 (1904).

traditional concepts, divorced from the actualities in their new locales. No juridical bridge of firmness could be built on so shaky a foundation.

The Supremacy of the Constitution

American influence on Asiatic constitutions, as was set forth at the outset, may be both on an abstract or conceptual level or in concrete or specific manifestations as evidenced by the adoption of provisions found in the United States Constitution or of doctrines based on them.

Insofar as the former is concerned, reference may be made to the fundamental postulate of the supremacy of a constitution, the idea of a higher law, one which has superior obligation and validity. As far back as 1803, in the landmark decision *Marbury* v. *Madison*,[17] Chief Justice Marshall, after taking note of "the province and duty of the judicial department to say what the law is," continued:

> So if a law be in opposition to the constitution; if both the law and the Constitution apply to a particular case, so that the court must either decide that case conformably to the law, disregarding the constitution; or conformably to the constitution, disregarding the law; the court must determine which of these conflicting rules governs the case. This is of the very essence of judicial duty. If then, the courts are to regard the constitution, and the constitution is superior to any ordinary act of the legislature, the constitution, and not such ordinary act, must govern the case to which they both apply. Those then who controvert the principle that the constitution is to be considered in court, as a paramount law, are reduced to the necessity of maintaining that courts must close their eyes on the constitution, and see only the law. This doctrine would subvert the very foundation of all written constitutions.[18]

That fundamental postulate of a fundamental law setting forth the criterion for the validity of any public act, whether proceeding from the highest official or the lowest functionary, is basic to the American system of a constitutional democracy. That is, to manifest fealty to the rule of law, with priority accorded to that which occupies the topmost rung in the legal hierarchy. The three departments of government in the discharge of the functions with which they are entrusted have no choice but to yield obedience to constitutional commands. Whatever limits are imposed must be observed. Congress in the enactment of statutes must ever be on guard lest the restrictions on its authority, whether substantive or formal, be transcended. The presidency in the execution of the laws cannot ignore or disregard what it ordains. In its task of applying the law to the facts as found in deciding cases, the judiciary is called upon to maintain inviolate what is decreed by the fundamental law. Even its power of judicial review to pass upon the validity of the acts of the coordinate branches in the course of adjudication is a logical

17. 1 Cranch 137. 18. Ibid., 176-177.

corollary of this overriding principle that the Constitution is paramount. Any governmental measure that fails to live up to its mandates falls to the ground. Thereby there is a recognition of its being the supreme law.[19]

The Function of Judicial Review

It is through the awesome and delicate power of judicial review, to follow the oft-quoted observation of Chief Justice Hughes made at a time before he became the chief magistrate, that while the United States is under a Constitution, "it is what the judges say it is."[20] For in discharging the task of inquiring into whether a challenged executive or legislative action is in conformity with, or repugnant to, its Constitution, the meaning attached to its provisions becomes authoritative when it is the United States Supreme Court that speaks. Such a pronouncement, Justice Jackson, in a work published when he was Attorney General, characterized as "the most understandable and comprehensive summary of American constitutional law. He pointed out, though, that there was no explicit constitutional grant of this power, that it was "left to lurk in an inference." At any rate, he continued, "Political evolution has supplied the omission, and the course of history has established that power in the Supreme Court."[21] It had its genesis in the aforesaid *Marbury* decision, where the doctrine was first enunciated and applied by the Supreme Court of the United States. It declined to issue the writ of mandamus to the then Secretary of State, James Madison, on the ground that it was not vested with such original jurisdiction under the Constitution of the United States. The authority conferred by a congressional act was not warranted by the fundamental law and hence was declared void. What is to be stressed is the absence in the Constitution of any such explicit grant of competence to annul statutes. It was merely an implied power, on the basis of the cardinal precept that the Constitution is paramount and thus overrides any statute that conflicts with its mandate.

The course of history, or "political evolution" in the words of Justice Jackson, has at any rate erased any doubts as to the existence of the power of judicial review. It did not take long. Justice Story, in his *Commentaries on the Constitution of the United States*, published in 1833, could speak of "the duty or course of justice to declare any

19. Cf. *Mutuc* v. *Commission on Elections*, L-32717, Nov. 26, 1970, 36 SCRA 228, 234-5.

20. Cf. W. B. Lockhart, Y. Kamisar, J. H. Choper, *Constitutional Law*, 3rd ed. (St. Paul, Minn.: West Pub. Co., 1970), p. 8, citing a speech of Chief Justice Hughes delivered on May 3, 1907.

21. Robert H. Jackson, *The Struggle for Judicial Supremacy* (New York: Knopf, 1941), pp. 3, 4, 5.

unconstitutional law passed by Congress or by State Legislature void."[22] Even as of that time, he could affirm that "the right of all courts, state as well as national, to declare unconstitutional laws void, seems settled beyond the reach of judicial controversy."[23] The power of judicial review was not again utilized to nullify an act of Congress until 1857 in the *Dred Scott* decision,[24] where the U.S. Supreme Court held that the act known as the Missouri Compromise was void, as Congress was without power to legislate on the issue of slavery. This attempt on the part of the Supreme Court to settle the slavery question proved singularly ineffective. It was in the crucible of the Civil War that the issue was decided. Nonetheless, Thomas Cooley in his *Constitutional Limitations*, first published in 1868, affirmed that "under some circumstances, it may become the duty of the courts to declare that what the legislature has assumed to enact is void, either from want of constitutional power to enact it, or because the constitutional forms or conditions have not been observed."[25] D. Watson, in his treatise on the Constitution of the United States, could by 1910 categorically state: "The Constitution does not confer authority upon the courts to declare an act of Congress to be in conflict with that instrument, yet from the beginning of the Government the courts have exercised such power, and will continue to do so."[26] W. W. Willoughby, in 1929, in his three-volume work on the Constitutional Law of the United States, could emphatically assert:

> The principle that statutory law, in order to be recognized as valid by the courts, must, in all cases, be in conformity with constitutional requirements, is a product of American law, and though now found in the jurisprudential systems of some other countries, has nowhere received the development and extended application that it has received in the United States.[27]

Judicial Review in the Philippines

In a leading case, the first of its kind after the effectivity of the 1935 Constitution, *Angara* v. *Electoral Commission*,[28] the Philippine Supreme Court stated that the power of judicial review "is granted, if not expressly, by clear implication from section 2 of Article VIII of our Constitution."[29] This Article stated that the Supreme Court was not to

22. Third ed., 1858, p. 645. 23. Ibid.

24. *Dred Scott* v. *Sanford*, 19 How. 393 (1857).

25. Thomas M. Cooley, *A Treatise on Constitutional Limitations*, 8th ed. (Boston: Little, Brown, 1927), vol. 1, p. 332.

26. D. Watson, *Constitution of the United States*, vol. 2 (Chicago: Callaghan, 1910), p. 1168.

27. W. W. Willoughby, *The Constitutional Law of the United States*, 2d ed. (New York: Baker Voorhis, 1929), p. 1.

28. 63 Phil. 139 (1936).

29. Ibid., 158. The opinion was penned by Justice José P. Laurel, the delegate who was the Chairman of the Committee on the Bill of Rights in the 1934 Convention.

be deprived of its jurisdiction "to review, reverse, modify, or affirm on appeal, certiorari, or writ of error, final judgments and decrees in . . . (1) All cases in which the constitutionality or validity of any treaty, law, ordinance, or executive order or regulation is in question." Then in a subsequent section, the number of votes required was provided for: "All cases involving the constitutionality of a treaty or law shall be heard and decided by the Supreme Court *en banc*, and no treaty or law may be declared unconstitutional without the concurrence of two-thirds of all the members of the Court" (Sec. 10). In the present Constitution, which became effective in 1973, with a Supreme Court of fifteen members, four more than was formerly the case, there were necessarily some changes. Thus: "All cases involving the constitutionality of a treaty, executive agreement, or law shall be heard and decided by the Supreme Court *en banc*, and no treaty, executive agreement, or law may be declared unconstitutional without the concurrence of at least ten Members" (Art. X, Sec. 2, par. [2]).

A brief historical background is not amiss. At the time when the United States acquired the Philippines from Spain in 1899, one of the principles of constitutional law binding on the territorial government established by her in the Philippines was this same principle of judicial review. It was natural for American lawyers admitted to practice in the Philippines to challenge the validity of statutes or executive orders, whenever the interests of their clients so demanded. The Filipino justices and judges, who with their American brethren administered justice, were soon made aware that the power to pass on the constitutionality of such statutes and executive orders was part of their judicial function. The Filipino lawyers vied with the American members of the bar in raising the question of constitutionality whenever appropriate. The American practice, therefore, of appealing to courts, by means of lawsuits, decisions reached by either the executive or legislative branches of the government, became a part of the accepted doctrines of constitutional law in the Philippines early in the period of American sovereignty.

Although it was not until March 22, 1907, that the Supreme Court of the Philippines set aside an act of the legislative branch in the case of *Casannovas* v. *Hord*,[30] as early as February 14, 1902, the Court in the case of *In re Prautch*,[31] dismissed as untenable the objection that there was an impairment of contractual obligation. A year later, on May 16, 1903, in *United States* v. *Dorr*,[32] it firmly rejected the assertion that the judgment of the lower court was void, as it did not provide for a jury trial as required by the American Constitution. In a disbarment proceeding in 1904, *In re Montagne*,[33] the plea by respondent attorney that

30. 8 Phil. 125. 31. 1 Phil. 132. 32. 2 Phil. 269. 33. 4 Phil. 1.

he was denied due process of law met with no sympathetic response from the Supreme Court. Various other cases could be cited to show the readiness with which counsel would seize upon an alleged infringement of constitutional rights and call upon the Court to exercise the power of judicial review.

Then came the period under the 1935 and the present constitutions. It may safely be asserted that the Philippine Supreme Court was and is ever alert to entertain constitutional questions. In the valedictory address before the 1934 Constitutional Convention, Claro M. Recto, its President, spoke of the trust reposed in the judiciary, in these words: "It is one of the paradoxes of democracy that the people at times place more confidence in instrumentalities of the State other than those directly chosen by them for the exercise of their sovereignty."[34] The assumption was that whenever a constitutional question was posed, the Court should act. It was expected that it would discharge such a task without regard to political considerations and with no thought except that of discharging its trust. Witness these words of the same Justice Laurel in an early landmark case, *People* v. *Vera*,[35] decided in 1937:

> If it is ever necessary for us to make any vehement affirmance during this formative period of our political history, it is that we are independent of the Executive no less than of the Legislative department of our government—independent in the performance of our functions, undeterred by any consideration, free from politics, indifferent to popularity, and unafraid of criticism in the accomplishment of our sworn duty as we see it and as we understand it.[36]

The hope, of course, was that such assertion of independence and impartiality was not mere rhetoric. There could not be the least doubt that what elicited the approval of the Filipino people was the belief that the judiciary is called upon to inquire into alleged breaches of the fundamental law to avoid its being infringed. To do so is merely to do what is expected of it. Thereby no invasion of spheres appropriately belonging to the political branches occurred. The judiciary had to act only when there was a suit with proper parties before it, wherein rights appropriate for judicial enforcement were sought to be vindicated. Nor would it approach constitutional questions with dogmatism or apodictic certainty. There was also the expectation that there would be the search for jural consistency and rational coherence. Once allowance is made for the fact that, for all its care and circumspection, a Supreme Court is manned by human beings fettered by fallibility, but nonetheless earnestly and sincerely striving to do right, it is easy to under-

34. VII *Proceedings of the Philippine Constitutional Convention* (S. Laurel, ed.), Appendix L, 800.

35. 65 Phil. 56 (1937). 36. Ibid., 96.

stand the public acceptance of its vigorous pursuit of the task of assuring that the Constitution be obeyed.

On a more specific level, reference may be made to an impressive number of cases to show that in the Philippines there had been neither judicial timidity nor reluctance in the exercise of the power of judicial review. In the period before the Japanese Occupation in 1942, the Supreme Court was called upon to rule on a dispute between two constitutional agencies, the National Assembly and the then Electoral Commission,[37] on the reorganization of the judiciary,[38] and on the extent of the supervisory power over local governments.[39] After liberation, controversies more momentous in their implications for the welfare of the country were taken to the Supreme Court for resolution. Again it had its hands full of cases decisive in their impact on the political and economic future of the Philippines. The presence of the United States Army in the Philippines introduced added complications. Instances of its none-too-tender regard for the liberties of individuals were called, in appropriate cases, to the attention of the Supreme Court.[40] The legality of proceedings against those Filipinos who worked with the Japanese with such intensity and enthusiasm as to qualify their collaboration as treasonable was dumped in its lap.[41] Thereafter came cases of equal significance, among them those involving the suspension of three Senators allegedly owing their election to terroristic activities of certain radical groups;[42] the sufficiency of the votes on the parity rights amendment to constitute a valid proposal, with three Senators and eight Representatives still under suspension and thus unable to participate;[43] the near-crisis brought about by well-nigh one-half of the Senators refusing to attend sessions after the incumbent Senate President was ousted by declaring the office vacant at a time when according to them there was no quorum;[44] the exercise by at least two Presidents (Roxas and Quirino) of the power to legislate under the Emergency Powers Act even after the return of normalcy with Congress actually in operation;[45] the independence of the Commission on Elections from the Executive,[46] and the scope of its authority to assure free and honest

37. *Angara* v. *Electoral Commission*, 63 Phil. 139 (1936).

38. *Zandueta* v. *De la Costa*, 66 Phil. 615 (1938).

39. *Planas* v. *Gil*, 67 Phil. 62 (1939), and *Villena* v. *Secretary of the Interior*, 67 Phil. 451 (1939).

40. *Raquiza* v. *Bradford*, 76 Phil. 50 (1945); *Tubb* v. *Griess*, 78 Phil. 249 (1947).

41. *Laurel* v. *Misa*, 77 Phil. 856 (1947).

42. *Vera* v. *Avelino*, 77 Phil. 192 (1946).

43. *Mabanag* v. *Lopez Vito*, 78 Phil. 1 (1947).

44. *Avelino* v. *Cuenco*, 83 Phil. 17 (1949).

45. *Araneta* v. *Dinglasan*, 84 Phil. 368 (1949), and *Rodriguez* v. *Gella*, 92 Phil. 603 (1953).

46. *Nacionalista Party* v. *Angelo Bautista*, 85 Phil. 101 (1949).

elections;[47] the legal consequence of there being a lone Senator from the opposition, thus tilting the balance in favor of the majority party in the Electoral Tribunal;[48] the limits that should be placed on presidential authority over local governments;[49] the legality of midnight appointments by the President, whether during the closing days of the Garcia[50] or the Macapagal[51] administration; the restrictions placed on political parties as well as civic groups to nominate candidates for the 1971 Constitutional Convention,[52] as well as the limits on the freedom of expression of candidates to such body;[53] and the piecemeal submission of proposals to amend the 1935 Constitution for ratification.[54]

How far the Supreme Court of the Philippines in the exercise of the function of judicial review could participate in the power process of the government was indicated by four cases arising from the present state of emergency. The first, *Lansang* v. *Garcia*,[55] overruled earlier Philippine decisions[56] by its pronouncement that the suspension of the privilege of habeas corpus is a judicial not a political question. It also held that the test of whether or not such power was unconstitutionally exercised is arbitrariness. There being no such showing, the 1971 suspension of the privilege by President Marcos was sustained. The next three decisions all were promulgated under a regime of martial law declared under the 1935 Constitution. *Aquino* v. *Ponce Enrile*[57] was a *habeas corpus* petition seeking the release of a detained Senator, one of the many filed by a number of those individuals who were detained after martial law for possible complicity in the insurrection, the main ground being the nullity of such proclamation.[58] The challenge was unsuccessful. Again there was no showing of arbitrariness, considering the Muslim rebellion by the Muslim Filipinos in the second biggest island in the Philippines, Mindanao, and the Maoist uprising in Luzon, where Manila is located. The validity of the martial law proclamation was thus upheld. The then Chief Justice Makalintal and seven other

47. *Nacionalista Party* v. *Commission on Elections*, 85 Phil. 149 (1949).

48. *Tañada* v. *Cuenco*, 103 Phil. 1051 (1957).

49. *Hebron* v. *Reyes*, 104 Phil. 175 (1958).

50. *Aytona* v. *Castillo*, L-19313, January 19, 1962, 4 SCRA 1 (1962).

51. *Guevara* v. *Inocentes*, L-25577, March 15, 1966, 16 SCRA 379 (1966).

52. *Imbong* v. *Ferrer*, L-32432, September 11, 1970, 35 SCRA 28 (1970).

53. *Badoy* v. *Comelec*, L-32546, October 17, 1970, 35 SCRA 285 (1970).

54. *Tolentino* v. *Comelec*, L-34150, October 16, 1971, 41 SCRA 702 (1971).

55. 42 SCRA 448.

56. *Barcelona* v. *Baker*, 5 Phil. 87 (1905), and *Montenegro* v. *Castañeda*, 91 Phil. 882 (1952). The latter case dealt with the suspension of the privilege under Philippine President Elipidio Quirino in 1950.

57. 59 SCRA 183 (1974).

58. Petitioner Aquino was the only political figure of consequence, being one of the leaders of the Liberal Party who was still under detention when the case was decided. Charges had been preferred against him, but there was still a pending action, *Aquino* v. *Military Commission*, to determine whether he could be tried by respondent body.

members of the Court spoke their minds on the crucial issue of martial law.[59] The presidential action under martial law was challenged in the two other petitions,[60] the first assailing the power of the President to call a referendum on crucial issues, and the second questioning the jurisdiction of a military commission to try petitioner, a civilian. Again, no constitutional infirmity was found. The unanimity that characterized the decision arrived at in the first case[61] was no bar to seven Justices submitting their considered views on the various constitutional aspects of the litigation.[62] It was again a divided Court in the latter suit,[63] with two outright dissents,[64] two concurring and dissenting opinions,[65] and one concurrence[66] to the main opinion. What clearly emerges is that even during a period of martial law, any order of the President, the Commander-in-Chief of the Armed Forces, could still be tested for alleged constitutional infirmity. The vitality of the institution of judicial review even during emergency times is thus evident.

Judicial Review in Other Asiatic Countries

Judicial review as a mode of assuring the supremacy of the Constitution is now an accepted legal institution in other Asiatic countries. The American influence is marked, as could be expected, in Japan and Korea. What is remarkable is that, even in those nations with previous ties to Great Britain, it has found acceptance. In that group may be included Burma, India, Malaysia, and Sri Lanka.

The Constitution of Japan is quite explicit: "The Supreme Court is the court of last resort with power to determine the constitutionality of any law, order, regulation or official act" (Art. 81). On this point, the words of a distinguished Japanese constitutionalist, Professor Masami Itō, are instructive:

59. The reference was to the eight other petitions docketed: L-35538, *Roces* v. *Ponce Enrile*; L-35539, *Diokno* v. *Ponce Enrile*; L-35540, *Soliven* v. *Ponce Enrile*; L-35547, *Voltaire Garcia* v. *Fidel Ramos*; L-35556, *Yuyitung* v. *Ponce Enrile*; L-35567, *Doronila* v. *Ponce Enrile*; L-35571, *Guiao* v. *Ponce Enrile*; L-35573, *Rondon* v. *Ponce Enrile*. Respondent in eight such suits is the Secretary of National Defense. In the other, the party against whom the action was brought, General Ramos, is the Chief of the Constabulary.

60. *Aquino* v. *Commission on Elections*, 62 SCRA 275, and *Aquino* v. *Military Commission*, 63 SCRA 546.

61. *Aquino* v. *Commission on Elections*, 62 SCRA 275 (1975). Justice Makasiar spoke for the Court.

62. Justices Castro, Teehankee, Barredo, Antonio, Fernandez, and Muñoz Palma, along with the writer, spelled out their thinking on the subject. The main opinion was penned by Justice Antonio.

63. *Aquino* v. *Military Commission No. 2*, 63 SCRA 546 (1975).

64. Justices Teehankee and Muñoz Palma dissented.

65. Justice Castro and the writer qualified their acceptance of the judgment of the Court.

66. It came from Justice Barredo.

> The Japanese Constitution legalizes the doctrine in two ways. In the first place, fundamental human rights receive strong guarantees against arbitrary exercise of any governmental power. Under the present Constitution, even a law enacted by the Diet, which under Article 41 of the Constitution is the highest organ of state power, shall not have legal force when it invades the constitutional area of individual freedoms and rights. In the second place, judicial review of legislation is recognized. Modeled after American constitutional practice, article 81 vests the courts, especially the Supreme Court, with the power to determine the constitutionality of any law, order, regulation, or official act. The power of judicial review seems to be the most universally typical institution embodying rule of law. "It was Coke's version of the supremacy of the common law principles as exemplification of rules of reason and of justice that served as a convenient precedent when American justices were confronted with the demand that limits must be placed on legislative powers in order to safeguard individual rights and privileges."[67]

In the Korean Constitution, there is a variant of the function of judicial review as traditionally known in the United States. Chapter VIII, Article 109, provides that it shall be vested not in its Supreme Court but in a Constitution Committee, which "shall judge the following matters: 1. The constitutionality of a law at the request of the Court. 2. Impeachment. 3. Dissolution of a political party." It is "composed of nine members, who are appointed by the President." Three of them are to "be appointed from persons selected by the National Assembly, and [three others from those] nominated by the Chief Justice . . . ." It is further provided: "(1) When the Constitution Committee makes a decision in the case of a constitutional violation, impeachment or dissolution of a political party, the approval of more than six members shall be required. (2) The organization, operation and other necessary matters of the Constitution Committee shall be determined by law" (Art. 111). Thus, instead of the Korean Supreme Court passing upon the constitutionality of any challenged legislation, the function is exercised by this Constitution Committee.

Then, there are the other Asiatic countries, Burma, India, Malaysia, and Sri Lanka, with their constitutional practices deriving mainly from English legal institutions. Nonetheless, as was noted, judicial review is now an accepted feature in their polity.

Great Britain, while lacking a written charter, is justly famed for its respect for constitutionalism. It is traceable, according to a number of scholars, to the Magna Charta. This is how Professor Dunham puts the matter:

67. Masami Ito, "The Rule of Law: Constitutional Development in Law in Japan," in *Law in Japan: The Legal Order in a Changing Society*, Arthur T. Von Mehren (ed.) (Cambridge: Harvard University Press, 1963), pp. 207-8.

> First of all, the Charter did help to stimulate and to sanction the formulation of the concept, the due process of law. It also preserved the medieval ideal of the law's supremacy and so promoted the principle of the rule of law. Furthermore, the fact of the Great Charter itself, following a century-old tradition of coronation charters—virtually, engagements between sovereign and subject—and the subsequent forty-four confirmations of the Charter, all these fostered the principle of contract, government by agreement. Also, the inviolability that men attributed to the Charter made of it a higher kind of law by which they might appraise the validity of ordinances and statutes. Thus Magna Carta, as a criterion of recognition of validity, inspired Englishmen eventually to create a set of principles that have assured the certainty in public law and the consistency in governance that form the quintessence of British constitutionalism.[68]

The view expressed by the late Professor de Smith in his work *The New Commonwealth and Its Constitution* would indicate that there is a fundamental agreement between the American and British concepts as to the significance of a constitution. According to him, a constitution

> defines and establishes the principal organs of government; it is the source of their authority, it prescribes the manner in which and the limits within which their functions are to be exercised, and it determines their interrelationship. In this sense, it is a body of fundamental law. It is, moreover, hierarchically superior to rules of law enacted by the legislature except insofar as they have been made in a manner and form which, in terms of the constitution itself, clothes them with validity.[69]

He had occasion to note that among

> the characteristic features of modern Commonwealth constitutions are the limitation of parliamentary sovereignty, guarantees of fundamental human rights, judicial review of the constitutionality of legislation, the transfer of the responsibility for terminating a superior judge's tenure of office from a legislative to a judicial forum, and the vesting of full control over the public service and the conduct of elections in the hands of independent commissions.[70]

Such an observation was repeated later in his work in the following words:

> Each country has a written constitution, the more important provisions of which cannot be altered except by a special procedure requiring more than a bare legislative majority vote, and in each of them the courts have jurisdiction to pronounce a measure void if it is repugnant to the constitution.[71]

More specifically, the Constitution of India has this provision:

68. Samuel E. Thorne et al., *The Great Charter* (New York: Pantheon, 1965), p. 41.

69. S. A. de Smith, *The New Commonwealth and Its Constitutions* (London: Stevens, 1964), pp. 109-110.

70. Ibid., pp. 107-108. 71. Ibid.

> (1) The right to move the Supreme Court by appropriate proceedings for the enforcement of the rights conferred by this Part is guaranteed. (2) The Supreme Court shall have power to issue directions or orders or writs, including writs in the nature of *habeas corpus*, *mandamus*, prohibition, *quo warranto*, and *certiorari*, whichever may be appropriate, for the enforcement of any of the rights conferred by this Part. (3) Without prejudice to the powers conferred on the Supreme Court by clauses (1) and (2), Parliament may by law empower any other court to exercise within the local limits of its jurisdiction all or any of the powers exercisable by the Supreme Court under clause (2). (4) The right guaranteed by this article shall not be suspended except as otherwise provided for by this Constitution. (Art. 32)

This other provision is equally relevant:

> (1) If at any time it appears to the President that a question of law or fact has arisen, or is likely to arise, which is of such a nature and of such public importance that it is expedient to obtain the opinion of the Supreme Court upon it, he may refer the question to that Court for consideration and the Court may, after such hearing as it thinks fit, report to the President its opinion thereon. (2) The President may, notwithstanding anything in the proviso to Article 131, refer a dispute of the kind mentioned in the said proviso to the Supreme Court for opinion and the Supreme Court shall, after such hearing as it thinks fit, report to the President its opinion thereon. (Art. 143)

The Constitution of Malaysia states the following:

> (1) The Federal Court shall, to the exclusion of any other court, have jurisdiction to determine: (a) any question whether a law made by Parliament or by the Legislature of a State is invalid on the ground that it makes provision with respect to a matter with respect to which Parliament or, as the case may be, the Legislature of the State has no power to make laws; and (b) disputes on any other question between States or between the Federation and any State. (2) Without prejudice to any appellate jurisdiction of the Federal Court, where in any proceedings before another court a question arises as to the effect of any provision of this Constitution, the Federal Court shall have jurisdiction (subject to any rules of court regulating the exercise of that jurisdiction) to determine the question and remit the case to the other court to be disposed of in accordance with the determination. (3) The jurisdiction of the Federal Court to determine appeals from a High Court or a judge thereof shall be such as may be provided by federal law. (Art. 128)

This power was characterized by Tun Mohamed Suffian bin Hashim, in these words:

> If Parliament is not supreme and its laws may be invalidated by the courts, are the courts then supreme? The answer is yes and no—the courts are supreme in some ways but not in others. They are supreme in the sense that they have the right—indeed the duty—to invalidate Acts enacted outside Parliament's power, or Acts that are within Parliament's power but inconsistent with the constitution. But they are not supreme as

> regards Acts that are within Parliament's power and are consistent with the constitution. The court's duty then is quite clear; they must apply the law in those Acts without question, irrespective of their private view and prejudice. If judges are free to inject personal prejudice into their duty, there will be grave disquiet.[72]

The Constitutuion of Burma provides for judicial review in this wise: "No law shall be enacted excepting from the appellate jurisdiction of the Supreme Court cases which involve questions as to the validity of any law having regard to the provisions of this Constitution" (Art. 137). Sri Lanka has a separate Constitutional Court. In the language of its Constitution:

> (1) There shall be a Constitutional Court for the performance of the functions assigned to it by the Constitution. The President shall appoint, for a term of four years, five persons to be members of the Constitutional Court. Whenever occasion arises for the determination of any matter arising under subsection (2) of this section or of section 55, three members of the Constitutional Court chosen in accordance with the rules of the Constitutional Court shall determine such matter. (2) Any question as to whether any provision in a Bill is inconsistent with the Constitution shall be referred by the Speaker or, when he is unable to perform the functions of his office, the Deputy Speaker to the Constitutional Court for decision if (a) the Attorney-General communicates his opinion to the Speaker under section 53; or (b) the Speaker receives within a week of the Bill being placed on the Agenda of the National State Assembly a written notice raising such a question signed by the leader in the National State Assembly of a recognized political party; or (c) the question is raised within a week of the Bill being placed on the Agenda of the National State Assembly and signed by at least such number of members of the National State Assembly as would constitute quorum of the National State Assembly; or (d) the Speaker or, when he is unable to perform the functions of his office, the Deputy Speaker takes the view that there is such a question; or (e) the Constitutional Court on being moved by any citizen within a week of the Bill being placed on the Agenda of the National State Assembly, advises the Speaker that there is such a question. (3) No proceedings shall be had in the National State Assembly in relation to a Bill referred to the Constitutional Court under subsection (2) of this section or of section 55 until the decision of the Constitutional Court under subsection (4) of this section or its opinion under section 55 has been given. (4) The decision of the Constitutional Court upon a reference under subsection (2) of this section shall bind the Speaker and shall be conclusive for all purposes. No institution administering justice and likewise no other institution, person or authority shall have the power or jurisdiction to inquire into, pronounce upon or in any manner call in question a decision of the Constitutional Court. (Art. 54)

72. Tun Mohamed Suffian bin Hashim, *An Introduction to the Constitution of Malaysia* (Kuala Lumpur, 1976), p. 18.

The Bill of Rights

The United States Bill of Rights

The United States Constitution, as drafted by the Philadelphia Convention in 1787 and as ratified, had no separate article on a Bill of Rights. Not that the subject was completely ignored. Article I, dealing with legislative power, explicitly provides: "The Privilege of the Writ of Habeas Corpus shall not be suspended, unless when in Cases of Rebellion or Invasion the public safety may require it" (Sec. 9, par. [2]). The very next paragraph reads: "No Bill of Attainder or ex post facto law will be passed" (par. 3). Moreover, as far as a State of the Union is concerned, it is prohibited from passing "any Bill of Attainder, ex post facto Law, or Law impairing the Obligation of Contracts . . ." (Sec. 10, par. [1]). It was not until 1791, however, when the first Ten Amendments were adopted, that the United States was thought to have a comprehensive Bill of Rights. (It was supplemented by the so-called Civil War Amendments: the Thirteenth, ratified in 1865, prohibited slavery and involuntary servitude, the Fourteenth, in 1868, provided for national citizenship and required the conformity of state action to the standards of due process and equal protection, and the Fifteenth, in 1870, assured the right to vote to any American citizen irrespective of race, color, or previous condition of servitude. The Nineteenth Amendment in 1920 extended the right of suffrage to women.) It is thus apparent that as of 1791 the prime safeguards of American freedom became part and parcel of the United States Constitution.

The civil liberties guaranteed in the original text and in the first eight Amendments identified, in Laski's formulation, "rights as boundary marks which traced out areas of conduct the state [is] not normally entitled to invade."[73] There was necessity, as far as the United States was concerned, for all ten of them. From the standpoint of the influence they were to exert in other lands and later times, only the First, Fourth, Fifth, Sixth, Seventh, and Eighth of these amendments call for further treatment. The First Amendment deserves to be quoted in full:

> Congress shall make no law respecting an establishment of religion or prohibiting the free exercise thereof; or abridging the freedom of speech, or of the press; or the right of the people peaceably to assemble, and to petition the Government for a redress of grievances.

Of equal importance for the rights of man is the due process amendment, the Fifth:

> No person shall be held to answer for a capital, or otherwise infamous crime, unless on a presentment or indictment of a Grand Jury, except in cases arising in the land or naval forces, or in the Militia, when in actual

73. Harold Laski, *The State in Theory and Practice* (New York: Viking, 1935), p. 35.

> service in time of War of public danger; nor shall any person be subject for the same offence to be twice put in jeopardy of life or limb; nor shall be compelled in any criminal case to be a witness against himself, nor be deprived of life, liberty or property, without due process of law, nor shall private property be taken for public use, without just compensation.

This guarantee, as was noted, applies to state action under the Fourteenth Amendment, which likewise assures equal protection. Moreover, the safeguards thrown around an accused include the prohibition against unreasonable search and seizure under the Fourth Amendment:

> The right of the people to be more secure in their persons, houses, papers and effects, against unreasonable searches and seizures, shall not be violated, and no Warrants shall issue, but upon probable cause, supported by Oath or affirmation, and particularly describing the place to be searched, and the persons or things to be seized.

The Sixth and Seventh Amendments safeguard the right to a speedy and public trial by an impartial jury with the assistance of counsel:

> In all criminal prosecutions the accused shall enjoy the right to a speedy and public trial, by an impartial jury of the State and district wherein the crime shall have been committed, which district shall have been previously ascertained by law, and to be informed of the nature and cause of the accusation; to be confronted with the witnesses against him; to have compulsory process for obtaining witnesses in his favor, and to have the Assistance of Counsel for his defence.
>
> In suits at common law, where the value in controversy shall exceed twenty dollars, the right of trial by jury shall be preserved, and no fact tried by a jury shall be otherwise re-examined in any Court of the United States, than according to the rules of the common law.

The Eighth Amendment provides:

> Excessive bail shall not be required, nor excessive fines imposed, nor cruel and unusual punishment inflicted.

It is thus rendered clear that what is found in a constitution is a recognition, not a grant, or rights—and, at that, not a comprehensive one either. There was thus acceptance of the view as far back as 1791 of their being possessed by every human being.

It was not too long ago (1963) that the New York University School of Law published a volume entitled *The Great Rights*, edited by the late Professor Edmond Cahn, containing the James Madison Lectures by four distinguished American jurists, Justices Hugo L. Black, William J. Brennan, Jr., Earl Warren, and William O. Douglas. The volume opens with Cahn's essay emphasizing the great debt owed Madison for the American Bill of Rights.

> Something daring and novel was in the wind which caught the finest minds of the time and inflamed them. To men like James Madison,

> the war against Britain was only the military aspect of an all-pervasive American Revolution and the question to be decided was not whether Americans should regain the rights that Englishmen had considered customary but whether for the first time in human history any man anywhere could enjoy the full political dignity to which all men were born. Though English notions of liberty were obviously useful, they were inadequate. What America promised must be nothing less than a new kind of society—fresh, equal, just, open, free, and forever respectful of conscience. (P. 3)

To the question of how "to implement this vision and find constitutional machinery" to lend it force and effectivity, he answered:

> The breakthrough came because Madison believed profoundly that in America the people were sovereign and the officials their mere trustees, agents and servants. He put it neatly: "In Europe," he wrote, "charters of liberty have been granted by power." And in America? "Charters of power granted by liberty." In Magna Carta where King John, though acting under coercion of powerful nobles, nevertheless spoke as monarch, "We will not" was deemed fitting (in Latin, of course, for the benefit of the common man.) In the English Bill of Rights where William and Mary, though accepting the conditions that Parliament had exacted, still spoke as sovereign, "ought not" was deemed bold enough for the protection of the rights of subject. But when the American people in 1789 prescribed the acts that their new Federal Government must either not do or do only in a particular manner, they were entitled to say "shall not," the language of command. Thus, the old flaccid promises and pious exhortations were at last toughened into imperative law. (P. 5)

What is embraced in the term "imperative law" is not limited to the literal language of the provisions as found, which in most cases are phrased in general terms allowing a great deal of discretion and flexibility in their application. Their history, of course, cannot be ignored. There is truth, moreover, in this observation of Justice Frankfurter: "Deeply imbedded traditional ways of carrying out state policy . . . are often tougher and truer law than the dead words of the written text."[74] The main reliance, though, in ascertaining the meaning rightfully attached to the constitutional commands should be on U.S. Supreme Court decisions. For the United States Constitution is not merely law, it is the supreme law. It is the judiciary, then, ultimately the Supreme Court, which, in the language of Charles G. Haines, "interpreted and applied its terms as they did the language of statutes so that matters of great political import were passed upon apparently with the same ease, simplicity, and procedure as the interpretation of a contract or the defining of the rights of persons under a will."[75] What is more, as

74. *Nashville C. & St. L. Railway* v. *Browning*, 310 U.S. 362, 369 (1940).

75. Charles G. Haines, *The Role of the Supreme Court in American Government and Politics, 1789-1835* (New York: Russell and Russell, 1960), p. 11.

Charles Fairman noted: "It has seemed far more consistent with our polity that for the protection of individual rights the citizen look to the Courts rather than be dependent upon the fluctuating views of the legislature."[76]

A careful and precise appraisal and study of such decisions and the opinions rendered would require a painstaking analysis, but the necessity for this is not apparent. Rather, viewed solely in terms of their impact on Asiatic constitutions, it may suffice to refer to the approach taken and the language employed to show adherence and fealty to the concept of fundamental rights, without ignoring, of course, the judgment rendered. It may be that the ideals professed rather than the ideals realized may in the end prove to be more influential as far as foreign lands are concerned. It will also have the merit of treading on grounds of a none-too-familiar terrain. More simply put, the peculiar and singular circumstances of each case may not be too apparent to a foreign observer. Even if the identical phraseology of the provisions as found in the U.S. Constitution is followed in the Asiatic nations to be referred to, there has to be an appreciation of the varying conditions and the flux of circumstances of each country involved. This is not to deny, however, that where no deviation of wording exists, there is at least a *prima facie* case for the persuasive character of the United States Supreme Court decisions in the interpretation of the provisions in question.

It only remains to be added that, considering the time when the Asiatic constitutions were framed, just after the close of World War II, aside from the deference and respect elicited by the majestic utterances of a Marshall, a Holmes, a Brandeis, or a Cardozo, the influence of the U.S. Supreme Court under the leadership of Chief Justice Hughes and Stone covering the period of 1930 to 1946 is quite apparent.[77] A word more about the present Constitution of the Philippines, which became effective on January 17, 1973. It was framed by the Constitutional Convention, which opened its session on June 1, 1971, and it was approved on November 30, 1972. It is not surprising, then, that traces of the Warren Court's leading decisions can be discerned in its Bill of Rights,[78] which, again not surprisingly, reiterated what was earlier

76. Charles Fairman, "The Attack on the Segregation Cases," 70 *Harv. Law Rev.*, 85 (1960).

77. The Constitutional opinions of both Chief Justices and, in the case of the latter, even those penned when he was an Associate Justice, received their due attention. From the late thirties and during this era, certain pronouncements on civil liberties by Justices Black, Douglas, Frankfurter, Jackson, Murphy, and Rutledge also came to be highly regarded.

78. In addition to those of Chief Justice Warren, the views of Justices Black and Douglas, as could have been expected, as well as others were duly taken into account by the framers of the Philippine Constitution.

contained in the Commonwealth Constitution of 1935. In that sense, the debt owed to the earlier Hughes and Stone eras must be acknowledged.

The fundamental rights to which further reference will be made insofar as they have found their way into Asiatic constitutions may be categorized into freedom of belief and expression, whether religious or secular, including freedom of assembly and of association in accordance with the First Amendment; the due process and equal protection guarantees, as ordained in the Fifth and Fourteenth Amendments, and in the case of the former, not only insofar as the procedural aspect is concerned but also insofar as it formerly constituted the main reliance for the protection of property interests; and the rights of an accused individual safeguarded by the Fourth, Sixth, Seventh, and Eighth Amendments. To repeat, while the rulings announced should be kept in mind, the aspect to be emphasized will be the constitutional objectives sought to be attained, even if, from a more detailed study of the technical and intricate questions raised, it may be difficult to resist the conclusion that, at times, performance did not match aspiration.

The Philippine Bill of Rights

The extent of the American influence in the Philippines so far as the liberties of the individual are concerned is easily discernible. All that needs to be done is to set forth the Bill of Rights as found in the 1935 Constitution, reproduced well-nigh *ipsissimis verbis* in the present fundamental law. It was embodied in a single section (Article III, Section 1) with the following paragraphs:

> (1) No person shall be deprived of life, liberty or property without due process of law, nor shall any person be denied the equal protection of the laws.
>
> (2) Private property shall not be taken for public use without just compensation.
>
> (3) The right of the people to be secure in their persons, houses, papers, and effects against unreasonable searches and seizures shall not be violated, and no warrants shall issue but upon probable cause, to be determined by the judge after examination under oath or affirmation of the complainant and the witnesses he may produce, and particularly describing the place to be searched, and the persons or things to be seized.
>
> (4) The liberty of abode and of changing the same within the limits prescribed by law shall not be impaired.
>
> (5) The privacy of communication and correspondence shall be inviolable except upon lawful order of the court or when public safety and order require otherwise.
>
> (6) The right to form associations or societies for purposes not contrary to law shall not be abridged.

(7) No law shall be made respecting an establishment of religion, or prohibiting the free exercise thereof, and the free exercise and enjoyment of religious profession and worship, without discrimination or preference, shall forever be allowed. No religious test shall be required for the exercise of civil or political rights.

(8) No law shall be passed abridging the freedom of speech, or of the press, or the right of the people peaceably to assemble and petition the Government for redress of grievances.

(9) No law granting a title of nobility shall be enacted, and no person holding any office of profit or trust shall, without the consent of the Congress of the Philippines, accept any present, emolument, office, or title of any kind whatever from any foreign state.

(10) No law impairing the obligation of contracts shall be passed.

(11) No ex post facto law or bill of attainder shall be enacted.

(12) No person shall be imprisoned for debt or non-payment of a poll tax.

(13) No involuntary servitude in any form shall exist except as a punishment for crime whereof the party shall have been duly convicted.

(14) The privilege of the writ of habeas corpus shall not be suspended except in cases of invasion, insurrection, or rebellion, when the public safety requires it, in any of which events the same may be suspended wherever during such period the necessity of such suspension shall exist.

(15) No person shall be held to answer for a criminal offense without due process of law.

(16) All persons shall before conviction be bailable by sufficient sureties, except those charged with capital offenses when evidence of guilt is strong. Excessive bail shall not be required.

(17) In all criminal prosecutions the accused shall be presumed to be innocent until the contrary is proved, and shall enjoy the right to be heard by himself and counsel, to be informed of the nature and cause of the accusation against him, to have a speedy and public trial, to meet the witnesses face to face, and to have compulsory process to secure the attendance of witnesses in his behalf.

(18) No person shall be compelled to be a witness against himself.

(19) Excessive fines shall not be imposed, nor cruel and unusual punishment inflicted.

(20) No person shall be twice put in jeopardy of punishment for the same offense. If an act is punished by law and an ordinance, conviction or acquittal under either shall constitute a bar to another prosecution for the same act.

(21) Free access to the courts shall not be denied to any person by reason of poverty.

Nothing can be clearer than that the bill of rights provision in the 1935 Constitution was patterned after that of the United States. That was the way the Filipinos wanted it, and it is easy to understand why. A great Filipino jurist, Claro M. Recto, as the President of the 1934 Constitutional Convention, observed how firm was the conviction held by so many leading delegates, products of the American system of education, that a constitutional democracy of the American type was the one most suited to Philippine conditions. Moreover, there was a practical reason. Care was taken by the Convention to avoid any radical departure from the United States constitutional system inasmuch as the Philippine Independence Act of 1934 contained a provision that the American President had to certify that the constitution drafted would provide for a republican form of government and contain a bill of rights. Without such certification, the Commonwealth of the Philippines could not be established. Since the long-sought independence was promised after a ten-year Commonwealth transition period, it was imperative, in the thinking of the Filipino leaders then, that there be no obstacle to its coming into existence as soon as possible, which might not be the case if the proposed constitution were to be indicted for unorthodoxy. There was, moreover, another consideration present in the mind of the delegates. Government, if viewed as a science, involves problems and difficulties formidable in character. If the technique of leadership by which it is carried out is looked upon as an art, it is baffling and complex. There is need then for caution and prudence, not the duty but the necessity (to paraphrase Holmes) to keep continuity with the past, to adhere to what has been insofar as it proved beneficial or to the extent that it has formed part of the people's accustomed ways. Nor can it be doubted that, from the inception of the American tutelage at the beginning of the century, and even earlier for that matter, the Filipinos were aware of the need for a bill of rights.

Moreover, by the time the Constitutional Convention met in 1934, the Supreme Court of the Philippines had for over three decades been busy at work construing the fundamental rights provisions of previous organic acts enacted by the United States for this country, with fundamental rights being embodied in nearly the very same language. That was an added reason for a bill of rights of a distinctly American cast.

The Filipino people were thus familiar with such guarantees, and their retention as worded would be most natural. Some intellectuals with a European background and a number of the surviving leaders of the revolution—first against Spain and thereafter against the United States in the early years of American rule, as was noted—were desirous of incorporating some changes. They had in mind certain provisions of the 1898 Malolos Constitution of the Philippines. In their opinion, that was more in keeping with Filipino tradition and would reflect greater responsiveness to local needs and conditions. While they were unable to persuade the Convention to go as far as they might wish, they met with some measure of success. By and large, though, the Bill of Rights of the 1935 Constitution adhered to what had been. Such a result, in light of what has been said, had almost the imprint of inevitability. There was a contributing factor: The draft was prepared by a committee headed by Delegate, later Justice, José P. Laurel, the leading Filipino authority on the subject of constitutional law and a Doctor of Civil Laws graduate of the Yale Law School. He sponsored the draft, and he pressed for its approval with all the persuasive powers at his command, arising from the breadth of his scholarship and his gift of oratory.

So much for the fundamental rights provision of the 1935 Constitution, which is no longer in force. The present Constitution of the Philippines was drafted by the 1971 Constitutional Convention. It came into force and effect on January 17, 1973. The amendments to the Bill of Rights (now Article IV of the Revised Constitution) are minimal. Two new rights have been added, one being an express recognition of the right of the people to have "access to official records and to documents and papers pertaining to official acts, transactions, or decisions . . . subject to such limitations as may be provided by law" (Sec. 6). The other new right assures the speedy disposition of cases "before all judicial, quasi-judicial, or administrative bodies" (Sec. 16). The promptness required in the disposition of cases may be looked upon as implied in the due process clause.

The search and seizure clause has been modified. It now reads:

> The right of the people to be secure in their persons, houses, papers, and effects against unreasonable searches and seizures of whatever nature and for any purpose shall not be violated, and no search warrant or warrant of arrest shall issue except upon probable cause to be determined by the judge, or such other responsible officer as may be authorized by law, after examination under oath or affirmation of the complainant and the witnesses he may produce, and particularly describing the place to be searched, and the persons or things to be seized. (Sec. 3)

Thus any possible ambiguity as to this guarantee being applicable to a warrant of arrest has been dissipated. The former language gave rise to doubts, as a literal reading would confine its scope only to search warrants. Now there is the express requirement that for such arrest to be constitutionally permissible there must be a "probable cause to be determined by the judge, or such other responsible officer as may be authorized by law. . . ." This last phrase is also an alteration. Where formerly it was only a judge who could do so, now legislation may be enacted vesting such competence in "such other responsible officer." This innovation may be fraught with undesirable consequences. With a judge, the element of impartiality is easier to attain: unlike a fiscal or some other executive official, he is under no pressure to have the party before him apprehended so that the prosecution can be started.

In the 1935 Constitution it was made clear that communication and correspondence "shall be inviolable except upon lawful order of the court or when public safety and order require otherwise" (Art. III, Sec. 1, par. [5]). A second paragraph has been added to Article IV, Section 4, in the present Constitution. It is therein explicitly provided: "Any evidence obtained in violation of this or the preceding section shall be inadmissible for any purpose in any proceeding." This is a most welcome feature of the new Constitution.

The present Constitution is likewise notable for the added vitality accorded the guarantee against self-incrimination. It now reads:

> No person shall be compelled to be a witness against himself. Any person under investigation for the commission of an offense shall have the right to remain silent and to counsel, and to be informed of such right. No force, violence, threat, intimidation, or any other means which vitiates the free will shall be used against him. Any confession obtained in violation of this section shall be inadmissible in evidence.[79]

The epochal American Supreme Court decision in *Miranda* v. *Arizona*[80] supplied the basis for this mandate in the present Philippine Constitution. If fully implemented, the opportunity for abusive practices committed against individuals interrogated under police custody would be minimized. Without such a safeguard, there were fears that their right against self-incrimination could be rendered futile.

There was also an addition to the provisions dealing with the rights of an accused at the trial: "However, after arraignment, trial may proceed notwithstanding the absence of the accused provided that he has been duly notified and his failure to appear is unjustified" (Sec. 19). Finally, it now suffices that the punishment be either cruel *or* unusual (Sec. 21), where formerly it had to be both, to be unconstitutional.

Social and Economic Rights in the Philippines

There is a feature of the 1935 Constitution of the Philippines, even more emphasized in the present Charter, that marked an advance in the field of fundamental freedoms. In addition to the traditional civil and political rights, there were provisions on social and economic rights, to which not much thought appeared to have been paid when the laissez faire theory was dominant. With the grave problem posed by the great number of the poor and the needy in the developing countries—and this observation would be applicable to most of the Asiatic nations, except possibly Japan—it was imperative that the State actively participate in its solution. Reliance on the free play of the market would not only be futile but would even exacerbate the problem of the rich becoming even

79. Art. IV, Sec. 20. Only the first sentence was found in the former Bill of Rights, Art. III, Sec. 1, par. (18).

80. 348 US 436 (1966).

more affluent and the poor becoming even more penurious. To avoid any constitutional question, it was thought best to adopt guarantees of a social and economic character, referring to those claims that have to be attended to by the government to assure the promotion of individual welfare and well-being. It is ironic to speak of the human dignity to which everyone is entitled when decent living conditions still elude so many of the poverty-stricken inhabitants of Asia.

In this regard, the American influence, as might have been expected, was minimal. While the United States can boast of a glorious tradition in the field of traditional political and civil rights expressive of the humanistic values that rightly elicited predominant judicial concern, social and economic rights hardly formed part of the judicial agenda. To repeat, in a developing country like the Philippines, that is a matter of urgency. Without such rights, constitutional democracy will fail of acceptance. So the 1934 Constitutional Convention believed, and it acted on such conviction. The 1935 Constitution represented a departure from, and to that extent could be said to be an improvement of, its American counterpart. That the Convention was moved to act thus was in large part due to the vigorous advocacy of Delegate Manuel Roxas, later the first President of the Republic of the Philippines. For him the Constitution that was to be drafted should have

> a definite and well defined philosophy, not only political but social and economic. A constitution that in 1776 or in 1789 was sufficient in the United States, considering the problems they had at that time, may not now be sufficient with the growing and ever-widening complexities of social and economic problems and relations. . . . If in this constitution the gentleman will find declarations of economic policy, they are there because they are necessary to safeguard the interests and welfare of the Filipino people because we believe that the days have come when in self-defense, a nation may provide in its constitution those safeguards, the patrimony, the freedom to grow; the freedom to develop national aspirations and national interests, not to be hampered by the artificial boundaries which a constitutional provision automatically imposes.[81]

One of the most vital national interests, an aspect of the country's aspirations, is the promotion of a social order truly concerned with the satisfaction of the primary needs of the common man. Accordingly, in the Declaration of Principles, an Article that was itself an innovation, it was expressly provided: "The promotion of social justice to insure the well-being and economic security of all the people should be the concern of the State" (Revised Constitution, Art. II, Sec. 5). This provision is supplemented by this requirement: "The State shall afford protection to labor, especially to working women and minors, and shall

81. *Proceedings of the Philippine Constitutional Convention*, vol. 3 (S. Laurel, ed.), pp. 177-178.

regulate the relation between landowner and tenant, and between labor and capital in industry and in agriculture. The State may provide for compulsory arbitration" (Art. IV, Sec. 6). The power of eminent domain was expanded to carry out the policy of transferring the ownership of lands to tenants: "The Congress may authorize, upon payment of just compensation the expropriation of lands to be subdivided into small lots and conveyed at cost to individuals" (Art XIII, Sec. 4). There was another manifestation of the enlarged sphere of governmental power (Art. XIII, Sec. 6):

> The State may, in the interest of national welfare and defense, establish and operate industries and means of transportation and communications, and, upon payment of just compensation, transfer to public ownership utilities and other private enterprises to be operated by the Government. (Art. XII, Sec. 6)

As for social and economic rights, the changes in the present Constitution are extensive. The social justice provision in the 1935 Constitution was limited to an expression of a general principle: "The promotion of social justice to insure the well-being and economic security of all the people should be the concern of the State" (Art. II, Sec. 5). There is a restatement of such a mandate in the present Charter less productive of doubts as to how far it can affect property rights:

> The State shall promote social justice to ensure the dignity, welfare, and security of all the people. Towards this end, the State shall regulate the acquisition, ownership, use, enjoyment, and disposition of private property, and equitably diffuse property ownership and profits. (Art. II, Sec. 6)

The duty cast on government as to its implementation is made explicit:

> The State shall establish, maintain, and ensure adequate social services in the field of education, health, housing, employment, welfare, and social security to guarantee the enjoyment by the people of a decent standard of living (Sec. 7).

The age-old evil of tenancy was likewise sought to be met frontally:

> The State shall formulate and implement an agrarian reform program aimed at emancipating the tenant from the bondage of the soil and achieving the goals enunciated in this Constitution. (Art. XIV, Sec. 12)

The constitutional policy on social justice in the 1935 Constitution was supplemented by the requirement that the State "shall afford protection to labor, especially to working women and minors" (Art. XIV, Sec. 6). The new fundamental law is much more definite:

> The State shall afford protection to labor, promote full employment and equality in employment, ensure equal work opportunities regardless of sex, race, or creed, and regulate the relations between workers and employers. The State shall assure the rights of workers to self-organiza-

> tion, collective bargaining, security of tenure, and just and humane conditions of work. The State may provide for compulsory arbitration. (Art. II, Sec. 9)

The Bill of Rights in Other Asiatic Countries

As far as the other Asiatic countries mentioned earlier are concerned, it may be said that the influence of the United States Constitution in their fundamental laws was not as considerable as in the case of the Philippines, for which, as was noted, there is a historical explanation. Of those nations, the constitutions of Japan and Korea contain a number of provisions of American origin. The fundamental laws of Burma, India, Malaysia, and Pakistan, to a lesser degree, bear traces of American concepts. The Constitution of Indonesia appears to have the least connection.

Of the cognate rights of due process and equal protection, which contributed much to the growth of American constitutional law, there is no mention in those constitutions whatsoever of the former. Such an omission may be due to the fears entertained that (as was the case for a rather long time in the United States) due process could be availed of to press the right to property to unreasonable extremes. That would indeed be regrettable, for in all these countries, except perhaps Malaysia, social and economic rights are a prominent feature.

The Constitution of Burma speaks of cultural and educational rights (Sec. 22) as well as economic rights (Sec. 23). India's Constitution in its Directive Principles of State Policy ordains: "The State shall strive to promote the welfare of the people by securing and protecting as effectively as it may a social order in which justice, social, economic and political, shall inform all the institutions of the national life" (Part IV, Sec. 38). Section 39 is specific:

> The State shall, in particular, direct its policy towards securing: (a) that the citizens, men and women equally, have the right to an adequate means of livelihood; (b) that the ownership and control of the material resources of the community are so distributed as best to subserve the common good; (c) that the operation of the economic system does not result in the concentration of wealth and means of production to the common detriment; (d) that there is equal pay for equal work for both men and women: (e) that the health and strength of workers, men and women, and the tender age of children are not abused and that the citizens are not forced by economic necessity to enter avocations unsuited to their age or strength; (f) that childhood and youth are protected against exploitation and against moral and material abandonment.

The Constitution of Indonesia provides for social welfare:

> Economy shall be organized cooperatively. Branches of production which are important to the State and which affect the life of most people, shall be controlled by the State. Land and water and the natural riches

> therein shall be controlled by the State and shall be exploited for the greatest welfare of the people. (Chap. XIV, Art. 33, Secs. 1-3)

The right to education is found in the Constitution of the Republic of Korea:

> (1) All citizens shall have the right to receive an equal education corresponding to their abilities. (2) All citizens who have children under their protection shall be responsible for at least their elementary education and other education as required by law. (3) Such compulsory education shall be free. (4) Independence and political impartiality of education shall be guaranteed. (5) Fundamental matters pertaining to the educational system and its operation shall be determined by law. (Art. 27)

The right as well as the duty to work comes next:

> (1) All citizens shall have the right to work. The State shall endeavor to promote the employment of workers through social and economic means. (2) All citizens shall have the duty to work. The contents and conditions of the duty to work shall be determined by law in conformity with democratic principles. (3) Standards of working conditions shall be determined by law. (4) Special protection shall be accorded to working women and children. (Art. 28)

Provision is then made for the right to association and collective bargaining:

> (1) The right to association, collective bargaining, and collective action of workers shall be guaranteed within the scope defined by law. (2) The right to association, collective bargaining, and collective action shall not be accorded to workers who are public officials, except for those authorized by the provisions of law. (3) The right to collective action may be either restricted or may not be recognized in accordance with the provisions of law for public officials and workers engaged in State, local, autonomous governments, state-run enterprises, public utility businesses, and enterprises which have serious influence on the national economy. (Art. 29)

What is more, there is recognition of the goal of decent human existence and social security:

> (1) All citizens shall be entitled to a decent human life. (2) The State shall endeavor to promote social security. (3) Citizens who are incapable of making a living shall be protected by the State in accordance with the provisions of law. (Art. 30)

The Constitution of Japan, after mentioning the right and obligation to work, requires that standards for wages, hours, rest, and other working conditions shall be fixed by law, and children "shall not be exploited" (Art. 27). Article 28 guarantees the "right of workers to organize and to bargain and act collectively."

So much then for substantive due process, which, as formerly interpreted by courts in the United States, could be attended with mischievous consequences for the welfare of those at the bottom of the economic pyramid. Procedural due process, however, even if not referred to by such term, is not ignored. The Constitution of Burma is quite clear: "No citizen shall be deprived of his personal liberty, nor his dwelling entered, nor his property confiscated, save in accordance with law" (Sec. 16). The same may be said of the Constitution of India: "No person shall be deprived of his life or personal liberty except according to procedure established by law" (Part III, Sec. 21). The Constitution of Japan is well-nigh identical: "No person shall be deprived of life or liberty, nor shall any other criminal penalty be imposed, except according to procedure established by law" (Art. 31). The Constitution of Korea is worded in a similar fashion: "All citizens shall enjoy personal liberty. No person shall be arrested, detained, seized, searched, interrogated, punished, subjected to involuntary labor, or branded as security risk except as provided by law" (Art. 10, par. [1]). The Constitution of Malaysia is categorical: "No person shall be deprived of his life or personal liberty save in accordance with law" (Part II, Art. 5, par. [1]). The same thought in language that is not distinguishable appears in the Constitution of Pakistan: "No person shall be deprived of life or liberty save in accordance with law" (Part II, Chap. I, Sec. 1).

Equality is an ideal highly prized by the Asiatic peoples. The Constitution of Burma is explicit on the matter: "All citizens irrespective of birth, religion, sex or race are equal before the law; that is to say, there shall not be any arbitrary discrimination between one citizen or class of citizens and another" (Sec. 13). Then: "There shall be equality of opportunity for all citizens in matters of public employment and in the exercise or carrying on of any occupation, trade, business or profession" (Sec. 14). After which comes a provision that is a step in the direction of sexual equality: "Women shall be entitled to the same pay as that received by men in respect of similar work" (Sec. 15). The Constitution of India has an expanded equal protection clause: "The State shall not deny to any person equality before the law, or the equal protection of the laws within the territory of India" (Part III, Sec. 14). The guarantee is made more specific:

> The State shall not discriminate against any citizen on grounds only of religion, race, caste, sex, place of birth or any of them. No citizen shall, on grounds only of religion, race, caste, sex, place of birth or any of them, be subject to any disability, liability, restriction or condition with regard to: (a) access to shops, public restaurants, hotels and places of public entertainment; or (b) the use of wells, tanks, bathing *ghats*, roads and places of public resort maintained wholly or partly out of State funds or dedicated to the use of the general public. Nothing in this article shall prevent the State from making any special provision for

> women and children. Nothing in this article or in clause (2) of Article 29 shall prevent the State from making any special provision for the advancement of any socially and educationally backward classes of citizens or for the Scheduled Castes and the Scheduled Tribes. (Sec. 15)

There is also equality prescribed for public service:

> There shall be equality of opportunity for all citizens in matters relating to employment or appointment to any office under the State. No citizen shall, on grounds only of religion, race, caste, sex, descent, place of birth, residence or any of them, be ineligible for, or discriminated against in respect of any employment or office under the State. Nothing in this article shall prevent Parliament from making any law prescribing, in regard to a class or classes of employment or appointment to an office under the Government of, or any local or other authority within, a State or Union territory, any requirement as to residence within that State or Union territory prior to such employment or appointment. Nothing in this article shall prevent the State from making any provision for the reservation of appointments or posts in favour of any backward class of citizens which, in the opinion of the State, is not adequately represented in the services under the State. Nothing in this article shall affect the operation of any law which provides that the incumbent of an office in connection with the affairs of any religious or denominational institution or any member of the governing body thereof shall be a person professing a particular religion or belonging to a particular denomination. (Sec. 16)

The concept of equality is set forth in the Constitution of Japan in these terms:

> All of the people are equal under the law and there shall be no discrimination in political, economic or social relations because of race, creed, sex, social status or family origin. Peers and peerage shall not be recognized. No privilege shall accompany any award of honor, decoration or any distinction, nor shall any such award be valid beyond the lifetime of the individual who now holds or hereafter may receive it. (Chap. III, Art. 14)

The Constitution of the Republic of Korea provides for the matter thus:

> (1) All citizens shall be equal before the law, and there shall be no discrimination in political, economic, social, or cultural life on account of sex, religion or social status. (2) No privileged castes shall be recognized, nor ever be established in any form. (3) The awarding of decorations or distinctions of honor in any form shall be effective only for recipients, and no privileged status shall be created thereby. (Art. 9)

The Constitution of Malaysia has an equal protection clause similar to that of India: "All persons are equal before the law and are entitled to the equal protection of the law" (Part II, Art. 8, par. [1]). The next three paragraphs of this article expand the guarantee thus:

> (2) Except as expressly authorized by this Constitution, there shall be no discrimination against citizens on the ground only of religion, race,

> descent or place of birth in any law or in the appointment to any office or employment under a public authority or in the administration of any law relating to the acquisition, holding or disposition of property or the establishing or carrying on of any trade, business, profession, vocation or employment. (3) There shall be no discrimination in favour of any person on the ground that he is a subject of the Ruler of any State. (4) No public authority shall discriminate against any person on the ground that he is resident or carrying on business in any part of the Federation outside the jurisdiction of the authority.

The Constitution of Pakistan, as does those of India and Malaysia, has a similar version of the equal protection clause: "All citizens are equal before the law and are entitled to equal protection of law" (Part II, Chap. 1, Art. 15). It also prescribes non-discrimination in respect of access to public places:

> In respect of access to places of public entertainment or resort, not intended for religious purposes only, there shall be no discrimination against any citizen on the ground only of race, religion, caste, sex or place of birth, but nothing herein shall be deemed to prevent the making of any special provision for women. (Art. 16)

By Way of Conclusion

Nothing can be clearer, therefore, than that the United States Constitution has had an impact, both deep-seated and profound, on the fundamental laws of practically all the Asiatic countries that have recently attained their statehood, as well as of Japan. That is easily understandable. The United States has the oldest living written Constitution. It has stood the test of time and circumstance. Through its judicious construction, it has been made adaptable to the constant flux of events. It has more than proven its worth. It is a living instrument. To paraphrase Justice Frankfurter, it is not a printed finality but a dynamic process.

There is this *caveat*, however. Necessarily, in view of the difference of conditions in Asiatic countries, there cannot be literal adherence in most cases to its leading constitutional law doctrines, even on the assumption that they are possessed of the highest merit. Environmental facts and the social milieu have to be taken into account. It cannot be denied, though, that the spirit that informs a constitution, namely, as the instrument to assure the welfare and well-being of the inhabitants of a country, has a significance that transcends national boundaries. To that extent, Asia has kept the constitutional faith.

More specifically, the Bill of Rights as a limitation on the powers of government is appreciated and to a great extent followed notwithstanding emergency or crisis conditions. Where judicial review is concerned, even now the landmark decision of *Marbury* v. *Madison* commands the utmost respect and provides an authoritative guide. Lastly, there may be need to mention anew that in the sphere of social and economic rights, in an area where the grave problems of poverty and disease continue to plague the governments, the reliance on American concepts is understandably not as great, the United States having the good fortune to have more than its share of the goods of existence and to be blessed with affluence.

IX

Singapore

Editorial Note

Singapore, roughly two-thirds the area of New York City, with two and one half million residents, generates well over twice the export income of Indonesia, whose population is sixty times greater. On a similar scale of contrast Singapore's approximate $6,000 per capita gross national product contrasts with Indonesia's $100. These statistics serve merely to illustrate the singularity of Singapore.

Autonomous in 1959, except for defense and foreign affairs, Singapore was subsequently coupled, reluctantly, with peninsular Malaya, Sarawak, and Sabah, to form the Federation of Malaysia in 1963. The vicissitudes of the Confrontation with Indonesia, exacerbated by Malay fears of potential domination of the Federation by Singapore Chinese, led to Singapore's severance and emergence as an independent nation two years later.

Beginning as Southeast Asia's preeminent entrepôt, independent Singapore under the tutelage of Lee Kuan Yew rapidly expanded processing, trade, manufacturing, and industrial sectors. Precision engineering, sophisticated electronics, shipbuilding, and textile manufacture represent the scope of exploitation of Singapore's only resource, labor.

Note: This chapter was written in December 1977.

The problems of miniscule territory, mushrooming population, and absence of natural resources contributed to partial movement away from democratic government and toward personalist rule and a one-party system. Communalist conflict, though hardly so severe as in Malaysia, reflects the division among 76 percent Chinese, 15 percent Malays, and 7 percent Indians. Elections today are aptly described as "Gallic referenda."

For treatment of the background of Singapore's legal apparatus, see the chapter on Malaysia.

May 1978 ROGER K. PAGET

The Singapore Constitution and the United States Constitution

S. Jayakumar
Dean of the Faculty of Law, University of Singapore

Introduction

A quick overview of Singapore's constitutional development is essential to our subsequent discussion.[1] Singapore's constitutional development can be separated into four phases. The first phase was the *colonial phase*. From the founding of Singapore in 1819 and until 1959, the British administered Singapore as a colony. Until the Japanese Occupation Singapore was part of the Straits Settlements, but after World War II, in 1946, Singapore was administered as a separate Crown Colony. The second phase was that of *self-government*. In 1959 Singapore achieved self-government and then received a new constitution from the United Kingdom providing for a wholly elected legislature having control over all matters except defence and foreign affairs and with a limited role in internal security. The United Kingdom was responsible for defence and external affairs. Third, there was the *Malaysian phase*, when Singapore (together with the two Borneo states of Sabah and Sarawak) became part of the Federation. Singapore, apart from now being subject to the Malaysian federal constitution, also received then a new state constitution. Singapore was part of Malaysia from September 16, 1963, until August 9, 1965. The final phase is the *post-independence era*. Due to various irreconcilable differences between the Singapore government and the Malaysian federal government, it was agreed by both sides that Singapore would separate and become an independent nation. This was effected through a mutual agreement, the Independence of Singapore Agreement, August 7, 1965.[2]

To the question of whether the Constitution of the United States has influenced the Singapore Constitution, the candid answer must be

1. For a brief introduction to Singapore constitutional law, see the writer's *Constitutional Law, with Documentary Materials* (No. 1 in Singapore Law Series), 1976.

2. Singapore Government Gazette Extraordinary No. 66 of 1965; also in International Legal Materials, 932 (1965).

in the negative. This, however, ought not be surprising, because (as was seen in the preceding paragraph) prior to independence as well as after independence there has not been a very intense relationship between the political and legal systems of the two countries.

If the constitutional systems of any other countries have influenced Singapore's Constitution, they are those of the United Kingdom and Malaysia. The United Kingdom's influence on Singapore's constitutional law can be appreciated in the light of the British colonial administration of Singapore over a long period, bringing with it the influence of the English legal system, legal concepts, and law. In today's independent Singapore, the legal system and much of the laws are still influenced by English parallels, and indeed in some areas English law is directly applicable. In the area of constitutional law, even though Singapore has a written constitution and the United Kingdom has not, English influence is nonetheless prominent, particularly in the parliamentary system of government which operates instead of a presidential system like that of the United States. Furthermore, Singapore courts have also been influenced by English judicial decisions in certain areas of constitutional law such as that concerning preventive detention. The facts that all the older-generation legal practitioners received their legal training in the United Kingdom and that several key political leaders studied in the United Kingdom are also important explanatory factors.

More recently, however, Malaysian influence on Singapore's constitutional development has been significant. One factor explaining this is that both Singapore and the states which make up the Malaysian federation were administered by Britain, and this common feature resulted in many similarities concerning the administration of law and legal systems. Even now when the two countries are separate independent sovereign states, it is quite common for courts in both countries to refer to each other's judicial decisions in various fields, including constitutional law. The Malaysian constitutional influence on Singapore came to a climax when Singapore was part of Malaysia from September 16, 1963, to August 9, 1965, during which period Singapore was governed by the federal Constitution. After Singapore separated from Malaysia, the Malaysian influence was maintained to a large extent because independent Singapore's legislature provided that certain Articles of the Malaysian Constitution would continue to have force in Singapore (including most of the provisions dealing with fundamental liberties). Therefore, Malaysian judicial decisions interpreting these provisions are also relevant to Singapore. For these reasons, much of what the Honourable Tun Mohamed Suffian, Lord President of Malaysia, has said in his chapter in this book would, *mutatis mutandis*, be applicable for Singapore, too, especially his comments on the scope of the provisions for fundamental liberties.

The relevance and extent of the Malaysian influence can best be illustrated by reference to the perspectives of the 1966 Constitutional Commission of Singapore. This commission, chaired by the Chief Justice, was appointed to make recommendations to the government, *inter alia*, on constitutional provisions to safeguard rights of minorities and to prevent discrimination. In its Report the Commission made it clear that, regarding fundamental rights, it was of the opinion that the preexisting influence of Malaysian constitutional provisions should in the main be maintained and in this connection stressed the "common destiny" of the peoples of the two countries:

> We approached this task bearing in mind that the provisions of Part II of the present Constitution of Malaysia—being provisions dealing with fundamental rights—were applicable to Singapore when it was a part of Malaysia and continue with one exception to apply in Singapore since its separation from Malaysia. We have looked at a large number of Constitutions which contain provisions dealing with fundamental rights and freedoms, but believing, as we do, that it would be wise, desirable and practical, having regard to the past, the present and the future, to preserve the common destiny of the peoples of Singapore and Malaysia, we do not propose in our recommendations on fundamental rights to depart, except where we think it is necessary and desirable, from the form and substance of similar provisions in the Malaysian Constitution.[3]

Notwithstanding such English and Malaysian influences, the constitutional law of Singapore has its unique characteristics, which will be brought out later in this chapter.

Extent of American Influence on Singapore's Constitutional Documents

One index of contemporary American influence would be the extent to which legislators and draftsmen, when addressing themselves to major constitutional questions, borrow ideas from the United States Constitution. The evidence that is available does not disclose any significant direct American influence on the drafting and development of Singapore's constitutional documents. Three different instances may be considered.

The 1963 Constitution for the State of Singapore, promulgated when Singapore joined Malaysia, was legally effected by a United Kingdom Order-in-Council.[4] It must, however, be viewed as a negotiated document, as the draft was annexed to the Malaysia Agreement. This 1963 Constitution, which with later amendments continues to be the republic's Constitution, does not reveal any special influence of the

3. Report of the Constitutional Commission 1966, par. 14.

4. *The Sabah, Sarawak and Singapore (State Constitutions) Order in Council* [1963] 2 U.K. S.I. 2656 (No. 1493).

U.S. Constitution apart from the "supremacy clause,"[5] which provided that statutes inconsistent with the provisions of the Constitution would be invalid. It cannot be disputed that this "supremacy clause," which can be found in the modern constitutions of many nations, owes its origins to the constitutional doctrine of supremacy of the Constitution and judicial review established by the United States Supreme Court in the classic case of *Marbury* v. *Madison*.[6]

Next, we may consider the Report of the 1966 Constitutional Commission. The Commission discussed in detail important questions of fundamental liberties, including the concepts of equality and equal protection. An American scholar might logically have thought that this would be a likely occasion where American constitutional concepts and doctrine might have been discussed. The Report, however, does not disclose this; there is no express reference to the provisions or position in the United States (although on other matters the Commission referred to the positions of Guyana and Scandinavian nations). It should be mentioned that the Commission recommended a new provision to deal with fundamental liberty:

> No person shall be subjected to torture or to inhuman or degrading punishment or other treatment.[7]

This bears a close resemblance to the Eighth Amendment to the United States Constitution, which prohibits "cruel and unusual punishments." The Commission did not say that it was borrowing from the U.S. Constitution, but it did say that it looked "at other written constitutions" and found this right to be acknowledged and protected in all of them.

It could well be that American constitutional provisions were discussed in the proceedings of the Commission, but, unfortunately, there is no published record of its detailed deliberations. (We should here recall that the Constitutional Commission in its Report revealed its inclination to maintain as much as possible of the provisions for fundamental liberties inherited from Malaysia).

It is also useful to consider the Singapore Parliament's debate on the Report of the 1966 Constitutional Commission, for that represents the latest major legislative debate in Singapore on constitutional questions. In this parliamentary debate at least twenty-five legislators

5. S. 52 reads "Any law enacted by the Legislature after the coming into operation of this Constitution which is inconsistent with this Constitution shall, to the extent of the inconsistency, be void."

6. 1 Cranch 137, 2 L.Ed. 60 (1803).

7. This, together with certain other recommendations of the Commission which were in principle acceptable to the government, has not yet been incorporated in the Constitution.

participated, including three Cabinet Members (Prime Minister, Foreign Minister, and Minister for Law). Here again the record of the legislative debate shows that *none* of the legislators who spoke on the Commission's proposals referred to provisions of the U.S. Constitution.

It is interesting, on the other hand, to note that several speakers referred to the American experience, especially with regard to the question of moulding a united nation out of a cosmopolitan population. That this should have been their preoccupation is understandable, since Singapore is multi-racial, and one of the specific matters dealt with by the Commission was the safeguarding of minority interests to ensure non-discrimination. Thus the Prime Minister, Mr. Lee Kuan Yew, referred to the American experience in making his point that the American multi-ethnic society was distinguishable from Singapore's multi-racial society:

> I am not suggesting that a multi-racial society is the ideal society in all circumstances. In fact, the great powers of this world today consist of nations which are ethno-centric in composition. True, both the Americans and the Russians have more than one single race or one single language group or one single religion. But there is in both countries one single race or ethnic group which shares one common language and whose culture is, by reason of its dynamism or aggressiveness, far in dominance over the others comprised in the nation. Be that as it may for aspirants to world powers, we are confronted, as a young migrant community, with the problem of continuing a tolerant, meaningful society for some two million people nearly all of whom cannot trace their links with the Republic for more than 150 years.[8]

Similarly, the Foreign Minister referred to the American multi-racial situation:

> If you were to read the history of modern nations, for example Britain—I used to read English history when I was a boy—you will discover that once upon a time, there was no such thing as "Britain." There were "English," "Saxons" and "Normans." They thought of themselves as minority groups. Only 100 years ago, there was no such thing as a German nation; there was no such thing as an Italian nation. In fact, there was no such thing as an American nation when Malacca was founded. There were Poles, immigrants of all kinds—just like us. Then over a period of years, the Americans had to constitute themselves into a nation. It was necessary. For example, the early settlers of America thought of themselves as Dutch, French, German, English and Irish and over a period of 100 years or more, they had learned to think of themselves as Americans. They have not yet completed the process, but today, a Dutchman or even a Japanese or Chinese or Negro from America will tell you that he is an American.[9]

8. *Parliamentary Debates, Republic of Singapore, Official Report*, Vol. 25, col. 1283.

9. Ibid., at col. 1363.

Influence of American Judicial Decisions

From what has already been said about the little influence of the United States Constitution on Singapore's constitutional concepts and institutions, it should not be surprising that American judicial decisions are seldom mentioned in judgments by Singapore courts in constitutional law cases. Because of the influences of the English legal system and the affinity with Malaysian constitutional provisions, Singapore courts are influenced more by United Kingdom and Malaysian judicial decisions. Indian constitutional law judgments are also heavily drawn upon as persuasive authorities; this is also the position in Malaysia. The explanation for the relevance of Indian judgments in Singapore and Malaysian courts is that the Malaysia and Singapore constitutional provisions in several respects have close similarity with the provisions of the Indian Constitution (concerning, e.g., public servants, fundamental liberties, emergency powers, and preventive detention). However, where the courts feel that the position here is different, they will not follow the Indian judgments.

The last reported instance when a Singapore court had to assess the relevance of American authorities was in *Lee Mau Seng* v. *Minister for Home Affairs, Singapore and Anor.*[10] Here a person detained under preventive detention legislation had been denied for twenty days after his arrest his constitutional right to counsel. In an application for *habeas corpus* it was argued that this amounted to an abuse of power justifying an order for release. United States and Indian authorities were cited.

Chief Justice Wee Chong Jin, who decided the case, held, however, that "*habeas corpus* is not an available remedy to a person who, after his arrest by the police and under lawful detention by the police under powers conferred [by the legislation], has been refused by the police his constitutional right under article 5 (3) of the Constitution to be allowed to consult a legal practitioner of his choice." The learned judge felt that some other available remedy ought to be sought.

In handling the American authorities cited by counsel, Chief Justice Wee Chong Jin distinguished them by saying:

> The American authorities all deal with the Sixth Amendment to the Constitution of the United States of America, the relevant provisions of which provide that "In all criminal prosecutions, the accused shall enjoy the right . . . to have the assistance of counsel for his defence." As I understand the law in America to be, it has been decided that under the Sixth Amendment, unless an accused at his trial has waived his right to be assisted by counsel, "compliance with this constitutional mandate is an essential prerequisite to a Federal Court's authority to

10. [1971] 2 Malayan Law Journal (hereinafter cited at M.L.J.).

deprive an accused of his life or liberty," so that a conviction of a person who did not effectively waive his constitutional right to counsel for his defence is void as having been rendered without jurisdiction thus entitling the accused person, to whom expiration of time has rendered relief by way of application for a new trial or by appeal unavailable, to *habeas corpus* as an available remedy (*Johnson* v. *Zerbst*[11]). In America, therefore, *habeas corpus* is available because a conviction being void, the convicted person's imprisonment is unlawful.[12]

In a recently decided Singapore constitutional law case, *Lee Keng Guan and Ors.* v. *Public Prosecutor*,[13] the Court of Criminal Appeal had to decide a significant argument on equal protection of the law. However, no American cases were referred to in the judgment; instead, the Court accepted certain principles enunciated in an Indian decision.

The Written Constitution

It could be said that Singapore's constitutional system is similar to that of the United States and Malaysia in that Singapore's Constitution also is in written form. However, unlike the United States or Malaysia, which have their constitutional provisions in one single composite constitution (at least their federal constitutions), this is not the case in Singapore. In Singapore there is a plurality of basic constitutional documents, and therefore reference has to be made to the following three basic constitutional documents: The Constitution of Singapore (including amendments made after Singapore's separation); The Republic of Singapore Independence Act 1965 (No. 9 of 1965); The Constitution of Malaysia, certain provisons of which were made applicable by The Republic of Singapore Independence Act 1965.[14]

The "Constitution of Singapore" refers to the state constitution which Singapore received when it joined Malaysia. When it separated from Malaysia, this continued to have legal effect, but being a state constitution it was inadequate in many respects for an independent nation. Since separation this document has been amended on several occasions. The Republic of Singapore Independence Act 1965 is a significant statute enacted by Singapore's legislature four months after separation to provide, *inter alia*, "that all existing laws shall continue in force on or after Singapore Day." But this was subject to "modifications, adaptations, qualifications and exceptions as may be necessary to bring them into conformity with this Act and with the independent status of Singapore upon separation from Malaysia." Certain provisions of the Constitution of Malaysia were made applicable in Singapore as a result of Section 6 of the aforementioned Republic of

11. 58 S.Ct. 1019. 12. [1971] 2 M.L.J. 141. 13. [1977] 2 M.L.J. 95.

14. The texts of these three documents are set out in the appendices in the writer's book *Constitutional Law* (cited in n. 1 above).

Singapore Independence Act, which prescribed that certain specified provisions of the Malaysian Constitution (including most of the provisions concerning fundamental liberties and emergency powers) would continue to have force in Singapore. This was because the Singapore state constitution lacked these provisions. Thus, although the Singapore Constitution was not expressly amended to incorporate these Malaysian provisions, there is no doubt that these Malaysian provisions are an integral part of Singapore's constitutional law. The Republic of Singapore Independence Act, in this regard, must be viewed not as routine legislation but as fundamental legislation enacted by Parliament in exercise of its constituent power.

In 1970 the government indicated that a new composite Constitution was in the making, but, as this has not yet been promulgated, the above mentioned plurality of constitutional documents continues.

Supremacy of the Constitution

The Singapore Constitution can be said to have a similarity with United States constitutional law in that it embodies the concept of the supremacy of the Constitution. Article 52 of the Constitution provides that "Any law enacted by the Legislature after the coming into operation of this Constitution which is inconsistent with this Constitution shall, to the extent of this inconsistency, be void."[15]

A constitutional lawyer, however, must recognize that the efficacy of the concept of the supremacy clause and of the general concept of a written constitution limiting legislative powers depends on several other factors. One such factor is whether the constitution can be easily amended.

In this regard the Singapore Constitution, with the exception of one Part, is very flexible. Article 90 provides that the Constitution can be amended "by a law enacted by the Legislature"; that is, the procedure for amending the Constitution is the same as that for amending any other law. The exception is that Part 2B of the Constitution (Protection of the Sovereignty of the Republic of Singapore) can be amended only if there is support of not less than two-thirds of the total number of votes cast by electors at a national referendum.

These provisions on amendment of the Singapore Constitution can provide an interesting basis for discussing the following remarks of Chief Justice Marshall in the celebrated American case of *Marbury* v. *Madison*:

> It is a proposition too plain to be contested, that the Constitution controls any legislative act repugnant to it; or, *that the Legislature may*

15. The date of coming into operation was September 16, 1963.

> *alter the Constitution by an ordinary act.* Between these alternatives there is *no middle ground.* The Constitution is either a superior paramount law, unchangeable by ordinary means, or it is on a level with ordinary legislative acts, and, like other acts, is alterable when the Legislature shall please alter it. If the former of the alternatives be true, then a legislative act contrary to the Constitution is not law; if the latter be true, then written Constitutions are absurd attempts, on the part of the people, to limit a power in its own nature illimitable. (Emphasis added.)[16]

The fascinating question is whether the Singapore Constitution is "middle ground," which Chief Justice Marshall claims can never exist. It is true that most of the provisions of the Singapore Constitution may be altered by the legislature "by an ordinary act." But this does not mean that the Singapore Constitution is "an absurd attempt . . . to limit a power in its own nature illimitable" because, as was pointed out, where a statute is in conflict with the constitutional provisions, Article 52 states that the statutory provision shall be void. The courts have proceeded on the basis that they can strike down a statute for invalidity.

However, if every statute that conflicts with the Constitution is to be regarded as an "implied amendment" to the Constitution, then the supremacy clause would be rendered otiose and the courts would never be able to strike down a statute as invalid for inconsistency with the Constitution. It is interesting to note that in the few occasions where the courts had to consider the constitutional validity of statutory provisions, the argument of implied amendment has not been raised.

Fundamental Liberties

In General

Most of the articles on fundamental liberties in the Malaysian Constitution are still applicable in Singapore. In view of this, much of what the Honourable Tun Suffian, the Lord President of Malaysia, has said (in his chapter on Malaysia) on fundamental liberties would be also descriptive of the position in Singapore. Therefore I shall not repeat all the points mentioned by him. There are, however, two important qualifications concerning the applicability of the Malaysian fundamental liberties provisions in Singapore.

The first qualification is that, in my view, the Malaysian constitutional provisions apply in Singapore as they stood on August 9, 1965, the date of separation and date of operation of the Republic of Singapore Independence Act, 1965, and I submit that this is the proper interpretation of the Act.[17] Thus, amendments to the Malaysian provisions made by the Malaysian legislature after the operative date do not

16. 1 Cranch 137 at 177.
17. See pp. 6 and 7 of the writer's *Constitutional Law.*

apply in Singapore. This point is important because after separation Malaysia amended some provisions of the Constitution, including those on fundamental liberties.

The second qualification is that one provision dealing with fundamental liberties found in the Malaysian Constitution was expressly declared by the Singapore legislature to cease to have effect in Singapore.[18] This was Article 13, which stated that no person shall be deprived of property "save in accordance with law" and that no law shall provide for compulsory acquisition or use of property "without adequate compensation." The statements made in Parliament suggest that the government was not in favour of this provision insofar as it allowed judicial review over the quantum of compensation.[19]

"Due Process of Law" and "In Accordance with Law"

The Honourable Tun Suffian has pointed out that while in America no person shall be deprived of his life, liberty, or property "without due process of law," the Malaysian Article 5 (1), which applies in Singapore, states that no person shall be deprived of his life or personal liberty "save in accordance with law."

In an article published ten years ago,[20] well before the provision was considered by Singapore or Malaysian courts, I considered the possible interpretation of the Malaysian provision and also considered an Indian case, *Gopalan* v. *State of Madras*,[21] and a Burmese case, *Tinsa Maw Naing* v. *Commissioner of Police, Rangoon*.[22] These two cases had interpreted "in accordance with law" in the Indian and Burmese constitutions to mean merely compliance with enacted law. I analyzed these cases and argued that "reliance on these cases is unwise in interpreting our provision," and stated that while "opposition to the adoption of a controversial concept such as the substantive due process" is understandable "*there appear to be no good reasons why Article 5 (1)* should be incapable of being interpreted to require any law (or executive act) depriving persons of life or personal liberty *to comply with the rules of natural justice*. It will be interesting to await the interpretation which the judges will give to this provision."[23]

In *Comptroller General of Inland Revenue* v. *N.P.*[24] and in *Arumugam Pillai* v. *Government of Malaysia*[25] the Malaysian courts

18. S. 6 (3) of the Republic of Singapore Independence Act 1965, Act No. 9 of 1965.

19. See statement of Minister for Law, Mr. E. W. Barker, *Singapore Parliamentary Debates, Official Report*, vol 25, col. 1054.

20. "Constitutional Limitations on Legislative Powers in Malaysia" (1967) 9 *Malaya Law Review* 96.

21. A.I.R. (1950) S.C. 27. 22. 1950 *Burma Law Rep.* 17.

23. "Constitutional Limitations . . . ," n. 20 at p. 101.

24. [1973] 1 M.L.J. 165. 25. [1975] 2 M.L.J. 29.

have indeed interpreted Article 5 (1), though not in a detailed manner. These two decisions suggest that the courts follow the Indian and Burmese cases in holding that "law" means only enacted law and that there was no scope for including rules of natural justice as a criterion with which to assess the validity of laws. It is most likely that, if the question arose in Singapore, the Singapore courts would take a similar approach.

Right to Counsel

The Singapore courts interpreted the Malaysian Article 5 (3) in the same way as the Malaysian courts (see the chapter on Malaysia). Thus, it was held in *Lee Mau Seng* v. *Minister for Home Affairs, Singapore and Anor.*[26] that:

> The language of Article 5 (3) of the Constitution is clear and simple. If a person who is arrested wishes to consult a legal practitioner of his choice, he is, beyond a shadow of doubt, entitled to have this constitutional right granted to him by the authority who has custody of him after his arrest and *this right must be granted to him within a reasonable time after his arrest.* (Emphasis added.)

Note that the Court did not say that the right must always be granted from the moment of arrest. Thus the position is different from the right to counsel in the United States.

Other Similarities and Differences

When the Singapore and United States constitutions or constitutional systems are compared, their other similarities and differences can be summarized as follows:

Absence of Federalism

Singapore is a unitary state, and the federal principle has never operated within Singapore, although Singapore had a taste of federalism when it was a constituent state within Malaysia. Therefore, all rules and concepts of American constitutional law turning on the federal-state division of powers find no analogy in Singapore.

Parliamentary System of Government

While the United States has the presidential system, Singapore, like Malaysia, is influenced by the United Kingdom and has the parliamentary system, whereby the Prime Minister and his Cabinet colleagues are members of the legislature and elected as such. Certain concepts which are unwritten conventions in England are expressly incorporated in the

26. [1971] 2 M.L.J. 137.

Singapore Constitution, such as the principle of the Cabinet's collective responsibility to Parliament.

It is true that in Singapore there is a President, but like the English, Indian, or Malaysian heads of state he has no major discretionary functions, and the general rule is that he must act on advice of the Cabinet.

Unicameral Legislature

Singapore, being a small, compact country, has always had a unicameral legislature and in this respect differs from the U.S., the U.K., Malaysia, and India, which have bicameral legislatures. It should be pointed out here that there exists a Presidential Council for Minority Rights,[27] which, while not part of the legislature, performs an advisory role to the legislature and is linked with the legislative process because the Council has to consider all legislative bills[28] and report whether there are any provisions which are discriminatory.

27. Part IV A of the Singapore Constitution.

28. But the following legislative bills are excluded: a money bill; a bill certified by the Prime Minister as being one which affects the defence or the security of Singapore or which relates to public safety, peace, or good order in Singapore; or a bill certified by the Prime Minister to be so urgent that it is not in the public interest to delay its enactment.

Biographical Sketches of the Asian Authors

Mr. Justice Abu Sayeed Chowdhury, BANGLADESH

Abu Sayeed Chowdhury was born in Tangail on January 31, 1921, during the British colonial period. He graduated from the Presidency College in Calcutta in 1940, and went on to earn his M.A. and Bachelor of Laws degrees from Calcutta University. In 1947 he was called to the English Bar from Lincoln's Inn. As a student he was General Secretary of the Presidency College Union and, in 1946, President of the British Branch of the All-India Muslim Students Federation.

The positions Mr. Justice Chowdhury has held include the following: Advocate-General of East Pakistan, 1960-61; Member of the Constitution Convention, 1960-61; Judge, Dacca High Court, 1961-1972; Member, United Nations Commission on Human Rights, 1971-74; Member or Leader of the Delegation of Bangladesh to many international conferences, including Leader of the Bangladesh Delegation to the 30th Session of the United Nations General Assembly in 1975; and Vice-Chancellor of the University of Dacca.

In 1971 he organized and led the Bangladesh liberation movement abroad, with headquarters in London. He was sworn in as the first President of Bangladesh on January 12, 1972. He was reelected by Parliament for a five-year term in the spring of 1973, but served in that capacity only until he took a position as Cabinet Minister on December 24, 1973. He was Foreign Minister of Bangladesh when a change of government in November 1975 led him to move to London, where he resides at present. He visited Bangladesh in 1977.

Mr. Justice Chowdhury married Begum Khurshid Chowdhury in 1948; they have one daughter and two sons. His hobbies are reading and gardening.

Professor Herbert Han-Pao Ma, REPUBLIC OF CHINA

Herbert H. P. Ma was born on November 27, 1926, in Hankow, Hupei Province, China. He attended National Futan University in Shanghai, China, from 1944 to 1947. He received his LL.B. degree from National Taiwan University in Taipei, Taiwan, in 1950. He conducted advanced research in law at Harvard University in 1964 and again during the 1975-76 academic year. Professor Ma taught in the School of Law of the University of Washington (Seattle) in 1971.

From 1966 to 1971 he was Executive Secretary, China Council on Sino-American Cooperation in Humanities and Social Sciences of the Academia Sinica. He held the appointment of Research Professor, National Science Council, Republic of China, 1969-71, and received the Distinguished Service Award of that nation's Ministry of Education in both 1967 and 1971.

Professor Ma is currently Professor of Law at National Taiwan University, and Member, Examination Yuan, Republic of China. His scholarly publications include such works as *Essays on Western Legal Thought* (in Chinese), *General Principles of Private International Law* (in Chinese), *Trade and Investment in Taiwan: The Legal and Economic Environment in the Republic of China* (in English), and numerous articles.

Dr. Pradyumna Kumar Tripathi, INDIA

P. K. Tripathi was born on May 24, 1924, in Bhanpura, Madhya Pradesh, British India. He graduated from Maharaja Shivaji Rao High School, Indore, in 1940, and then attended Holkar College in Indore, from which he received a diploma in intermediate science (1942), a B.S. (1944), and his LL.B. (1946). In 1949 he earned the LL.M. degree from the University of Delhi, and completed his work for the J.S.D. at Columbia University in New York in 1957. In the same year he married Kusum Tendulkar; they have one son, Pradar.

In his academic career, Dr. Tripathi progressed from Lecturer (1949-59) to Reader in Law at the University of Delhi (1959-61), to Professor and Head of Department (University of Allahabad, 1961-65; University of Delhi, 1965-71). From 1971 until late 1977 he served as a Member of the Law Commission of India and its Executive Committee and then returned to his professorial duties at the University of Delhi. He was Parker Fellow at the Law School of Columbia University (1955-56), visiting Professor of Law at the University of Singapore (1963), and Leverhulm Visiting Fellow at the Law School of the University of Melbourne, Australia, in 1971. Dr. Tripathi is also a member both of the Legal Education Committee of the Bar Council of India, and of the Executive Committee of the Indian Law Institute. He was National Lecturer for Law, 1971-72, and was the first Indian academic lawyer to present the Kashinath Trimbak Telang Endowment Lectures in 1971. His lectures were published by Bombay University as *Some Insights into the Fundamental Rights*. Besides his other book, *Spotlights on Constitutional Interpretation* (Bombay, 1972), he has published many papers in Indian journals and in American legal periodicals.

Chief Justice Dr. Oemar Seno Adji, INDONESIA

Oemar Seno Adji was born in Solo, Central Java, on December 5, 1915, when most of present Indonesia was the Dutch East Indies. He earned his degree from the Faculty of Law, Gajah Mada University, Yogyakarta, in 1949. In 1964 Dr. Seno Adji visited the United States on an Eisenhower Exchange

Fellowship. Before assuming his present duties as Chief Justice of the Supreme Court of the Republic of Indonesia, Dr. Seno Adji served as Minister of Justice (1966-1974) and Professor and Dean of the Faculty of Law, University of Indonesia, Jakarta. He represented Indonesia at the United Nations Conference on Crime Prevention. Among his writings are *Innovation in Criminal Justice in Indonesia*, "Indonesia Rechstaat," "Press Freedom, Mass Media, and the Law," and publications on criminal law. He is married and has eight children.

Professor Nobushige Ukai, JAPAN

Nobushige Ukai was born on March 9, 1906, in Tokyo, Japan. He received his B.Juris. degree from Tokyo Imperial University in 1930, and taught at Seoul Imperial University in Korea from 1931 to 1946, except for studies at Harvard Law School and teaching at Carleton College in 1940. He received his D.Juris. degree from the University of Tokyo in 1955, where he was Professor from 1947 until 1961, and Director of the Social Science Research Institute in 1952 and 1953. In this country, he has lectured extensively, at such schools as Southern Illinois University, the Fletcher School of Law and Diplomacy of Tufts University (1960-61) and Stanford University (1956-57). He served as President of International Christian University in Tokyo from 1961 to 1967, and returned to teaching at Seikei University (1968-75) and Senshu University (1975). Professor Ukai has been President of the Japan Public Law Association, and member of such agencies as the Experts Committees of the Ministry of Local Autonomy and the National Personnel Authority of Japan, the Library Committee of the Supreme Court, and the Public Safety Commission of the Tokyo Metropolitan Government. He has also been associated closely with the work of the Grew Foundation, the Bancroft Foundation, and the American Studies Foundation of Japan.

Among Professor Ukai's numerous publications in Japanese are books on Japan's constitutional law, administrative law, local government system, public employee laws, civil liberties, and judiciary, as well as on America's jurisprudence. His writings in English on civil liberties, politics, and law in Japan have appeared in several American law and social science journals.

Lord President Tun Mohamed Suffian bin Hashim, MALAYSIA

Tun Mohamed Suffian was born on December 11, 1917, at Kota Lama Kiri near Kuala Kangsar, Malaysia. ("Tun" is a title conferred by His Majesty the King of Malaysia.) He was educated at Clifford School (Kuala Kangsar, Perak). From Gonville and Caius College, Cambridge University, he earned his M.A. and LL.B. degrees. He became Barrister-at-Law in 1941 after studies at the Middle Temple, London. Tun Suffian served as a radio announcer on All-India Radio (1942-45) and on BBC (London, 1945-46). He was in the Malayan Civil Service in 1948 and the Malayan Judicial and Legal Service from 1949 to 1961. In international service, he was Malayan delegate to the U.N. Conferences on the Law of the Sea in Geneva in 1960 and 1961. He was awarded an Eisenhower Exchange Fellowship in 1964, and the Ramon Magsaysay Award (the Philippines) in 1975.

Tun Suffian played a notable role as advisor in the drafting of the Malayan constitution (1956), and was honorary advisor on constitutional matters to the Sultan of Brunei in 1959. He has served as President of the Council for the Promotion of Higher Education in Malaysia (1973-76), and Pro-Chancellor of the University of Malaya (1963-). Before assuming the position of Lord

President of the Federal Court of Malaysia in 1974 (the equivalent of the U.S. Chief Justice), he was Solicitor General (1959-61) and a member of the appellate bench. He is author of *An Introduction to the Constitution of Malaysia*, and the famous "Suffian Report," as Chairman of the Royal Commission on Salaries in the Public Service. Tun Suffian has long been an active member of the Advisory Editorial Board of *The Malayan Law Journal*. He is married to Toh Puan Bunny.

Senior Associate Justice Enrique M. Fernando, THE PHILIPPINES

Enrique M. Fernando was born in 1915 during the period when the Philippines was under American sovereignty. He earned his law degree, *magna cum laude*, at the University of the Philippines in 1938, and obtained his LL.M. degree in 1948 after studying as the first Filipino Sterling Fellow at Yale University. While serving on his nation's highest tribunal, he retains his positions as George A. Malcolm Professor of Constitutional law at the University of the Philippines, and Professor of Law in the Lyceum of the Philippines, and Santo Tomas University. His past positions of responsibility have included the following: legal advisor to three Filipino Presidents (R. Magsaysay, C. P. Garcia, and F. E. Marcos); Philippines' representative to four United Nations Southeast Asian Regional Seminars on Human Rights; Co-Chairman, Philippine Delegation, U.N. Conference on the Law of Treaties, Vienna, 1968; Member, Philippine Delegation to the United Nations, 1977. Justice Fernando has twice been chosen Chairman of the Civil Liberties Union of the Philippines. He has written and spoken frequently on human rights and the Constitution of the Philippines, in recent years under a martial law situation. He was a major speaker at the World Peace Through Law Conference in Washington, D.C., in 1975, and in Manila in 1977, when he was Chairman of the Resolutions Committee. He was invited to present the First Tun Razak Memorial Lecture in Kuala Lumpur, Malaysia, in 1977. He is the author of a treatise on the Constitution of the Philippines.

Justice Fernando is married to Emma Quisumbing, also a member of the Philippine Bar; they have five children.

Dean S. Jayakumar, SINGAPORE

S. Jayakumar is Associate Professor and Dean of the Faculty of Law, University of Singapore, where he has been teaching since 1964. He earned his law degrees from the University of Singapore (LL.B.) and Yale University Law School (LL.M.). From 1971 to 1974 he served as Singapore's Permanent Representative to the United Nations and as High Commissioner to Canada with the rank of Ambassador Extraordinary and Plenipotentiary.

His articles and notes on issues of constitutional law, international law, and legal education in various law journals are many. He has published three books: *Public International Law Cases from Malaysia and Singapore* (1974); *Constitutional Law Cases from Malaysia and Singapore* (1976, 2nd ed.); and *Constitutional Law*, No. 1 in the Singapore Law Series (1976).

Short Bibliography on Law and Constitutionalism in Asia

General

Bayley, David H. *Public Liberties in the New States* (Chicago: Rand McNally & Co., 1964).

Carey, John. *UN Protection of Civil and Political Rights* (Charlottesville: University of Virginia Press, 1971).

Claude, Richard P., ed. *Comparative Human Rights* (Baltimore: Johns Hopkins University Press, 1976).

Duchacek, Ivo. *Power Maps: Comparative Politics of Constitutions* (Santa Barbara: ABC Clio Press, 1973).

Ehrmann, Henry W. *Comparative Legal Cultures* (Englewood Cliffs, N.J.: Prentice-Hall, 1976).

Groves, Harry E. *Comparative Constitutional Law* (Dobbs Ferry, N.Y.: Oceana Publications, 1963).

Hooker, M. B. *Legal Pluralism: An Introduction to Colonial and Neo-Colonial Laws* (Oxford: Clarendon Press, 1975).

Lawasia. Journal of the Law Association of Asia and the Western Pacific, c/o Faculty of Law, University of New South Wales, Kensington, N.S.W. 2033, Australia.

Spann, R. N., ed. *Constitutionalism in Asia* (Bombay: Asia Publishing House, 1963).

Studies in the Law of the Far East and Southeast Asia (Washington, D.C.: Washington Foreign Law Society, 1956).

Universal Human Rights: An International Scholarly Journal of Law, Philosophy and the Social Sciences (New York: Earl M. Coleman Publishers).

Weeramantry, C. G. *Equality and Freedom: Some Third World Perspectives* (Colombo: Hansa Publishers Ltd., 1976).

East Asia

Cohen, Jerome A. *Criminal Processes in the People's Republic of China, 1949-1963* (Cambridge, Mass.: Harvard University Press, 1968).

———, ed. *Contemporary Chinese Law: Research Problems and Perspectives* (Cambridge, Mass.: Harvard University Press, 1970).

Hahm, Pyong-choon. *The Korean Political Tradition and Law* (Seoul: Hollym Publishers, 1967).

Henderson, Dan Fenno, ed. *The Constitution of Japan: Its First Twenty Years, 1947-67* (Seattle: University of Washington Press, 1969).

Henderson, Gregory. *Korea: The Politics of the Vortex* (Cambridge, Mass.: Harvard University Press, 1968).

Itoh, Hiroshi, and Lawrence W. Beer. *The Constitutional Case Law of Japan: Selected Supreme Court Decisions, 1961-1970* (Seattle: University of Washington Press, 1978).

Law in Japan: An Annual, Japanese American Society for Legal Studies, Seattle and Tokyo, c/o Asian Law Program, University of Washington, Seattle, Washington 98195.

Laws of the Republic of Korea (Seoul: The Korean Legal Center, 1975). Translations of 101 laws, including the six Codes.

Li, Victor H. *Law without Lawyers* (Stanford: Stanford Alumni Association, 1977).

Maki, John M. *Court and Constitution in Japan: Selected Supreme Court Decisions, 1948-1960* (Seattle: University of Washington Press, 1964).

Tsao, W. Y. *The Constitutional Structure of Modern China* (Melbourne: Melbourne University Press, 1947).

Southeast Asia

Badgley, John, et al. *The Future of Burma in Perspective* (Columbus: Ohio State University Press, 1978).

Brown, B. J., ed. *Fashion of Law in New Guinea: Being an Account of the Past, Present and Developing System of Laws in Papua and New Guinea* (Sydney: Butterworths, 1969).

Butler, William J., et al. *The Decline of Democracy in the Philippines* (Geneva: International Commission of Jurists, 1977).

Fernando, Enrique M. *Reflections on the Revised Constitution* (Manila: Supreme Court Press, 1974).

———. *The Rule of Law under Martial Law: The Philippine Experience* (Manila: Supreme Court Press, 1975).

Jayakumar, S. *Constitutional Law (with Documentary Materials).* Singapore Law Series, No. 1 (Singapore: Malaya Law Review, 1976).

———. *Constitutional Law Cases from Malaysia and Singapore* (Singapore: Malayan Law Journal Pte. Ltd., 1976, 2nd ed.).

Lev, Daniel S. *Islamic Courts in Indonesia* (Berkeley and Los Angeles: University of California Press, 1972).

Steinberg, Joel, ed. *In Search of Southeast Asia* (New York: Praeger Publishers, 1971).

Suffian bin Hashim, Tun Mohamed. *An Introduction to the Constitution of Malaysia* (Kuala Lumpur: Government Printer, 1976, 2nd ed.).

———, H. P. Lee, and F. A. Trindade, eds. *The Development of the Constitution of Malaysia in Its First Twenty Years: 1957-1977* (Selangor, Malaysia: Oxford University Press, 1978).

Ter Haar, B. *Adat Law in Indonesia* (New York: Institute of Pacific Relations, 1948).

South Asia

Choudhury, G. W. *Constitutional Development in Pakistan* (London: Longman, 1969, 2nd ed.).

______. *The Last Days of United Pakistan* (Bloomington: Indiana University Press, 1974).

______. *India, Pakistan, Bangladesh, and the Major Powers* (Riverside, N.J.: The Free Press, 1976).

Cooray, Joseph A. L. *Constitutional and Administrative Law of Sri Lanka (Ceylon)* (Colombo: Hansa Publishers, 1973).

Jahan, Rounaq. *Pakistan: Failure in National Integration* (New York: Columbia University Press, 1972).

______. "India, Pakistan, and Bangladesh." In Gregory Henderson et al., eds., *Divided Nations in a Divided World* (New York: David McKay, 1974), pp. 299-399.

Lal, Jagdish. *The Constitution of India, as Amended by Forty-Second Amendment* (Delhi: Delhi Law House, 1977).

Pylee, M. V. *Constitutional Government in India* (Bombay: Asia Publishing House, 1975, 3rd ed.).

Tripathi, P. K. *Some Insights into Fundamental Rights* (Bombay: University of Bombay, N. M. Tripathi, 1972).

Ziring, Lawrence, et al. *Pakistan: The Long View* (Durham, N.C.: Duke University Press, 1977).

Index

Designer:	Carolyn Bean
Compositor:	U.C. Press
Printer:	Braun-Brumfield, Inc.
Binder:	Braun-Brumfield, Inc.
Text:	Compset Times Roman
Display:	Compset Times Roman
Cloth:	Holliston Roxite B 53543
Paper:	50 lb. P&S Offset Vellum B32